THE
HISTORY
BOOK

**LONDON, NEW YORK,
MELBOURNE, MUNICH, AND DELHI**

Senior editor Julie Ferris
Senior art editor Jim Green

Project editors Francesca Baines,
Jenny Finch, Niki Foreman, Fran Jones
Designers Spencer Holbrook, Katie Knutton, Philip Letsu,
Hoa Luc, Stefan Podhorodecki, Marilou Prokopiou, Smiljka Surla

Editors Hazel Beynon, Steven Carton
Additional design Sheila Collins, Johnny Pau,
Owen Peyton Jones, Samantha Richiardi, Nihal Yesil

Managing editor Linda Esposito
Managing art editor Diane Thistlethwaite

Commissioned photography Stefan Podhorodecki
Creative retouching Steve Willis
Picture research Nic Dean

Publishing manager Andrew Macintyre
Category publisher Laura Buller

DK picture researchers Lucy Claxton, Rose Horridge,
Emma Shepherd, Romaine Werblow
Production editor Andy Hilliard
Production controller Pip Tinsley

Jacket design Laura Brim
Jacket editor Mariza O'Keeffe
Senior design development Yumiko Tahata
Design development and jacket manager
Sophia M Tampakopoulos Turner

First published in hardback in Great Britain as Take Me Back in 2008
This paperback edition first published in 2009 by
Dorling Kindersley Limited,
80 Strand, London, WC2R 0RL

A CIP catalogue record for this book
is available from the British Library

Hardback edition ISBN: 978-1-40533-253-8
Paperback edition ISBN: 978-1-40534-932-1

Colour reproduction by Altaimage.co.uk
Printed and bound by Toppan, China

Discover more at
www.dk.com

Take me back to the beginning...

Contributors: Samone Bos,
Laura Buller, Ian Harrison,
Susan Kennedy, Philip Parker,
Sally Regan, Anne Rooney

wait for me

WHAT'S INSIDE...

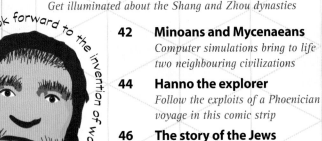

Look forward to the invention of waxing strips!

What did he say?

Dunno, it's all Greek to me!

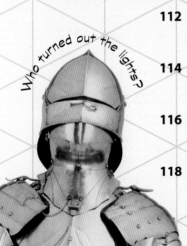

Who turned out the lights?

I used to vandalize church doors, but now I'm a reformed character.

156 All change

Aaargh! It's true what they say about farting in a spacesuit!

210 Fast forward

284 The end bit

Across Europe, Stone-Age people build structures (**p20**) to celebrate or communicate with their gods.

The Minoans and Mycenaeans (**p42**) and the Phoenicians (**p44**) explore and trade in the Mediterranean, and beyond.

Hunter-gathers in the great plains of North America hunt mastodons and bison (**p14**).

The Olmec civilization in Mexico develops a form of writing (**p26**).

Early people (**p14**) make flint tools and decorate cave walls with paintings.

In the Americas, Australasia, most of Africa, Europe, and parts of Asia, most people still live as hunter-gatherers (**p14**) until about 3000 BCE.

How it all started

The beginning of the story – from the first rather rough humans to a bit of civilization.

While all the other chapters in this book together deal with about 3,000 years of history, this one covers an incredible 4.5 million years. It begins with "prehistory", the story, pieced together by archaeologists from human remains, of the evolution and survival of *Homo sapiens* – that's us! The first humans were nomads, but eventually they learned to farm and settled along the fertile land around great rivers. Then civilizations developed as people learned new skills, like writing. The invention of writing marks the beginning of true "history" – the story of the past told in the words of people alive at the time.

The farming life: Learning how to farm – especially with the help of inventions like the plough – means there's enough food for everyone, which gives people time to do other things, such as pottery, writing, maths, and more inventing.

New forms of transport: Boats open up new horizons for early people, and the invention of the wheel really gets trade rolling.

Art: As soon as people have time to do anything other than hunt, gather, or survive, they get arty, creating paintings and sculptures.

Belief systems: Even the earliest people seek to understand the world, in order to make it a slightly less scary place. All the first great civilizations have complex belief systems, with gods ruling over life and death.

Going up

People settle in the Fertile Crescent (**p18**), an arc of land that stretches from the Mediterranean up through Turkey and into modern Iraq.

Early people discover how to make tools, first of stone and later with metals – copper, bronze, and iron (**p22**).

The events in this chapter took place a very long time ago – so long ago that some dates may be followed by the letters "MYA", short for "million years ago". Other dates have "BCE" and "CE" after them. These are short for "before the Common Era" and "Common Era". The Common Era began with the birth of Jesus.

Empires battle it out in the Middle East (**p34**), and the Jewish people settle in Israel (**p46**).

The Shang and Zhou dynasties rule over Bronze-Age China (**p40**).

Farming and the first civilization begins in Mesopotamia (**p24**), on the land between the Tigris and Euphrates rivers.

Low sea levels mean that nomads are able to cross from Asia into America across a bridge of land called Beringia (**p16**).

A great civilization grows up along the banks of the River Nile (**p28**) in Egypt and lasts 3,000 years (**p30–33**).

Hinduism – the world's oldest religion – is formed as tribes from the north move into India (**p38**) and share their beliefs and ideas.

Our earliest human ancestors (**p10**), and later the first of our species, *Homo sapiens* (**p12**), evolve in East Africa and spread out across the globe (**p16**).

Large planned towns with wide, straight streets, are built by the people of the Indus Valley civilization (**p36**).

The first humans travel to Australia from Asia in small boats (**p16**).

Going down

Stone tools: The discovery of metals, such as copper, bronze, and iron, spells the beginning of the end for stone.

A solitary life: People discover that a crowd is good for hunting large prey and that living and working together in villages, towns, and even cities is much more fun.

Animal skins: This attire is never going to go completely out of fashion, particularly in cooler climes, but woven textiles offer a more sophisticated look.

Take me back to 4.5 million years ago and on to 601 BCE

UNUSUAL SUSPECTS

Who are the ancestors of modern humans? Clues lie in fossilized remains and stone tools that have been unearthed around the world. In 1859, English naturalist Charles Darwin published his theory that species evolve by "natural selection". This is the idea that living things best adapted to their environment tend to survive and pass on their features to their offspring, while those less well-adapted die out. Based on Darwin's work, scientists concluded that humans and apes share a common ancestor. If any of the early and pre-human suspects lined up here for identification look familiar, it's because our species, *Homo sapiens*, is related to them all.

ARDIPITHECUS RAMIDUS

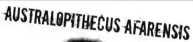

AUSTRALOPITHECUS AFARENSIS

HOMO HABILIS

Lived: 4.5–4.3 MYA
Location: Africa
Brain size: About 26per cent of modern human brain

Lived: 3–2.4 MYA
Location: Africa
Brain size: 34 per cent of modern human brain

Lived: 2.5–1.8 MYA
Location: Africa
Brain size: 41 per cent of modern human brain

Little is known about this very early forest-dwelling suspect, though his name means "ground ape at the root of human origins". Shares many characteristics with the

Do not be deceived by this petite 1-m- (3.3-ft-) tall suspect, nicknamed "Lucy". She may be working with a gang of taller male accomplices in Afar, Africa. Has short limbs and walks on

Suspect last spotted in Africa. Known in some circles as the "handy man", *Homo habilis* is thought to be the first species to make its own tools. Easily identified by his

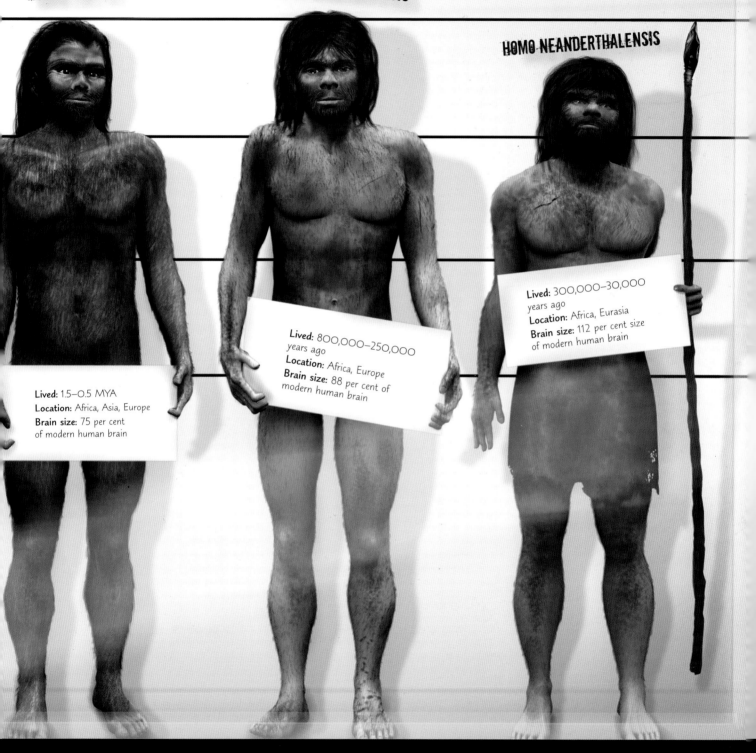

HOMO ERECTUS

HOMO HEIDELBERGENSIS

HOMO NEANDERTHALENSIS

Lived: 1.5–0.5 MYA
Location: Africa, Asia, Europe
Brain size: 75 per cent of modern human brain

Lived: 800,000–250,000 years ago
Location: Africa, Europe
Brain size: 88 per cent of modern human brain

Lived: 300,000–30,000 years ago
Location: Africa, Eurasia
Brain size: 112 per cent size of modern human brain

This suspect is recognizable by his large face, powerful build, and upright gait (from which he gets his name). Has strong limbs and a large brain, which may account for

First spotted in Heidelberg, Germany, this suspect may have connections with the *Homo neanderthalensis* Has a strong brow ridge and a very large brain. Is known

A cave dweller and an expert hunter, this suspect is thought to have lived alongside our species, *Homo sapiens*. Known to hang out in the Neander valley, Germany. Short and robust,

Quiz Just how Homo sapiens are YOU?

Worried about your protruding brow? Concerned your teeth are far too big? Prefer the greeting "URGH! URGH! HMMRGH!" to a simple "Hello"? Over the past 1.9 million years, there have been many types of human species swinging from our family tree, yet today just one remains. The prehistoric race for the survival of the fittest decided who was hot and who was not, with ape-like flat foreheads OUT, and the smaller, higher forehead IN. Today, an astonishing 100 per cent of people are Homo sapiens (wise man). Are you Homo sapiens? To find out, try this fun quiz.

Q1. BRAIN BOX

Your favourite aunt knits you a very smart hat for the coming winter. She reassures you that it's an average size. You:

- ☐ a. Slam Auntie a high-five. It's a perfect fit for your neat and rounded skull.

- ☐ b. Find it a very tight squeeze for your wide and sloping head, and not a flattering look with your prominent brow and big nose.

- ☐ c. Use it as a kneecap warmer. There's no way that tiny thing is going to fit your massive melon!

Q2. BODY BEAUTIFUL

Which of the following features do you consider most important for a thriving species?

- ☐ a. A low lingual bone in your throat. This is the one that makes sophisticated speech possible, so you can pass on helpful information, such as: "DON'T LOOK NOW, BUT THERE'S A SABRE-TOOTH TIGER CREEPING UP BEHIND YOU!"

- ☐ b. Loads and loads of hair... all the better for getting through a chilly Ice Age. Brrrrrrrr!

- ☐ c. Large jaws and teeth to chew the tougher bits of raw hippo hide. (Sadly, rare meat is your only menu option until you work out how to keep the fire from the last lightning strike burning.)

Q3.

FOOD, GLORIOUS FOOD!

It's dinner time and you have been wandering out in the wild, a long, long way from your nearest supermarket. To fill your growling belly, you:

- ☐ a. Creatively chisel a variety of scrapers, knives, and borers from flint to help you in your hunt for food.

- ☐ b. Choose a large stone and replicate the exact same pointed spear your ancestors made 250,000 years ago. Why mess with a classic, eh?

- ☐ c. Go scavenging for fresh kills made by lions and other predators. If you meet any competing carnivores, drive them away by throwing rocks, screaming, and beating your chest.

Q4.

ART AND CULTURE

Please complete the following sentence: "Art is...

- ☐ a. ...a highly imaginative way of thinking about the world, and even feelings, in terms of symbols." Go on, pass me that piece of charcoal and I'll draw you what I mean.

- ☐ b. ...you... repeat... question?"

- ☐ c. ...er?"

Q5.

ADAPTABILITY

The temperature has dropped, and you find yourself very chilly and in need of immediate shelter. You:

- ☐ a. Set up a working bee of relatives. Build a hut out of handy mammoth bones, cover it in animal skins for insulation, and sew yourselves a stylish wardrobe of matching fur cloaks.

- ☐ b. Run for the nearest cave and hide.

- ☐ c. Oh dear. This has never happened before. Um? Hmmmrgh!

ANSWERS:

Mostly As

Congratulations! You are one highly evolved human being. Like the rest of the world's human population, you too are a Homo sapiens. Rejoice in the knowledge that you are creative, adaptable, and probably not all that hairy.

Mostly Bs

Are you one of those 60,000-year-old Neanderthal dudes that scientific types keep finding frozen stiff in marshy swamps? You need to sharpen up, or that's where you'll end up.

Mostly Cs

You must be a really early human species. In fact, it's a wonder you're not extinct already. Sorry, but you're just not going to make it.

HUNTER-GATHERER
THEME PARK

The daily grind of roaming around, hunting wild animals and foraging for food can be a real drag. So why not gather up the tribe and head to the theme park? We've taken all the tedious chores you do every day and made them terrific fun.

MASTODON DRIVE
Test your hunting skills by driving a mastodon (big, hairy prehistoric elephant) round the path and into the swamp. Then, while it's stuck, finish it off with stones and flint spears. All beasts must be skinned on site.

WILD BERRY MAZE
Ladies, bring a basket and pick an assortment of wild berries, grasses, and low-growing fungi for a vitamin boost. Rest assured that no fruits or mushrooms in the maze are poisonous.

WOLF PETTING
Raised as orphan pups, our dogs have a howl worse than their bite. There's a big future for dogs as man's best friend, but please supervise small children closely.

HONEY TRAP
Calling all daredevils! If you can climb the tree, soothe the angry insects with smoke, and shove your hand into the nest, you'll get a taste of sweet liquid gold.

STORY CAVE

Gather round, listen, and learn as storytellers recount magical tales of creation. Flaming torches set the mood in the cave, and drawings by talented rock artists bring the stories to life.

SHELTER CHALLENGE

Fancy an upgrade from the leafy lean-tos you build time and time again? Using techniques pioneered in Siberia, experts show you how to create a cosy shelter with mammoth tusks, bones, and hides.

SPEAR-A-FISH

The lagoon brims with fish for the taking, but how good is your aim? All spears have barbs made of obsidian, the glassy rock that's the latest technology. Then pick up some tips for preserving your catch by smoking and drying.

GIFT SHOP

Looking for the perfect souvenir? We have animal-skull masks for the kids, flint in all shapes and sizes, and treated elk hides, ready to be stitched for clothing and home furnishings.

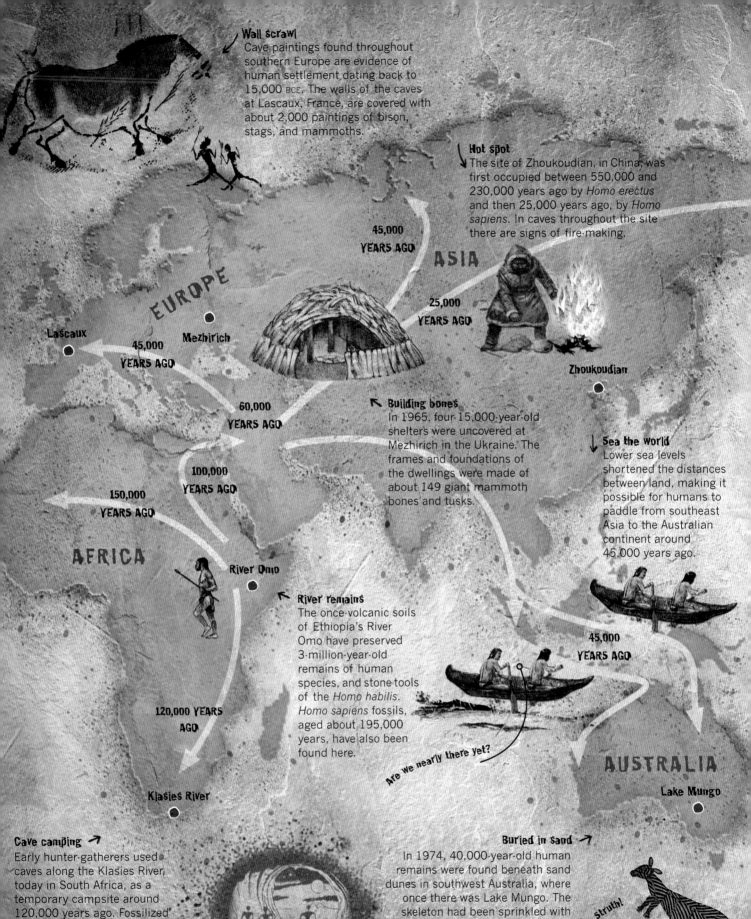

Wall scrawl
Cave paintings found throughout southern Europe are evidence of human settlement dating back to 15,000 BCE. The walls of the caves at Lascaux, France, are covered with about 2,000 paintings of bison, stags, and mammoths.

Hot spot
The site of Zhoukoudian, in China, was first occupied between 550,000 and 230,000 years ago by *Homo erectus* and then 25,000 years ago, by *Homo sapiens*. In caves throughout the site there are signs of fire-making.

45,000 YEARS AGO

ASIA

25,000 YEARS AGO

EUROPE

Lascaux

Mezhirich

45,000 YEARS AGO

60,000 YEARS AGO

Zhoukoudian

Building bones
In 1965, four 15,000-year-old shelters were uncovered at Mezhirich in the Ukraine. The frames and foundations of the dwellings were made of about 149 giant mammoth bones and tusks.

Sea the world
Lower sea levels shortened the distances between land, making it possible for humans to paddle from southeast Asia to the Australian continent around 45,000 years ago.

100,000 YEARS AGO

150,000 YEARS AGO

AFRICA

River Omo

River remains
The once-volcanic soils of Ethiopia's River Omo have preserved 3-million-year-old remains of human species, and stone tools of the *Homo habilis*. *Homo sapiens* fossils, aged about 195,000 years, have also been found here.

120,000 YEARS AGO

45,000 YEARS AGO

Are we nearly there yet?

AUSTRALIA

Lake Mungo

Klasies River

Cave camping
Early hunter-gatherers used caves along the Klasies River, today in South Africa, as a temporary campsite around 120,000 years ago. Fossilized remains suggest they feasted on shellfish, seals, penguins, antelope, and other humans.

Buried in sand
In 1974, 40,000-year-old human remains were found beneath sand dunes in southwest Australia, where once there was Lake Mungo. The skeleton had been sprinkled with powdered red rock, which suggests he was given a ritual burial – the earliest example of such a ceremony.

Struth!

Closer continents

A bridge of land, called Beringia, once connected what is now eastern Siberia with Alaska. It is thought that humans followed animals across the grassy plains, reaching the Americas about 15,000 years ago.

15,000 YEARS AGO

NORTH AMERICA

12,000 YEARS AGO

Game for anything

The people of Folsom (today in New Mexico) killed their prey with light stone blades. They hunted big game, such as bison, which they usually ambushed at watering holes.

Folsom

Clovis

Wish you were spear

Dating back to 11,500 BCE, the nomadic Clovis people are thought to be North America's earliest inhabitants. They developed fine leaf-shaped flints to spear mammoth, mastodon, and giant sloth species.

This really is life at the sharp end

12,500 YEARS AGO

SOUTH AMERICA

OUT of AFRICA

No one knows why our species, Homo sapiens, began to spread out of their original homeland in Africa, but the ability to master fire and craft hunting tools may have helped them on their journey. This map shows the migration of Homo sapiens across the world as lower sea levels made it possible for people to cross into new continents in search of food.

Going nuts

Remains of a 12,500 year old settlement in Monte Verde, central Chile, suggest that up to 30 people lived in a communal tent. They used stone tools to grind tough seeds and nuts.

I wish someone would hurry up and invent polyester

Monte Verde

WELCOME

Hunter-gatherers, it's time to settle down and put your feet up. Don't keep trudging around chasing after the next meal, discover the farming life! Be the envy of all your friends, build a permanent home, and produce food from your own plot in the glorious Fertile Crescent!

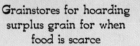

Grainstores for hoarding surplus grain for when food is scarce

TRY THE FARMING LIFE

Join dozens of other happy families in our small agricultural communities. Settle into the farming life with your own mudbrick hut, handy grainstores, and a corral (pen) for keeping your animals safe at night. You'll be surprised how quickly villages grow once there's enough food to feed a big family.

B-A-A-A

HARVEST CROPS

Grow tasty plants so you don't have to go looking for them. There's now a range of grasses cultivated to have bigger ears of seeds than ever seen before. Harvest the grains with cool new tools - we've flint-bladed antlers and wooden sickles.

TAME FLOCKS

Imagine having your own cows, goats, and sheep ready to milk or eat whenever you want. Discover new beasts that have been bred to be smaller and easier to handle than their wild cousins, and without those dangerous pointy horns.

to the FERTILE CRESCENT

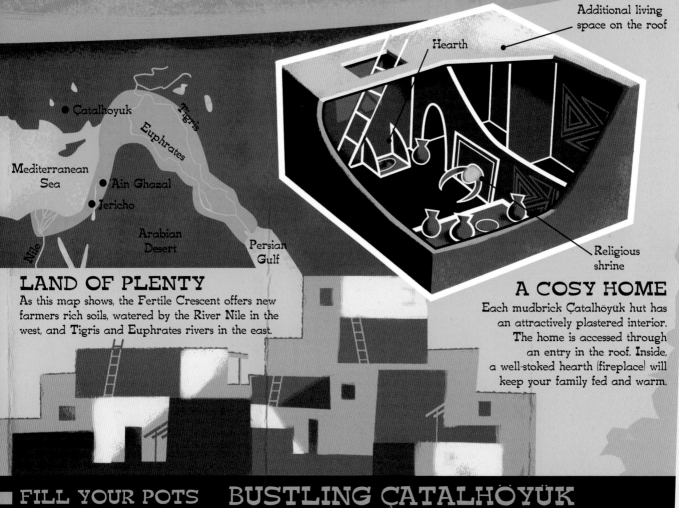

Additional living space on the roof

Hearth

Religious shrine

LAND OF PLENTY

As this map shows, the Fertile Crescent offers new farmers rich soils, watered by the River Nile in the west, and Tigris and Euphrates rivers in the east.

A COSY HOME

Each mudbrick Çatalhöyük hut has an attractively plastered interior. The home is accessed through an entry in the roof. Inside, a well-stoked hearth (fireplace) will keep your family fed and warm.

FILL YOUR POTS

BUSTLING ÇATALHÖYÜK

Farming women just love the convenience of pottery. Coil pots can be used to carry liquids, boil food, and store grain. Crafted from strips of soft clay, the pot is baked hard in a roaring fire.

If you prefer the hustle and bustle of a big city, why not move north to the settlement of Çatalhöyük (population 5,000)? Not everyone here needs to grow food all year round, so some farmers work part-time as potters, or become shamans (priest-like figures believed to have magic powers). Others trade obsidian - a black volcanic glass used to make cutting tools. Discuss it with your family - the choice is yours.

BUILDING BIG

It's the Neolithic ("new stone") Age. Farming is taking off, and stone is big. You're head of the tribe, and have weapons, tools, and all the animal skins you can wear. What's left to do? How about building something monumental to make your mark? Or designing an impressive tomb, so you won't be forgotten? Check out these hot properties across Neolithic Europe for ideas.

For maximum effect, Stonehenge rises out of a plain (a level landscape)

PILLARS OF SOCIETY

Special "standing stones" are extremely popular, and one of the finest examples is the stone circle at Stonehenge, with picturesque views of Wiltshire, England. Sturdily built, the ditch and bank date from 2950 BCE, with construction completed by about 2500 BCE. Not only is Stonehenge a great place for Sun worship, but each gigantic stone can be dedicated to a dead ancestor.

Outer circle of stones

Blocks were probably moved on wooden rollers, and raised with ropes and posts

Inner horseshoe of trilithons

BIRD'S EYE VIEW
Five trilithons (two upright stones with one on top) make a horseshoe, encircled by 80 blocks. Sunlight pours into the centre at midwinter sunset and midsummer sunrise.

Sunlight shines through these two stones and into the circle

HEAVY WORK
Construction of a stone circle should not be undertaken lightly. The blocks at Stonehenge weigh up to 45 tonnes. A first set of blue sandstone blocks from Wales, 385 km (240 miles) away, was later replaced with grey sandstone blocks from a quarry 30 km (19 miles) away.

All the stones, including the "Giant" were hewn from local rock

STONES IN ROWS
If you prefer stones in lines to circles, visit Carnac, France, where about 3,000 stones were arranged in orderly rows some time between 4500 and 3300 BCE. Why lines, and why so many stones? Who knows? Keep them guessing.

SEEN FROM THE SKY
There are three major alignments (groups of lines) in the Carnac area, at sites in Menec, Kermario, and Kerlescan. An aerial view of some of the stones at Kerlescan shows an attractive pattern of straight lines.

Standing stones at Menec

MIGHTY MENHIR
If you haven't got a big budget, why not go for a single stone, or menhir. Looming over the Kerlescan alignment, the "Giant" is a whopping 6.5 m (21.3 ft).

PASSAGE GRAVE

Looking for something special in the Irish countryside? Dating back to 3200 BCE, Newgrange is a grassy mound with a secret. Inside, a 19-m- (62-ft-) long passageway leads to a cross-shaped inner burial chamber.

From the mound, ancestors watch over the land

A cross-section view through the grave shows the passage

Grassy mound

Bones are placed in the inner chamber

GRASS AND STONE

Newgrange's turf-covered mound stretches 76 m (250 ft) across and is 12 m (40 ft) high. Ninety-seven large stones surround the structure, supporting an outer wall. Inside, the roof of the burial chamber rises 6 m (20 ft).

HIDDEN SECRETS

An overhead cross-section view reveals the passage is shaped like a cross. To ensure the Sun returns to shine for another year, a ceremony is held here at dawn on the winter solstice (the shortest day of the year), as sunlight floods into the inner chamber.

Inner chamber

Light passes through a hole in the stones

LAKE LIFE

Perhaps you're sick of stone and fancy a lakeside residence? The Dispilio lakeside village has a number of wooden dwellings dating from 5260 BCE. This delightful Greek settlement is ideally located for a buyer interested in fishing, hunting, and agriculture.

TIMBER HUT

Each hut is built of local timber. A communal fire, protected by an earth cover, meets all your outdoor kitchen needs.

Fish from your own hut on the lake shore

ISLAND PARADISE

The Dispilio community is located on the southern shore of Lake Kastoria. All the dwellings are built on an artificial island connected by wooden walkways. Residents share use of simple canoes, made of hollowed-out tree trunks.

Overhead view showing the layout of the six huts – only two still available!

Copper

Raise your fists in the air for the copper axe! Around 5000 BCE, parts and people in the Middle East began making lumps of copper ore (green metal malachite) in kilns at high temperatures. The liquid metal was poured into moulds to make tools and weapons.

Copper Axe

BRONZE FOR BATTLE

BRONZE FOR BATTLE
Bronze-heads in Anatolia, (modern-day) by metal, sang in the Bronze Age (2000 BCE to 900 BCE) by Turkey, mixing 90 per cent copper with 10 per cent tin. This strong alloy was cast in clay moulds to create weapons and tools. Bronze was an armour. Bronze battle tool as easily effective didn't blunt as it as copper.

TMB CONCERTS PRESENTS:
HEAVY METALS

Dude, if you thought the stone age rocked, things got even heavier when early metal was swept the world at bronze! The world at 7000 BCE, began metal and iron times. Around Turkey, copper different fans in Çatalhöyük, from ore metal-bangers in jewellery, much brainier crafting simple centuries later, metal from down nuggets. metal-heads extracted. Head down (mineral as we count hits! unite as metal's greatest hits!

SILVER AND GOLD

By 5000 BCE, gold was a symbol of rich metal dudes. A grave discovered in Varna, Bulgaria, contained 1,000 golden rings and beads. By 3000 BCE, silver was mined in Asia Minor (modern-day Turkey). It was probably the first metal to be minted as coins.

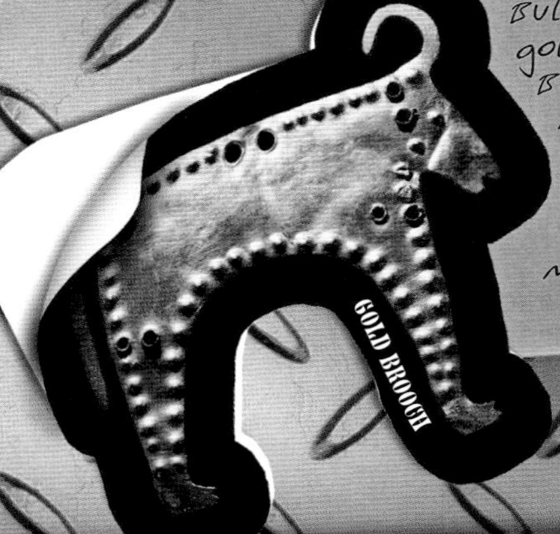

Gold
Coins

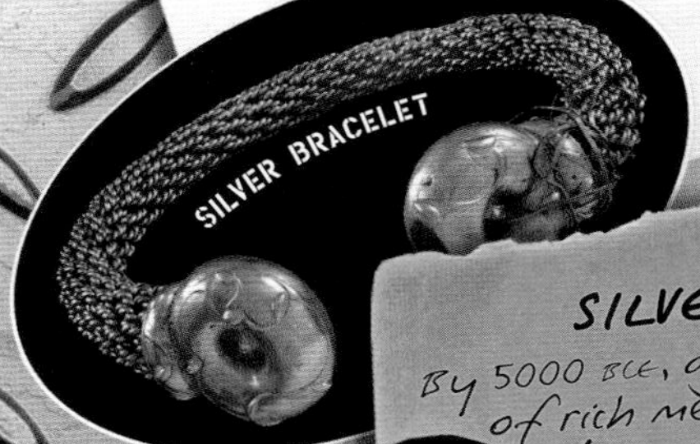

SILVER BRACELET

GOLD BROOCH

SECTION
ROW/BOX SEAT
SEAT

IRON

Metal got seriously heavy when iron-making spread between 1550 BCE and 700 BCE. Iron ore called ore and then was forged (hammered) by a metalworker called a smith. The smith heated the ore and then beat it over a large block called an anvil. After repeated heating, beating, and cooling, the iron piece eventually took shape.

THE BRONZE BEAUTIES

2000 BCE EUROPEAN TOUR

BRONZE BLING

When the Iron Age dawned, bronze lost its hardcore status in warfare and became a decorative metal used for sculptures, jewellery, buckles, and hair accessories. Other uses of bronze were later made in moulded vessels (such as cups or jars), tiles, and sewing needles.

MESOPOTAMIA

Settle down, class. Today we're looking at the world's first civilized people, the Mesopotamians. "Civilized" means "with a high level of cultural and technological development", so listen and learn. Between 4000 and 3000 BCE, these farming folk settled in villages, which grew into towns and then the first-ever cities.

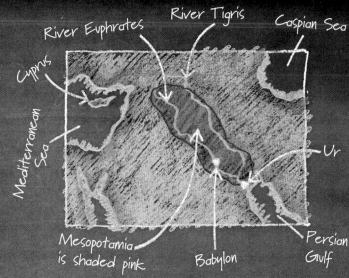

River Euphrates · River Tigris · Caspian Sea · Cyprus · Mediterranean Sea · Ur · Mesopotamia is shaded pink · Babylon · Persian Gulf

THE FIRST KINGS

Each city had a god, and a king ruled on the god's behalf – possibly the first kings in history. Priests were also powerful because they were believed to communicate with the gods.

A king was always shown really big

Priest

WHERE WAS MESOPOTAMIA?

Known as the "land between two rivers", Mesopotamia lay between the Tigris and Euphrates – today largely in Iraq. Good rainfall meant fertile soils in the north, while annual floods watered the dry southern plains.

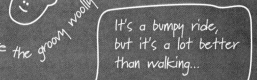

I like the groovy woolly skirts

It's a bumpy ride, but it's a lot better than walking...

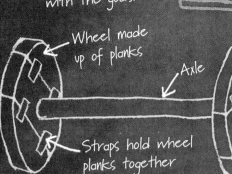

Wheel made up of planks

Axle

Pin secures axle to the wheel

Straps hold wheel planks together

INVENTING THE WHEEL

Things really got rolling when the Mesopotamians invented the wheel around 3200 BCE. Until then, people relied on sledges and log rollers to drag heavy goods. The wheel, together with the earliest carts, revolutionized transport and trade.

Wheel shape reduces friction

Staircases up three huge steps led to the temple at the top

WHAT'S A ZIGGURAT?

By 2000 BCE, all the big Mesopotamian cities had built their god a massive mudbrick temple, called a ziggurat. This ziggurat was dedicated to Nanna, the Moon god of the city of Ur.

Do you think he knows what he's doing?

B

A

C

THE PLOUGH

The Mesopotamians domesticated oxen to carry out farm work, and made the first simple plough to till the soil. They also invented the seeder plough, which helped them seed and plough at the same time.

TRICKY MATHS

You can thank the Mesopotamians for mind-boggling algebra. They invented it to solve complex problems, such as how many people were needed to build a canal on time. They also divided hours into minutes and seconds, and circles into 360 degrees.

WRITING

Scribes were highly valued for their record-keeping skills. Using simple pictures and signs (pictograms) at first, they recorded basic information about crops on clay tablets. Later, a script called cuneiform was developed to record trade, taxes, astronomy, and literature.

← Wild asses pulled chariots and carts

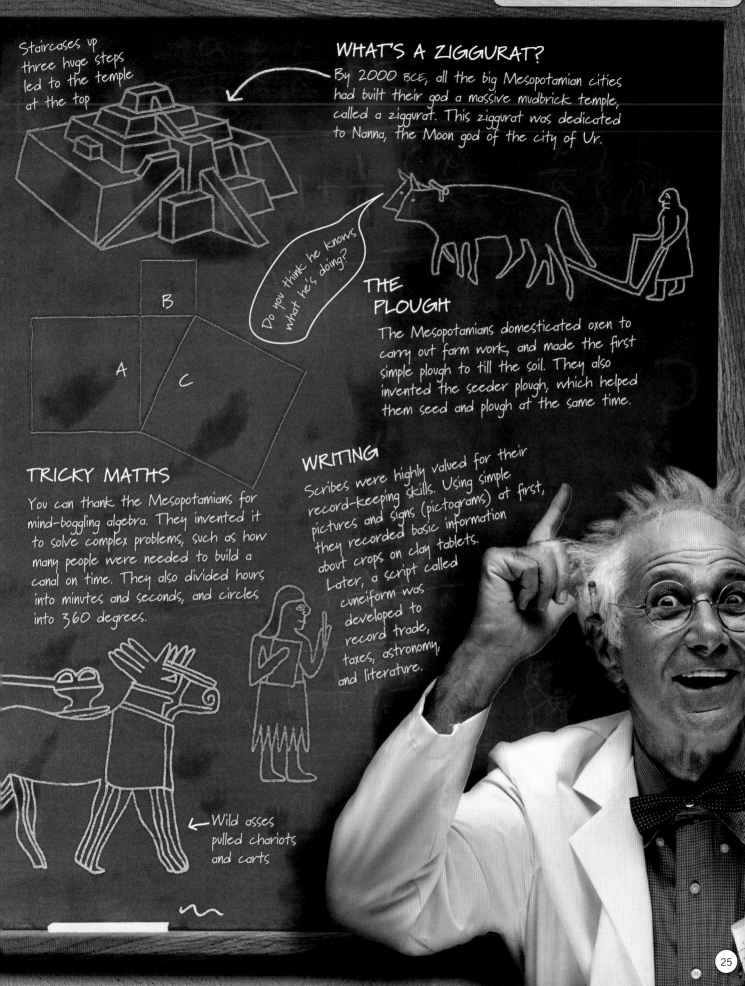

Voices from the past

The editor of this newspaper has received a heavy postbag in response to Tuesday's article, *The writing on the wall*, about how "history" officially begins with the invention of writing, which allows us to hear voices speak to us from the past. Some ancient readers were annoyed that their writing systems had been misunderstood, so today's *Letters to the Editor* gives them the opportunity to answer back.

The first and the best?

Sir, Your article suggested that writing has "evolved" since Ancient Egyptian hieroglyphs. I am not so sure. Other scripts may be quicker to write, but I do not feel they can match the sheer beauty of hieroglyphs. More than 2,000 symbols for objects, sounds, and ideas – this is the script of a truly great civilization. OK, so only a handful of people can read or write them, but are you going to decorate your tomb with drab Phoenician scribble? I don't think so.
Tasteful of Thebes

Counting sheep

Sir, As a Mesopotamian farmer living near Ur, I would like to tell your readers how cuneiform script has changed my life. Before the blunt reed and clay tablet, I found it impossible to keep track of sales and orders for sheep and barley. Now, when I go to market, I pay a scribe to record the day's business in pictograms (picture signs). My wife is not happy about the number of tablets mounting up at home, but even she admits that the farm is running much more smoothly.
Enthusiastic of Ur

Simply misunderstood

Sir, I wish to clear the air here. In your recent article about the story of writing, the author dismissed my culture's brief and elegant text as indecipherable! It could not be more simple. In the Indus Valley, we combine signs and pictures, reading from right to left. We might not have lengthy text, but our script of hundreds of different signs has served our civilization well, labelling seals, pottery, and copper wares. I would suggest that the problem lies with the limited brainpower of your reporter, not with the script.
Indignant of the Indus Valley (Pakistan)

"Cuneiform script has changed my life"

EGYPTIAN HIEROGLYPHS, FROM 3200 BCE

CUNEIFORM SCRIPT, FROM 3100 BCE

INDUS VALLEY SCRIPT, FROM 2600 BCE

History begins in the library

Heaven and Earth

Sir, Much in the way that oracle bone script communicates between heaven and Earth, I am writing to you from China. I had considered etching the shoulder blade of an ox, but thought this turtle shell had more room for my pictograms. I felt that your article did not explain the purpose of our script. I'm sure your readers would be interested to know that we write questions to the gods on ox bones and turtle shells, and then burn them. A priest studies the cracks that appear to give the gods' reply.

Chatty of China

An international alphabet

Sir, It will take all 22 letters of my alphabet to say how much I enjoyed your article on the key role of the Phoenician alphabet in the development of writing. The potential of a system of signs to represent sounds, may seem obvious now, but it was the Phoenicians who really made it work. I don't like to brag, but so many scripts, such as Arabic and Hebrew, are descended from the Phoenician alphabet, we deserve proper recognition.

Proud of Carthage

Olmec outrage

Sir, I was outraged at your reporter's suggestion that the civilizations of Central and South America were slow to take up writing. If he had done his research properly, your reporter would have discovered that we Olmec have a symbolic script, which we believe to be the first in this area of the Americas. Rock is pretty rare in these parts, so we often inscribe on less permanent materials, like wood. However, just because there is little evidence of our script does not mean it did not exist. I would recommend your reporter take a trip to Cascajal, near San Lorenzo, where I know they have been working in stone since 900 BCE. Ha!

Miffed of Mexico

We regret we cannot return any clay tablets, papyrus scrolls, stones, bones, or shells.

CHINESE ORACLE BONE SCRIPT, FROM C1500 BCE

PHOENICIAN ALPHABET, FROM 1050 BCE

OLMEC SCRIPT, FROM 900 BCE

Kingdom of the Nile

Five thousand years ago, the great civilization of Ancient Egypt grew up out of a desert. Through the parched land snaked the longest river on Earth – the Nile. Each year the river flooded to deposit fertile soil along the banks where people were able to grow enough food to support craftsmen, soldiers, priests, and powerful kings, called pharaohs. The first period of the Ancient Egyptian civilization, when the pyramids were built, is known as the Old Kingdom. It was a time of peace and prosperity, and the Nile affected every aspect of life and death.

Lower Egypt

Giza •
Memphis •

Great pyramid for Khufu

Not quite so great pyramids on either side, for his successors

AN AWESOME TOMB

One of the biggest inventions of the Old Kingdom was the pyramid – a vast tomb fit for a pharaoh. The biggest of them all was the Great Pyramid of Pharaoh Khufu at Giza, overlooking the Nile. It is made up of more than 2 million limestone blocks, each weighing between 2 and 70 tonnes, and took about 20 years to build. Inside is a passage leading to a burial chamber where the pharaoh was buried with everything he needed in the afterlife.

MAN, GOD, OR BIRD?

The life-giving annual flooding of the Nile led the Egyptians to believe that the world was ordered by gods. There were many different gods, and the first pharaohs were thought to be a living version of the god Horus – a god with the head of a hawk.

THE FIRST PHARAOH

Early Egypt was divided into two kingdoms. The ruler of Upper Egypt in the south wore a red crown; the ruler of Lower Egypt in the north wore a white crown. Around 3000 BCE, King Narmer united the two kingdoms. He got to wear a double crown, plus he was the first to go by the grand title of pharaoh.

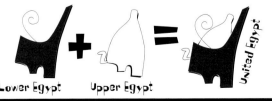

Lower Egypt   Upper Egypt   United Egypt

INTERNATIONAL TRADE

Trade with Africa and across the Mediterranean made Egypt rich. They swapped grain, gold, linen, and papyrus for copper, silver, olive oil, wood, and a precious perfume called incense. Over land, the transport was by donkey, so the Nile route was usually quicker!

NILE FACTS

〜〜 The Nile is 6,825 km (4,100 miles) long.

〜〜 63 per cent of the inhabited area of Egypt lay in the Nile delta (where the river splits to meet the sea).

〜〜 In the dry season it took two months to sail from Thebes to Memphis, but on the fast flood-waters it took just two weeks.

〜〜 Along the river, carved rocks or posts, called nilometers, were used to measure the flood levels closely.

THE EGYPTIAN YEAR

There were three seasons in the Egyptian year, based on the cycle of the Nile. The first was Akhet, the season of flood, when water rushed down from the highlands to submerge the farmland. When the waters retreated they left behind a layer of rich mud.

Next was Peret, the season of planting and growth, when the farmers got busy preparing the soil, sowing seeds, and digging ditches to hold the remaining floodwater.

Finally, there was Shemu, the season of harvest and drought, when everyone worked hard to bring in the crops, with the help of nifty tools, such as sickles, seen in action here.

WONDER PLANT

In the marshes grew a reed called papyrus. This was an incredibly valuable and versatile plant, because wood was very scarce. The stalks were used for making boats, paper, pens, mattresses, furniture, mats, baskets, sandals, and rope, just for starters. The root was used for food, medicine, and perfume.

RIVER WILDLIFE

The Nile was full of life, some good, some not so good. Tasty fish and river birds were the good news, but only the rich got to eat them. To be avoided were the crocodiles, known to attack cattle as they drank at the water's edge and even women washing clothes in the river. Hippos usually left people alone but often trampled crops – and who was going to stop them?

GETTING AROUND

The Nile was like a motorway leading from one end of Egypt to the other, and the only way to get around was by boat. River traffic included wealthy traders in large wooden sailing ships, fishermen in reed boats, and barges transporting stone for building pyramids. And of course the only way to reach the afterlife and the Kingdom of the Dead was a boat trip to transport your mummified body across the Nile.

• Thebes

Upper Egypt

EGYPT

THE NEW KINGDOM

Egypt gained great wealth and political influence at the height of the New Kingdom (1569–1069 BCE). It was a time of lavish art and architecture, as extravagant pharaohs built temples and monuments to celebrate themselves and their gods. After their deaths, pharaohs were buried in tombs at the Valley of the Kings in Thebes. The empire seemed untouchable.

NOW SHOWING

US EGYPTIANS SURE KNOW HOW TO MAKE AN EXHIBITION OF OURSELVES!

PHARAOH
SUPREME RULER OF MIGHTY EGYPT

EGYPTIAN PHARAOHS WERE REGARDED AS GOD-LIKE. THEY HAD TOTAL CONTROL OVER ALL THE LAND. THOUGH HIS GOLDEN MASK IS A FAMOUS SYMBOL OF EGYPT, TUTANKHAMUN WAS A MINOR PHARAOH. THE TREASURES REVEALED WHEN HIS TOMB WAS OPENED IN 1922 ONLY HINT AT THE RICHES THE MORE POWERFUL PHARAOHS MUST HAVE ENJOYED.

THE GOLDEN DEATH MASK OF EGYPT'S BOY KING

UNMISSABLE
THE ORIGINAL GLAMOUR QUEENS

QUEENS OF EGYPT

NEFERTITI (1370 BCE – 1330 BCE)

IF PHARAOHS WERE SYMBOLS OF NEW KINGDOM GLAMOUR, THEIR QUEENS WERE EVEN MORE SO! QUEEN NEFERTITI, WIFE OF AKHENATEN, IS OFTEN SHOWN IN WARRIOR-LIKE POSES BESIDE THE PHARAOH. QUEEN HATSHEPSUT WAS A FEMALE PHARAOH. SHE RULED FOR 22 YEARS.

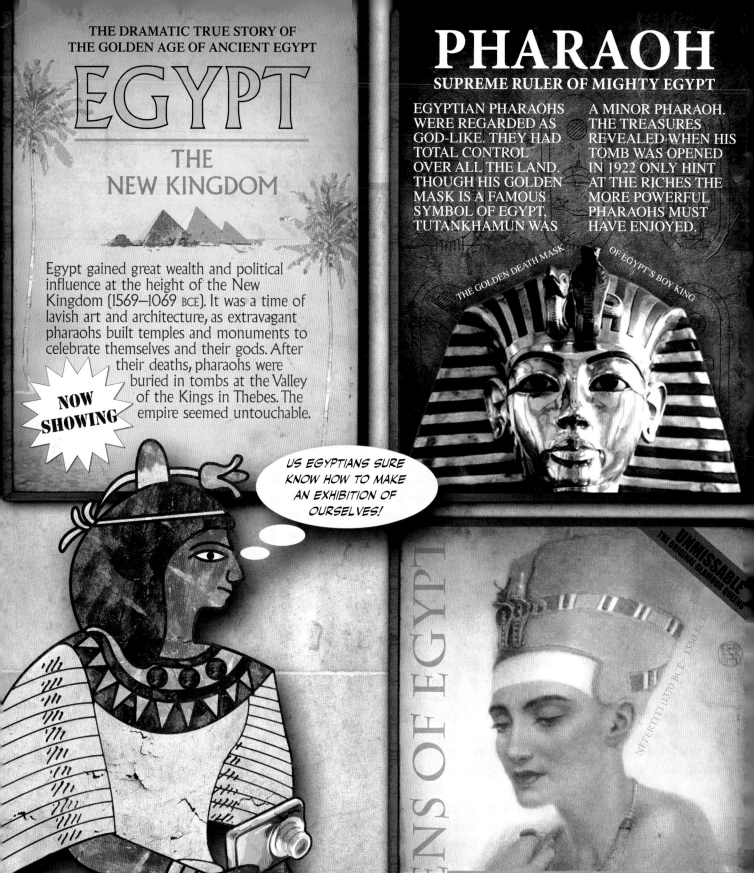

REALM OF THE GODS

CONTROLLING LIFE, DEATH, AND LIFE AFTER DEATH

OSIRIS   HORUS   ANUBIS

The Ancient Egyptians honoured many gods, including Osiris (god of the underworld), Horus (patron of the Sun and sky), and Anubis (protector of the dead). In the New Kingdom, the Sun god Amun-Ra was worshipped as the king of the gods. Pharaohs often called themselves "sons of Ra".

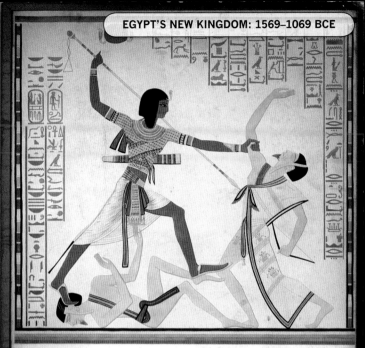

EMPIRE

Rameses II (1279–1213 BCE) was the greatest pharaoh of the New Kingdom, exercising tight control over his lands. Throughout the Middle East he was respected as a diplomat and feared for his military might. Rameses was a fearless warrior, dead set on expanding his empire. This mural from Abu Simbel shows him in combat.

THE BACKBONE OF THE NEW NATION
POWER OF THE PEOPLE

WITH NEW TRADE LINKS AND GREAT WEALTH, LIFE IMPROVED FOR ORDINARY EGYPTIANS. TECHNOLOGY HELPED FARMERS TO CHANNEL WATER INTO DRY AREAS. SCRIBES MEASURED THE FIELDS WITH ROPE TO ASSESS HOW MUCH GRAIN WAS DUE AS TAX.

BUILDING FOR ETERNITY

Abu Simbel was carved into a mountainside on the west bank of the River Nile. Rameses II built the twin rock temples to honour himself, his wife, and the gods. The monumental entrance to the Greater Temple displays four 20-m (66-ft) seated statues of Rameses, with a frieze of 22 baboons worshipping the rising Sun.

BONUS POINTS

THE FINAL TEST

Anubis, the dog-headed protector of the dead, leads the pharaoh on to the final stage of the challenge. His heart will be placed on one side of the scales of justice. On the other side sits the feather of truth. Will his heart be pure and light, or heavy with bad deeds?

JUDGEMENT DAY

Thoth, the Ibis-headed god, and chief scribe, oversees the weighing ceremony. What is the pharaoh's fate? If his heart is as light as a feather, and the scales balance, go straight to the Kingdom of Osiris. If his heart is too heavy, it's a trip to the Devourer of the Dead, and a sticky end.

TESTED BY THE GODS

Gods also challenge the pharaoh along the way. Here, the lion-headed god Sekhmet delivers a tough quiz. Has your pharaoh been a good student? Does he know right from wrong? He can only move up to the final level if he gets the answers right.

egyptian afterlife

GAME ON. An Ancient Egyptian pharaoh has died, but this doesn't mean the end... it's the beginning of the afterlife, and his fate lies in your hands. With danger lurking at every turn, can you lead the pharaoh through the different levels of the underworld to the ultimate goal – eternal life in the Kingdom of Osiris, god of the dead? Or will it be **GAME OVER** as he meets a grisly end in the jaws of the Devourer of the Dead?

MUMMIFICATION

Take the pharaoh to a tent of purification. Preserve his organs in canopic jars, then dry the corpse in salt for 40 days and stuff with sawdust. Perfume the body, and fill wounds with wax. Seal with molten resin, and bandage with fine cloth. Don't forget amulets (protective charms)!

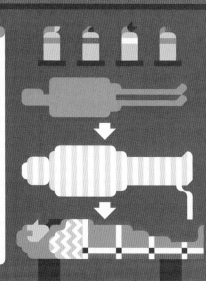

KINGDOM OF OSIRIS

Well done! You have safely led the pharaoh to the Kingdom of Osiris. He has been judged worthy of eternal life in the universe of the gods.

GAME OVER

DEVOURER OF THE DEAD

Bad news. The feather of truth has deemed the pharaoh's heart to be heavy with sin. His heart is thrown to Ammut, a creature part lion, crocodile, and hippopotamus, and all of them hungry.

GAME DEFINITELY OVER

BOOK OF THE DEAD

To pass safely across the lake of fire, and the demons, serpents, and crocodiles trying to thwart him, the pharaoh must chant hymns, recite spells, and follow carefully all instructions written in the "Book of the Dead".

ALIVE AGAIN

The pharaoh emerges alive in the underworld, home of terrifying monsters and dangerous beasts. He will not survive without powerful magic. Go back a level if you didn't bury the "Book of the Dead", his book of spells, in the tomb.

FUNERAL BARGE

The pharaoh is now a mummy. Cover his face with a death mask and place the coffin on a funeral barge. Sail along the River Nile, while priests waft incense and shake sistrums (rattles) and women wail.

INTO THE TOMB

Place the mummy in a tomb. To ensure his comfort in the afterlife, furnish the tomb with gold, jewels, slaves, food, furniture, clothing, wigs, perfumes, and all luxuries befitting a pharaoh.

BONUS POINTS

SARGON STATISTICS BOX

TITLE: KING OF AKKAD

DATES: 2296–2240 BCE

FIGHTS: RULER OF THE FIRST EMPIRE IN HISTORY

"Mighty Sargon, a legend in the Middle East, is surely the favourite to win tonight. He came from nowhere – they say that as a baby his mother set him adrift on the river in a basket. But he was rescued and raised in the royal court, and began fighting his way to the top.

"Ouch! He's slugged Nebuchadnezzar with a powerful left hook.

"This is the guy that built himself a city at Akkad, on the River Euphrates in Mesopotamia, and then conquered the surrounding lands until the Akkadian Empire stretched from the Mediterranean Sea in the west to the Persian Gulf in the east.

"The crowd's going wild! Sargon's got his opponent up against the ropes. No wonder this guy held onto his empire to the end and passed it onto his sons. I think he's going to hold on to this heavyweight title too."

TAKE THAT!

BLUE CORNER

"Get ready to rumble! This unique event brings two former kings back from the dead, to fight for the title of heavyweight emperor of the Middle East. In the blue corner is Sargon of Akkad, mighty emperor of Mesopotamia, and in the red corner is Nebuchadnezzar II, crushing king of Babylon."

SOK!!

UNHHH--!

NEBUCHADNEZZAR STATISTICS BOX

TITLE: CHALDEAN DYNASTY, KING OF BABYLONIA

DATES: 605–561 BCE

FIGHTS: DEFEATED EGYPTIANS AND CAPTURED JERUSALEM

RED CORNER

"You shouldn't write off the battling Babylonian yet. He's a fighter and a schemer, and isn't afraid of playing dirty.

"The Babylonians took over in the Middle East after two centuries of Assyrian domination. While the Assyrians squabbled, the Babylonians moved in. Big Neb carried on the good work, defeating the Egyptians, invading Judea, capturing Jerusalem in 597 BCE, and rebuilding the city of Babylon to its former glory.

"Aiieeh! He's taking a pasting. Let's hope the brutal Sargon doesn't ruin the Babylonian's good looks. The ladies want Neb to win. What girl wouldn't swoon for a man who built his foreign wife the Hanging Gardens of Babylon – one of the Seven Wonders of the Ancient World – to remind her of home.

"He's down! But look, he's getting up and smiling at the crowd. The fight's not over yet!"

Great civilizations website of the year 2044 BCE

INDUSVALLEY ONLINE

" Once you've shopped in Mohenjo-daro you'll never shop anywhere else. "
Harappan Housekeeping   **click here to send your views**

INDUS ART
Visit the famous River Gallery in Mohenjo-daro to see examples of the finest Indus art, such as this statue, called the "Priest King".

A TRIP TO TOWN

Welcome to Indus Valley Online, the Internet home of southern Asia's first great civilization. This region's hottest spots are its cities, and our roving guides have been on the streets to help you make the most of your next trip to town. There are so many great cities to choose from – cosmopolitan Mohenjo-daro (our largest city), busy Harappa, or magnificent, fortified Dholavira – there's something for everyone in the ancient Indus Valley.

find a town

useful information

+

- Don't come shopping for weapons here, you won't find any. We're a peace-loving people and don't even have an army.
- Ours is the first civilization to develop precise weights and measures, so you'll get all you pay for in the shops.
- If you're planning to settle in the region and build a home, don't forget all bricks must be of the uniform shape and size.

more

useful information

−

key Indus dates

+

- ⌄ **7000 BCE** Farming begins in the area of modern-day Pakistan and northwest India.
- ⌄ **3300 BCE** The village of Mohenjo-daro is settled on the banks of the Indus River.
- ⌄ **2800 BCE** The Indus people develop their own form of writing.
- ⌄ **2600–1900 BCE** Height of Indus Valley civilization. Cities become great centres of craft and trade.
- ⌄ **1700 BCE** Indus Valley civilization mysteriously declines – theories include possible flooding, invasion, earthquake, or disease.

more

INDUS VALLEY

River Indus

Harappa

Dholavira

Mohenjo-daro

ASIA

Indus Valley civilization

LIFE ON THE FLOODPLAIN

Our civilization thrives along the Indus River, which floods each year to produce rich silt for the surrounding farmland. After harvest, wheat, barley, and rice are stored in the cities before distribution throughout the valley.

MOHENJO-DARO

BUILT TO PLAN

Mohenjo-daro (population 40,000) is the pride of the Indus Valley. It's a prosperous city that has thrived on trade along the river. With modern baked-brick architecture, our town planners – possibly the first in the world – have designed an elegant grid of streets and sweeping avenues 10 m (33 ft) wide.

MOHENJO-DARO STREET BY STREET

UPPER AND LOWER TOWNS

There are two parts to Mohenjo-daro. The upper town, or citadel, is the centre of government and religion. Surrounded by high walls and built on a mound, the citadel looks over the lower town, where people live. It's easy to find your way round the lower town, with houses laid out in orderly blocks off the main streets.

CLEAN STREETS

Mohenjo-daro prides itself on its clean streets. Floodwater and rain drain away through brick channels, while fresh water is found in wells protected by high walls.

UPPER TOWN

LOWER TOWN

First Street

POTTERY PARADISE

Looking for a souvenir from your visit to the Indus Valley? The terracotta (clay) figurines from Pottery Paradise are the ideal keepsake. This female figure is a charming memento of the best of Indus fashion, with belt, necklaces, and stunning fan-shaped headdress.

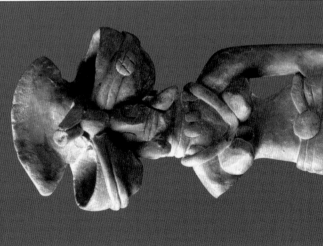

WRITERS' CENTRE

Having trouble making sense of script? Drop by our friendly Writers' Centre for help decoding the mysterious Indus Valley script. With more than 400 signs to choose from, you'll soon be writing on your own steatite (soft stone) seal, which will then be baked while you wait. There's a wide range of seal pictures for you to choose from, including the ever popular unicorn.

click here for more info

○ THE TEMPLE

⭐⭐⭐ The dome of the stupa, or Buddhist temple, is a later addition to the sights of the citadel, and dates from the 2nd century CE. It was built by one of the local cultures that emerged after the mysterious disappearance of the Indus people about 1700 BCE. Well worth a visit for the wonderful views across the city.

○ THE GREAT BATH

⭐⭐⭐⭐⭐ No one should leave Mohenjo-daro without seeing the Great Bath. At 12 m (39 ft) long and 7 m (23 ft) wide, it plunges 2.5 m (8 ft) deep and is completely watertight. On special days, watch priests preside over sacred bathing ceremonies here. Check our website for ceremony dates.

HORIZON TRAVEL

Do you ever wonder what lies over the horizon for your business? Well now you can find out. Visit our offices on First Street and we'll discuss the trips we offer on long-distance ships travelling across the Indian Ocean. Don't stay at home – discover fantastic trading opportunities in such exotic locations as Mesopotamia, Iran, and Afghanistan.

HINDU RELIGION

Hindus believe in a cycle of birth, death, and rebirth governed by karma (the good and bad deeds a person performed in past lives). Many devas (gods) and devis (goddesses) are worshipped, with each person praying to the deity they find most useful. A farmer, for example, might pray to Shiva, lord of the beasts. These deities include Brahma (top left), Shiva (top right), Vishnu (centre), Krishna (bottom left), and Rama (bottom right).

5 HOLY RIVER
Hindus worshipped in temples, but also believed other places were sacred. The River Ganges is very important in the Hindu religion. Believers worship it as a goddess and bathe in it to cleanse themselves of sin. The Kumbh Mela festival, when millions go to bathe there, has its roots in Vedic legend.

6 SACRED WRITING
The Vedas are the earliest Hindu texts. Hindus believe they were dictated to scribes by the gods. For many generations, the Vedas were passed down through Hindu families as stories. The most ancient Veda, the Rig Veda, dates back to 1200 BCE and contains 1,028 hymns.

1 ARYANS INVADE
The Aryans came from the steppes (grassy plains) of central Asia. They invaded Persia and then pushed on to settle in the Indus Valley. Their religious texts, the Vedas, are the earliest basis of Hinduism, and the warlike gods they tell of reflect the Aryans' warrior culture.

2 WARRIOR TRIBES
The earliest period of Aryan settlement in India (1500–1000 BCE) is named after the Rig Veda, the holiest Vedic text. In this period, society was organized into small tribes called *jana*, each headed by a warrior chief, and Vedic civilization completely replaced the earlier culture of the Indus Valley.

HINDU INDIA

Hinduism is the world's oldest religion. It developed from about 1500 BCE by the River Indus in what is now Pakistan, when a group of nomadic warriors from central Asia settled in the Indus Valley. These warlike people called themselves Aryans, meaning "nobles". They brought with them a belief in many gods, ruled over by supreme god Indra, and are referred to as the Vedic civilization after their sacred literature, the Vedas. Over the centuries their religion evolved into the Hindu faith.

7 THE EPICS

As well as the sacred Vedas, moral tales are important to Hindus. Written between 500 BCE and 100 BCE, the Mahabharata and the Ramayana are stories that praise the gods as central to human life, and remind worshippers that good ultimately triumphs over evil.

8 SANSKRIT

The language of the Hindu religion, Sanskrit, is one of the oldest languages still in use today. It dates back to around 1500 BCE, and the Vedas were written in an ancient form of the sacred script. Although Sanskrit is one of India's 23 official languages, it is no longer spoken.

3 FARMING THE LAND

From 1000 to 500 BCE, the Vedic civilization spread across northern India to the fertile lands by the River Ganges. The nomads turned to farming and the nature of their religion began to change. Priests came to dominate society and rituals were introduced that controlled all aspects of people's lives.

4 CLASS SYSTEM

By 1000 BCE, a rigid class system had formed, with four "varnas" (castes). Most important were the Brahmins (priests), followed by Kshatriyas (warriors and nobles), Vaishyas (farmers and merchants), and Shudras (servants). Outside the system were social outcasts called untouchables.

生思
胜水

Until oracle bones were found in 1899, it was believed that the Shang Dynasty existed only in myth. Oracle bones had writing on them – the earliest known form of Chinese writing – and Shang rulers used them to communicate with their dead ancestors. The writing tells us about life during the Shang period, and over time it developed into the Chinese characters used today.

EARLY CHINA

The Shang and Zhou dynasties of early China were both known for their highly organized armies and the beautiful objects they made of bronze. The Shang kings first began their rule in northern China in 1600 BCE. Their kingdom soon included eight royal capitals protected by fortified walls. Then, in 1046 BCE, the neighbouring Zhou clan conquered the Shang. The Zhou became China's longest-serving dynasty, and were replaced by the Qin in 226 BCE.

ANCESTOR WORSHIP

The ancient Chinese believed that when a family member died, their spirit could either help or punish their living descendents. To keep these powerful ancestors happy, the Shang honoured them with regular offerings of food and drink, and ritual sacrifices.

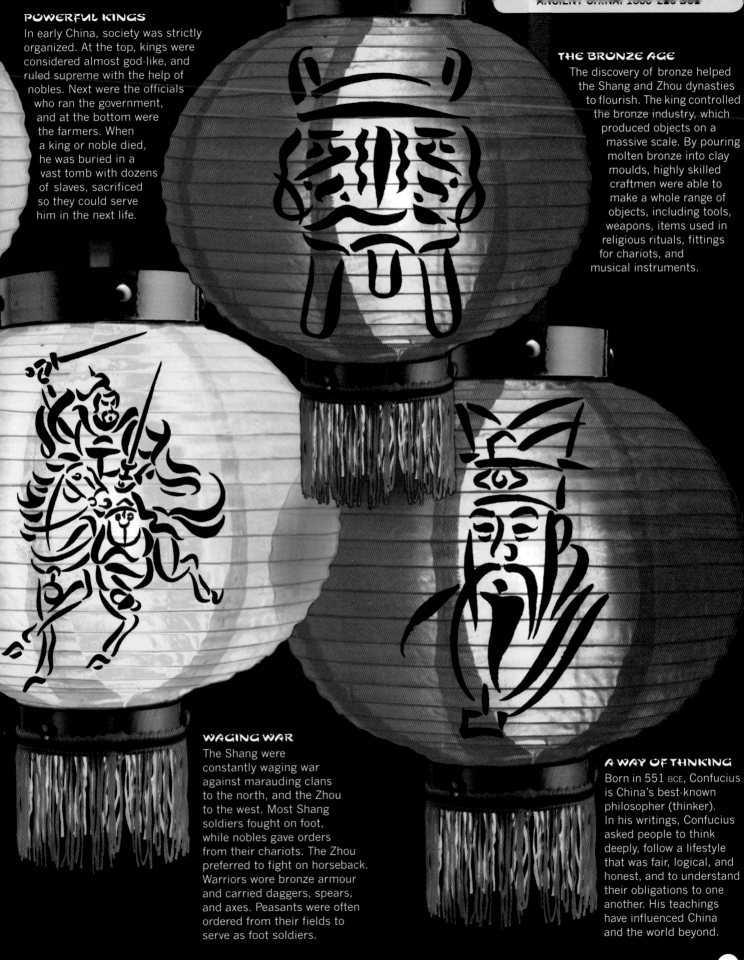

POWERFUL KINGS

In early China, society was strictly organized. At the top, kings were considered almost god-like, and ruled supreme with the help of nobles. Next were the officials who ran the government, and at the bottom were the farmers. When a king or noble died, he was buried in a vast tomb with dozens of slaves, sacrificed so they could serve him in the next life.

THE BRONZE AGE

The discovery of bronze helped the Shang and Zhou dynasties to flourish. The king controlled the bronze industry, which produced objects on a massive scale. By pouring molten bronze into clay moulds, highly skilled craftsmen were able to make a whole range of objects, including tools, weapons, items used in religious rituals, fittings for chariots, and musical instruments.

WAGING WAR

The Shang were constantly waging war against marauding clans to the north, and the Zhou to the west. Most Shang soldiers fought on foot, while nobles gave orders from their chariots. The Zhou preferred to fight on horseback. Warriors wore bronze armour and carried daggers, spears, and axes. Peasants were often ordered from their fields to serve as foot soldiers.

A WAY OF THINKING

Born in 551 BCE, Confucius is China's best-known philosopher (thinker). In his writings, Confucius asked people to think deeply, follow a lifestyle that was fair, logical, and honest, and to understand their obligations to one another. His teachings have influenced China and the world beyond.

Minoans

PROFILE: It is 1600 BCE on the island of Crete. The who's who of Minoan society has gathered at a palace in the city of Knossos for a sophisticated afternoon of song, dance, and conversation. But how long will the good times last? The volcano on the nearby island of Thera is starting to rumble, and some unwelcome guests have arrived...

LOVE OF WAR:

LOVE OF CULTURE:

Yes, we Minoans are known for our seafaring skills. For years, I've sailed around the Mediterranean selling gold jewellery and pottery. Cups, jugs, urns – you name it, I've sold it.

Uh-oh. Have you seen this smoke?

Ever wondered what would happen if that volcano over on Thera erupted? Just think of the massive tidal wave. Our naval fleet would be sitting ducks! The cities would be rocked to ruins, and the ash would poison our crops. The Minoans would be wiped out of existence.

Stop being so gloomy, Stavros. Chill out and enjoy the party.

I must say, Linear A is the best script around. With our fine scribing, the Minoan economic records will last for years and years! Please fetch some more clay tablets from the stationery cupboard, Petros.

The Snake Goddess is my favourite Minoan god. Your statuette will protect the palace. Girl power!

Hooray for the mother goddess! Isn't it great that all of our gods are female? Strike up another tune on your lyre, Eleni, we have a lot more worshipping to do. If I'm to stand any chance of winning the bull-leaping contest tomorrow, I need to loosen up my muscles today. Let's boogie!

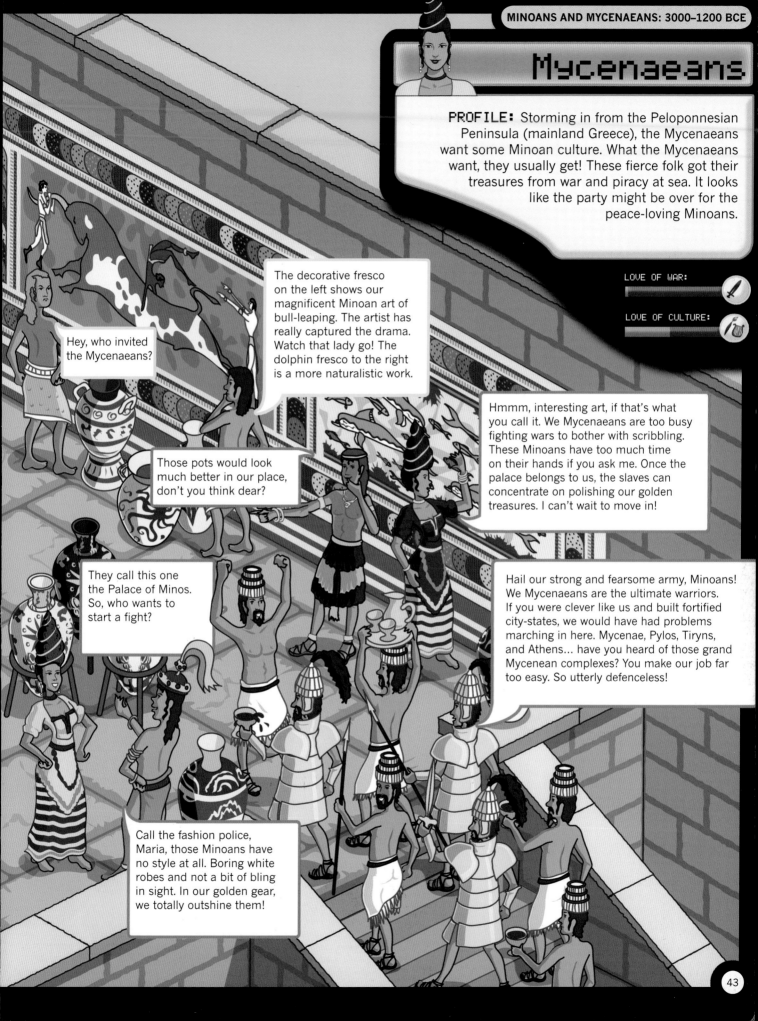

Mycenaeans

PROFILE: Storming in from the Peloponnesian Peninsula (mainland Greece), the Mycenaeans want some Minoan culture. What the Mycenaeans want, they usually get! These fierce folk got their treasures from war and piracy at sea. It looks like the party might be over for the peace-loving Minoans.

LOVE OF WAR:

LOVE OF CULTURE:

The decorative fresco on the left shows our magnificent Minoan art of bull-leaping. The artist has really captured the drama. Watch that lady go! The dolphin fresco to the right is a more naturalistic work.

Hey, who invited the Mycenaeans?

Hmmm, interesting art, if that's what you call it. We Mycenaeans are too busy fighting wars to bother with scribbling. These Minoans have too much time on their hands if you ask me. Once the palace belongs to us, the slaves can concentrate on polishing our golden treasures. I can't wait to move in!

Those pots would look much better in our place, don't you think dear?

They call this one the Palace of Minos. So, who wants to start a fight?

Hail our strong and fearsome army, Minoans! We Mycenaeans are the ultimate warriors. If you were clever like us and built fortified city-states, we would have had problems marching in here. Mycenae, Pylos, Tiryns, and Athens… have you heard of those grand Mycenean complexes? You make our job far too easy. So utterly defenceless!

Call the fashion police, Maria, those Minoans have no style at all. Boring white robes and not a bit of bling in sight. In our golden gear, we totally outshine them!

HANNO THE EXPLORER

THE LAND OF PHOENICIA LAY IN THE AREA THAT IS NOW LEBANON, SYRIA, AND ISRAEL. THE ANCIENT PHOENICIANS WERE GREAT SEAFARERS AND FROM ABOUT 1200 BCE BEGAN TO BUILD A NETWORK OF TRADE ROUTES AND SETTLEMENTS ACROSS THE MEDITERRANEAN. THE CENTRE OF THEIR TRADING EMPIRE WAS THE CITY OF CARTHAGE, IN NORTH AFRICA. IT WAS FROM CARTHAGE, SO THE STORY GOES, THAT AN EXTRAORDINARY EXPEDITION, LED BY A MAN NAMED HANNO, SET OFF IN THE 6TH CENTURY BCE TO EXPLORE THE COAST OF AFRICA.

EUROPE

PHOENICIA AND CARTHAGE

BLACK SEA

ANATOLIA (TURKEY)

CARTHAGE

STRAITS OF GIBRALTAR

MEDITERRANEAN SEA

CYPRUS

PHOENICI

BYBLOS
SIDON
TYRE

NORTH AFRICA

AROUND 600 BCE

THE PHOENICIAN TRADING EMPIRE BEGAN IN THE CITIES OF TYRE, BYBLOS, AND SIDON. IN THE PORTS, SHIPS WERE LOADED WITH GOODS TO TRADE – CEDAR AND PINE WOOD, WINE, GLASS, SALT, AND FINE LINENS.

PURPLE DYE, MADE FROM ROTTING SEA SNAILS, WAS ANOTHER VALUABLE PHOENICIAN EXPORT. THE ROMANS AND OTHER ANCIENT CIVILIZATIONS USED THIS COLOUR FOR THEIR NOBLE AND CEREMONIAL ROBES.

PEEEEEUUUUW! THAT STINKS.

I BELIEVE THIS SHIP STOPS AT CYRENE. CAN YOU PASS THIS TO MY SON THERE?

PHOENICIAN TRADING POSTS WERE QUICKLY ESTABLISHED ACROSS THE MEDITERRANEAN. NOT ONLY DID THE PHOENICIANS EXPORT THEIR GOODS, BUT ALSO THEIR LANGUAGE AND CULTURE.

THE PHOENICIANS WERE ALSO GREAT EXPLORERS AND IN THE 6TH CENTURY BCE ADMIRAL HANNO SET OFF FROM CARTHAGE TO MAP NEW AREAS OF AFRICA. SIXTY BOATS, EACH WITH 50 OARS, CARRIED 30,000 BRAVE FOLK THROUGH THE STRAITS OF GIBRALTAR...

ONWARD-HO TO THE WESTERN WILDS OF THE ATLANTIC. ROW, MEN, ROW!

I WONDER WHAT STRANGE PEOPLE AND CREATURES AWAIT US, MOTHER.

NO ONE KNOWS, CHILD. LET'S HOPE THE LANDS WE FIND ARE FULL OF GOODS TO TRADE.

WITH THE HELP OF THE NORTH STAR I CAN READ THE STARRY SKIES.

AS THEY SAILED, THE SAILORS ALWAYS KEPT LAND IN SIGHT. AT NIGHT, THEY NAVIGATED BY THE NORTH STAR.

SOME CALL IT "THE PHOENICIAN STAR"!

TWO DAYS TRAVEL BEYOND GIBRALTAR, THE PHOENICIANS WENT ASHORE. IT WAS A FLAT AND BARREN LAND. HERE THEY FOUNDED THE CITY OF THYMIATERION. HANNO THEN LED THE FLEET WESTWARD TO A LEAFY GREEN PROMONTORY THEY CALLED SOLOEIS. THERE THEY BUILT A TEMPLE DEDICATED TO A SEA GOD.

SAILING ON, THE FLEET CAME TO A MARSH TEEMING WITH MARVELLOUS BIRDS AND BEASTS.

LOOK, MOTHER! SEE HOW THOSE CREATURES DRAW THE WATER THROUGH THEIR LONG NOSES.

HANNO LED THE FLEET ONWARDS, FOUNDING MANY CITIES ALONG THE WEST COAST OF AFRICA.

THESE KIND CATTLEMEN HAVE WARNED OF A HOSTILE TRIBE LIVING CLOSE BY, IN THE MOUNTAINS. IT IS SAID THEY RUN FASTER THAN HORSES!

I WILL KEEP A WATCHFUL EYE, SIR.

ARRIVING AT THE RIVER LIXOS, THE PHOENICIANS ANCHORED. NOMADS, KNOWN AS THE LIXITES, BEFRIENDED THE VISITORS. ENJOYING THE HOSPITALITY, THE PHOENICIANS STAYED A WHILE.

WITH SOME LIXITE NOMADS AS INTERPRETERS, HANNO SAILED ON TO KERNE. SOME OF THE SEAFARERS DECIDED TO STAY BEHIND AND SETTLE IN A BAY OF SMALL ISLANDS.

NOW, SON, FIRST WE MUST BUILD OUR SHELTER. GATHER ANY WOOD YOU FIND.

SURE, DAD.

WE WILL NEED KINDLING, TOO. YOUR SISTERS AND I WILL PREPARE A FIRE.

BACK AT THE FLEET...

GO AWAY, CURSED SEA MONSTERS! LEAVE! BE OFF WITH YOU! NOW!

WHAT ARE THEY SAYING TO US IN THAT WILD GIBBERISH, MY LIXITE FRIEND?

I SUGGEST WE DO NOT ANCHOR, ADMIRAL.

AAAARGH! OUCH! YOW!

NOTHING TO SEE HERE. KEEP ROWING, MEN!

SAILING ONWARD, HANNO'S FLEET PASSED THE RIVER CHRETES BEFORE REACHING A LARGE BAY. ON THE SHORE AN ANGRY TRIBE, DRESSED IN ANIMAL SKINS, AWAITED THEM – THE PHOENICIANS WERE NOT WELCOME!

NEXT THE FLEET REACHED A RIVER OF HIPPOPOTAMUSES AND CROCODILES...

HERE, NAPPY! ARE YOU HUNGRY?

STOP! DO YOU WISH TO LOSE YOUR HAND?

THOSE HIPPOS ARE JUST AS LETHAL AS THE CROCS, SON. IF YOU FALL IN, THEY'LL CHARGE YOU IN A SECOND. BAM! SQUISHED! DEAD!

THE FLEET JOURNEYED SOUTH FOR ANOTHER 12 DAYS. HERE THE COAST WAS INHABITED BY PEOPLE THE LIXITE INTERPRETERS COULD NOT UNDERSTAND. THE FLEET PASSED AROMATIC WOODLANDS, AND SAW FIRES BURNING.

MUU-UUM, I'M SCARED!

HUSH, LITTLE ONE. WE'RE SAFE HERE, I PROMISE.

WISE ADMIRAL, THE GODS SAY THAT WE MUST SAIL AT FIRST LIGHT. THOSE EERIE JUNGLE RUMBLINGS ARE THE VOICE OF... THE DEVIL!

AFTER A FURTHER WEEK, HANNO REACHED THE HORN OF THE WEST. THERE, HE ORDERED THE FLEET TO ANCHOR. BY DAY, ALL THAT COULD BE HEARD WAS THE SOUNDS OF THE FOREST, BUT AT NIGHT, THE BEATING OF DRUMS AND WAILING OF FLUTES HAUNTED THE PHOENICIANS' VERY SOULS...

FOUR DAYS LATER, THE FLEET WERE ASTONISHED TO SPY A TOWERING MOUNTAIN THAT SEEMED TO BE ABLAZE – AN ERUPTING VOLCANO! THEY CALLED IT "THE CHARIOT OF FIRE".

THE PHOENICIANS' GREAT JOURNEY ENDED AT THE HORN OF THE SOUTH. IN THE BAY LAY AN ISLAND INHABITED BY STRANGE HAIRY PEOPLE WHO BEAT THEIR CHESTS. THEY CAPTURED THREE OF THE WOMEN... THESE WERE OF COURSE GORILLAS!

HAVING RUN OUT OF SUPPLIES, THE PHOENICIANS TURNED THEIR SHIPS FOR HOME. ON HIS RETURN TO CARTHAGE, HANNO WAS WELCOMED AS A GREAT HERO.

STRAITS OF GIBRALTAR

CARTHAGE

THYMIATERION

AFRICA

KERNE

HORN OF THE WEST

HORN OF THE SOUTH

GLORY OF THE PHOENICIANS!

AN ADMIRABLE ADMIRAL!

HURRAH!

OUR GREAT HERO!

The story of the Jews

In Mesopotamia, in about 1900 BCE, a man named Abraham sowed the seeds of the Jewish faith when he began a religion that followed just one god.

The Twelve Tribes of Israel

In the Hebrew Bible, or Old Testament, it is said that God promised Abraham that all the nations of the world would be blessed through his children. So Abraham took his followers, known as the Israelites, from Mesopotamia to found a new civilization in Canaan, the lush area between the River Jordan and Mediterranean Sea. Abraham had 12 great-grandsons and each formed their own tribe. These were the Twelve Tribes of Israel, and each one ruled over a separate territory. The tribes were named after each great-grandson: Asher, Benjamin, Dan, Gad, Issachar, Joseph, Judah, Levi, Naphtali, Reuben, Simon, and Zebulun.

The Israelites were cruelly treated by the Egyptian slave masters

Forced to flee

Drought forced the Israelites to leave Canaan for Egypt. The Egyptians were suspicious of this new religious group, and the Israelites were condemned to suffer years of slavery. Then, in 1200 BCE, an Israelite leader named Moses led his people back to Canaan, known as the "Promised Land". According to the Bible, on the way, he raised his staff and the Red Sea parted, allowing the Israelites to cross. When the Egyptian army followed, Moses raised his staff again, and the sea crashed down, drowning them. After a 200-year struggle, the Twelve Tribes were reunited under Saul, the first Israelite king, and then David, a young Judean warrior.

After the Israelites crossed the Red Sea safely, the sea crashed down on the Egyptian army

The First Temple

It was David's son, Solomon, who captured Jerusalem and reunited the Hebrew nation in 990 BCE. There, he built the magnificent First Temple, the first place of worship for the Hebrew God. The Twelve Tribes of Israel split – the two southern tribes formed Judah and 10 northern tribes formed Israel. The people of the tribe of Judah became known as the Jews.

King Solomon ordered the construction of a temple in Jerusalem

Jewish exile

By 722 BCE, the Assyrian army from the north of Mesopotamia had conquered the northern kingdom of Israel. Then, in 586 BCE, the Babylonians destroyed the First Temple and killed the Jewish leadership. The surviving Jews were forced into exile in Babylon, starting what is known as the "diaspora" – the scattering of Jewish communities outside the Promised Land. When the Persians conquered Babylon in 539 BCE, some Jews returned to Jerusalem, while others remained in exile.

The Second Temple

The King of Syria outlawed Judaism in 168 BCE. For years, a revolutionary Jewish movement called the Maccabees staged a rebellion, eventually rebuilding the temple in Jerusalem. Today, their 164 BCE revolt is celebrated as the Jewish festival of Hanukkah. The Maccabees soon founded the Hasmonean Dynasty, where they ruled as high priests and kings. In 37 BCE, the Romans captured Jerusalem and installed Herod as king. By 20 BCE, Herod had built Jerusalem's Second Temple, using 1,000 priests as labourers. In 6 BCE Judea became a Roman province.

The Assyrian army attacked the cities of Judah

The Romans took over the city of Jerusalem in 37 BCE

Certainly civilized

Going up

Gory fun: In the Roman Empire, popular entertainment includes gladiators and wild animals fighting to the death in arenas, and hair-raising chariot races, which take place in circuses (oval-shaped tracks).

Long poems: Epics, such as the *Iliad* and the *Odyssey*, are recited throughout the Greek-speaking world. They tell of wars and gods. In China, the *Shi jing*, ("Book of Songs") is produced.

Democracy: The Greeks devise a system of government in which laws are decided by popular vote. Who knows – it might catch on?

Rational thought: Greek, Roman, and Arab philosophers put forward ways of explaining the world that do not rely on myth or religion, providing the foundations for modern science.

The Celts **(p60)** spread their warrior culture across Europe.

Great civilizations, such as the Maya **(p68)**, flourish in Central America.

From the 8th century BCE, the village of Rome grows into an important town. Initially a republic **(p54)**, it goes on to be ruled by a succession of emperors **(p56)**. With an army that is virtually unbeatable **(p58)**, Rome dominates Europe for 500 years. In the 4th century CE, the Empire is split into east and west, and the western part goes into decline **(p76)**.

Going down

Bronze: The metal of choice in the previous era, bronze is increasingly replaced with iron. Stronger and more durable, iron also bends more easily, as the Celts find out on the battlefield.

Body odour: The Romans build baths in all their major towns. The Greeks clean themselves with olive oil, scraped off with a tool called a strigil.

Lots of gods: The Romans and Greeks believe in a whole range of gods, but by the end of the period, Christianity is the religion of the Roman Empire and comes to dominate Europe.

Taking the long way round: The Romans build a network of famously straight roads. They don't avoid obstacles, but find ways around them using bridges and tunnels.

Alexander the Great of Macedonia (**p66**) conquers Greece and the Persian Empire.

Ancient Greek city-states like Athens and Sparta (**p50**) colonize the Mediterranean. Greeks thinkers (**p52**) develop ideas in science, philosophy, and the arts that still influence society today.

The Persian Empire (**p64**) reaches its height under the rule of the Achaemenids.

A new religion, based on the teachings of Jesus Christ (**p74**) develops in the Middle East.

In India, a new religion called Buddhism (**p62**) is born.

The warring states of China are united under Qin Shi Huang (**p70**) in 221 BCE.

Polynesian navigators (**p72**) spread vast distances across the Pacific, settling on thousands of far-flung islands.

Take me back to the years 600 BCE– 399 CE

Great civilizations are like buses. You hang around for thousands of years and then five come along at once. First up is Ancient Greece – an assortment of city-states, each with their own ways of life. Greece gives way to Rome, a city-state in Italy that grows into a vast empire. In Persia, a golden age is brought crashing to an end by the military mastery of Alexander the Great. Meanwhile, the Mayans make merry down Mexico way and Qin Shi Huang unites China.

Time to marvel (or should that be marble?) at the amazing achievements of some of history's all-time great civilizations.

YOUR CITY-STATE NEEDS YOU

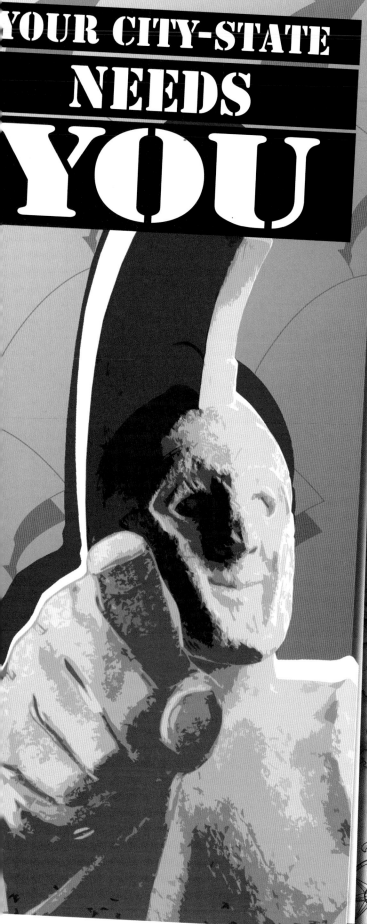

JOIN THE SPARTAN ARMY

The Ancient Greek mainland and islands are ruled by hundreds of different city-states, all struggling for supremecy. Obviously, Sparta is the best, and you're privileged to be able to defend it.

WHY JOIN UP?

Because you have to! Our system of rule by aristocrats and kings leaves no room for confusion – or wimps. Unlike Athens, a city packed with useless culture and wishy-washy liberal ideals like democracy, we know what's important. We have strong leadership and a stunning tradition of military excellence. All male citizens of Sparta must serve.

A life of excitement lies ahead. Living with a band of tough hoplites (foot soldiers), you'll eat, sleep, train, and fight. State slaves will farm your land while you're away, so if you survive you'll have a comfortable retirement.

You'll travel to many of the Greek city-states. Most tours of duty will see you heading towards Athens, but you could be engaged around the Mediterranean coast of North Africa or even in a battle against the Persians.

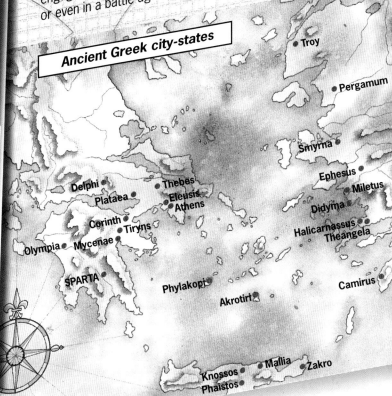

Ancient Greek city-states

KNOW YOUR ENEMIES

- **Spartan enemy no. 1: Athens**
  Our sworn enemy. They have a strange system of government called "democracy", where the laws are decided by popular vote.

- **Troublesome tyrants**
  Many city-states are run by tyrants (strong leaders). Sparta is proud to run a tyrant-eradication scheme.

- **Pesky Persians**
  The Persians have been attacking Greek territories for years. Working with Athens (for once) we defeated them in 480 BCE – but you can bet they'll be back for more!

WE'LL MAKE A MAN OF YOU!

Our training regime is the most rigorous in the world. It's harsh – but you'll become one of the elite. Be prepared to:

- leave home aged seven and train until you're 20

- manage without sleep for days

- be beaten

- have little food and no home comforts

STRICTLY NO HOME VISITS – WE DON'T WANT WEAKLINGS!

FIGHTING FORM

Spartan hoplites fight in a phalanx – a block of soldiers marching together. This formation lets each soldier engage in hand-to-hand fighting with the enemy while protected by the shield of the man on his right.

BATTLE KIT Q & A

Q WHAT WEAPONS DO I GET TO USE?
A A short spear and a sword.

Q IS THERE A STYLISH UNIFORM?
A You'll have 30 kg (70 lb) of bronze armour to protect your head, body, and lower legs. A distinctive red cloak and long hair will show you're a Spartan.

Q WHAT DO I WEAR WHEN I'M NOT FIGHTING?
A A thin tunic and no shoes – so no dreary washing or boot-polishing.

GAMES TIMES

When we're not at war, you'll have a chance to compete in the Olympic Games, one of four "Panhellenic Games" contests with competitors from all over Greece. A tradition that's been going since 776 BCE, it's great training for war, and fun, too.

A GREEK EPIC

Competitors, gods, and friendly spectators alike, welcome one and all to the Festival of Zeus, also known as the Olympic Games. Don't worry about getting here – all wars are put on hold so that we can travel safely. The Olympics are always much more than a sporting event, but this year there's a twist. On the bill we have some of the inspiring thinkers from Athens, the centre of Greek culture. Since 509 BCE, the Athenians have governed themselves with a new system they call "democracy" (that's "people power" to you and me). Enlightening stuff, I tell you.

HEADS IN THE CLOUDS

We Greeks worship an array of gods (Zeus is their king), each with many an exciting story of love and war. Offerings are given to the gods, who each rule over a particular area of life, such as war and marriage. We use oracles and offerings to ask them what's on the horizon and what we should do. You have to be good at seeing patterns in sacrificed chicken guts to get the message!

LET'S HEAR IT FOR THE GREEKS. WOO!

GAME FOR ANYTHING

Athletes at the Olympic Games compete in a wide variety of events, including running, jumping, discus throwing, wrestling, and chariot racing.

I HAVE THE WINNING FORMULA

A TRUTHFUL HISTORY

Make way for Thucydides and his epic *History of the Peloponnesian Wars,* about the wars between Greece and Sparta. His rigorous analysis of the plain and simple facts set the standard for future historians.

A EUREKA MOMENT

Next up is Archimedes, one of the greatest mathematicians ever. When he noticed the water level in his bath rise as he stepped in, he suddenly realized how to measure the volume of objects. He was so excited he ran naked into the street shouting "Eureka!"

ARISTOTLE VS PLATO

And now for the sparring match between Plato and Aristotle. Both of these great philosophers wanted to use reason to find out how the world works, but Aristotle also believed in using facts to back up his theories.

MEDICINAL PURPOSES

Hippocrates is the bright bod credited with establishing medicine as a scientific discipline. Rather than seeing illness as a punishment from the gods, he bases his treatments on observing people's symptoms.

A REAL PLAYER

Next gallops in Euripides. If we're lucky, he might quote a snippet from his play in honour of Dionysus, god of drama, wine, and partying. The Greeks invented theatre, and Euripides helped shape the great tradition of Greek tragedy.

A TRUE DIAMOND

Later on the bill we have Hippodamus. This architect designed towns by grouping people into different categories (soldiers, farmers, and crafts people) and dividing land into public, sacred, and private areas. His ideal city was diamond-shaped.

SOCRATES VS SOPHISTS

Hang fire for this fight between intellectual heavyweights. Founder of debating, Socrates believed in questioning everything, while the sophists ("wise men") simply sought to persuade others of their own views.

SENATE MUSEUM

Toga Tours are pleased to welcome you to the senate – the Ancient Roman seat of power. When Rome was founded it was a monarchy. The senate, or council of elders, held a powerful role alongside the king. In 509 BCE, Rome ditched its monarch and became a republic, leaving the senate to rule, headed by two annually elected consuls. Don't forget to visit the souvenir shop on your way out.

SENATE TOUR

The tour visits the site of the Curia Hostilius, where senate meetings were held during the Republic. The Curia Hostilius burned down and was rebuilt several times, and fell out of use by 29 BCE, but it was here that senators drawn from the patricians (city elite) debated and decided Roman laws and policy. The senate was led by two consuls, who were elected annually and supported by magistrates, who put the laws into practice.

FOUNDATION OF ROME: FACT AND FICTION

Legend has it that Rome was founded in 753 BCE by Romulus, who, along with his brother Remus, had been raised by a wolf. It's true that Rome's first king was called Romulus – but his background was probably amongst the neighbouring Etruscan hill tribes rather than wolves! This exhibition explores the facts behind the myth.

ROMAN TERRITORY

ITALY
Rome
GREECE
SYRIA
Athens
Carthage
Mediterranean Sea
EGPYT
AFRICA

■ 197 BCE ☐ 133 BCE ☐ 1 CE

EXHIBITION OF ENGINEERING

Many great Roman buildings, from temples to aqueducts, are supported by arches. Ancient Roman engineers perfected the construction of the arch and the use of fired bricks, stone, and concrete. Check out their engineering marvels in this new show.

WHO WERE THE SEVEN KINGS OF ROME?

Visit this waxwork parade to find out about the kings who ruled Rome from 753 BCE. All seven are there, along with a replica of their throne. After the last king, Tarquinius Superbus, was overthrown in 509 BCE the senate declared Rome a republic.

HOW DID ROME EXPAND?

Rome's location on major trade routes brought wealth and contact with other peoples. By 264 BCE the Roman Republic had taken over all of Italy. The army's march across the western world looked unstoppable – by 30 BCE the whole of the Mediterranean had become Roman territory.

FREE ADMISSION

PEOPLE OF ROME T-SHIRT
Look like a leader in our funky T-shirt! The motto of Rome, SPQR, stands for "the senate and the people of Rome". The people of Rome were divided though: plebeians farmed the land and manned the army, while patricians owned the land and made up most of the senate.

MVSEVM

PUNIC WARS SOUVENIR MUGS
These super souvenir mugs show scenes from Rome's wars against the Carthaginians of North Africa. There were three conflicts, known as the Punic Wars. In the second (218–201 BCE), the Carthaginian general Hannibal Barca famously led his war elephants over the Alps, but was finally defeated.

JULIUS CAESAR AND THE END OF THE ROMAN REPUBLIC
Have your photo taken with the man who ended it all! Julius Caesar rose through the army to command Roman forces in France. Disobeying instructions to disband his troops, he marched on Rome and had himself appointed dictator. Goodbye Republic!

The class of Imperial Rome has been an eventful one! From Julius Caesar, the general turned dictator-for-life, to Constantine, tipped to take the capital from Rome to Byzantium, here are some faces we'll all remember for years to come.

JULIUS CAESAR

TERM IN OFFICE: 44 BCE
INTERESTS: Military pursuits; claiming land for Rome
GOALS: Conquer Europe
VOTED MOST LIKELY TO: Rise to power in the military; appoint himself dictator for life, effectively ending the Republic; get assassinated soon after
IF NOT MILITARY DICTATOR, WOULD BE: Unofficial emperor

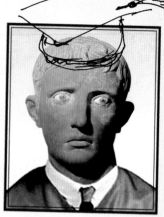

OCTAVIAN

REIGNED: 27 BCE– 14 CE
INTERESTS: Urban renewal
GOALS: To be recognized as the first emperor and a god
VOTED MOST LIKELY TO: Pretend to restore the Republic but become emperor, taking the title "Augustus" in 27 BCE; create lasting prosperity for Rome
IF NOT EMPEROR, WOULD BE: Administrator or accountant

CLEO 4 JULIUS

CLEOPATRA

This visiting student from Egypt made her mark on Imperial Rome High — falling for Julius Caesar AND his rival Mark Antony. Famed for her beauty and intelligence, this chick is ambitious — she says she plans to fight Rome and take over the world. If it goes wrong, she's ready to end it all with a poisonous snake.

CLAUDIUS

REIGNED: 41–54 CE
INTERESTS: History, writing
GOALS: Invade Britain, subdue barbarians; reform Roman systems along liberal lines
VOTED MOST LIKELY TO: Stammer during speeches; make a foolish marriage; swing between tolerance and cruelty
IF NOT EMPEROR, WOULD BE: Scholar, historian

NERO

REIGNED: 54–68
INTERESTS: Poetry competitions; killing Christians
GOALS: Make Rome beautiful; further the arts; splash the cash on entertainment; abolish taxes
VOTED MOST LIKELY TO: Murder his own wife and mother; fiddle while Rome burns
IF NOT EMPEROR, WOULD BE: Sectioned in a psychiatric ward

JULIA AGRIPPINA

ROLE: Empress; power behind the throne
INTERESTS: Toxic mushrooms; avoiding assassination attempts by her son Nero
GOALS: Marry Claudius; give birth to Nero; absolute power
VOTED MOST LIKELY TO: Scheme and manipulate; marry for power; murder her husband so her son can succeed to the throne

HIGH

IMPERIAL ROME
HIGH SCHOOL

SCHOOL

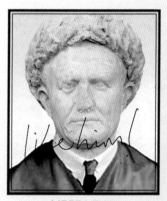

VESPASIAN

REIGNED: 69–79
INTERESTS: The simple life; hard work; soldiering; buildings
GOALS: Restructure and renew the Roman economy; acheive peace for the Empire
VOTED MOST LIKELY TO: Start ambitious construction projects – a colosseum, for example
IF NOT EMPEROR, WOULD BE: Soldier

TRAJAN

REIGNED: 98–117
INTERESTS: Social welfare; empire-building in the east
GOALS: Expand the Empire; encourage public building in the provinces
VOTED MOST LIKELY TO: Help the poor; start a building project outside Rome
IF NOT EMPEROR, WOULD BE: Philanthropist

HADRIAN

REIGNED: 117–138
INTERESTS: Travel, art, law
GOALS: Consolidate the Empire, strengthening its borders; give back some of the ungovernable land won by Trajan; visit all corners of the Empire
VOTED MOST LIKELY TO: Build a very large wall in Britain
IF NOT EMPEROR, WOULD BE: Architect

MARCUS AURELIUS

REIGNED: 161–180
INTERESTS: Philosophy, writing, scholarship, law
GOALS: Subdue the Germanic people who threaten the Empire in the north; overhaul the legal system
VOTED MOST LIKELY TO: Write a book of philosophy
IF NOT EMPEROR, WOULD BE: Philosopher

JULIA DOMNA

ROLE: Wife of Emperor Severus and mother of emperors Geta and Caracalla
INTERESTS: Philosophy; writing; mixing in scholarly circles
GOALS: To be recognized as "the mother of the senate and of the fatherland"
VOTED MOST LIKELY TO: Fail to instill suitable values in her son Caracalla

CARACALLA

REIGNED: 211–217
INTERESTS: Military campaigns
GOALS: Be a ruthless dictator
VOTED MOST LIKELY TO: Grant citizenship to all freemen in order to raise money in taxes; assassinate his brother and wife; carry out a massacre in a tantrum
IF NOT EMPEROR, WOULD BE: Serial killer

DIOCLETIAN

REIGNED: 284–305
INTERESTS: Traditional family values; social justice
GOALS: Restore order and efficiency to the army, the economy, and society
VOTED MOST LIKELY TO: Persecute Christians; share the Empire with three other rulers
IF NOT EMPEROR, WOULD BE: A god

CONSTANTINE

REIGNED: 306–337
INTERESTS: Christianity; religious tolerance; building churches
GOALS: Establish a new city to govern the Empire from the east, and name it after himself
VOTED MOST LIKELY TO: Have his wife and eldest son killed; convert to Christianity
IF NOT EMPEROR, WOULD BE: A Christian saint

FEARSOME FORCE

The army of the Roman Republic was staffed by volunteers, but as the Empire expanded a professional fighting force became necessary. By the 1st century CE, the troops had become a well-organized and virtually unbeatable standing army with career soldiers who each served for 25 years.

STANDARD

Each legion (army unit) had a unique emblem, or standard, that it carried into battle. Choose one of your legionnaire models to be the standard-bearer. And don't forget he needs a wolf skin* over his shoulders to look extra fearsome!

LEAD YOUR LEGION
INTO BATTLE

* WOLF SKIN SOLD SEPARATELY

CENTURION

ABLE TO
MARCH
ALL DAY

COMMANDS
80 SOLDIERS

CARRIES A
30-KG (65-LB) KIT BAG

This great new action figure from Trajan Toys™ comes complete with armour, shield, and a *vitis* (short staff) that shows his authority. In the Roman army, a centurion was in charge of a century of 80 men, and was chosen for his strength and toughness.

COLLECT THE SET

WHERE YOUR FIGURE FITS IN

A centurion commanded a century of 80 men. Six centuries made a cohort, 10 cohorts made a legion, and the whole army had 28 legions in all.

YOU'VE GOT THE MOVES

Discipline and training were key to the success of the Roman army. Your poseable centurion can be moved into all the main training positions, including running, marching, swimming, wrestling, and throwing.

ON LOCATION

The Roman army had outposts all over Europe, North Africa, and parts of Asia. They battled red-headed Celts, Hannibal's savage Carthaginians, and the vicious Germanic barbarians.

SPECIAL SKILLS

The army got around on foot, marching for days on end, and didn't budge in the face of obstacles. Skilled soldiers constructed forts, built bridges across rivers, and cut roads through hills.

CREATE AN ARMY AND FORM A TESTUDO

TOUGH

IMPENETRABLE

STRONG

UNSTOPPABLE

INTIMIDATING

DEFENSIVE

BATTLE FORMATIONS

Roman soldiers fought in tight formations. For this defensive *testudo* (tortoise) the men stood in a bloc, with their shields facing outwards and upwards. Attacking formations included the wedge, where the men stood in a V-shape.

FANTASTIC ROMAN FORT

Collect four tokens and this fantastic scale model of a Roman fort can be yours. The Romans built forts across their Empire as military bases and to keep the locals in check. Pose your soldiers at the gates, in the barracks (living quarters), or even in the commandant's house.

ONE TOKEN   **ONE TOKEN**

WEAPONS

Arm your centurion to the teeth with this bumper pack of fighting tools. The *gladius* is the soldier's weapon of choice, while the *pugio* comes in handy for close combat. The *pilum* is designed to break on impact so it can't be thrown back.

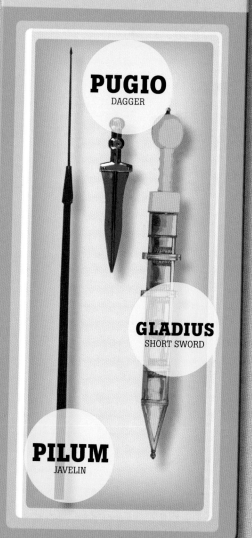

PUGIO
DAGGER

GLADIUS
SHORT SWORD

PILUM
JAVELIN

PINBALL CELTS

In this game you're a Celt, whizzing around Europe about 400 BCE. The Celts were a group of tribes who shared a common culture and spread all over Europe, taking their warrior society and skill in metalworking with them. They were no match for the Roman legions though, and by the 1st century CE controlled only the British Isles. But maybe you'll fare better. Start at the flippers and try your luck at Pinball Celts!

HOME SWEET HILL

To keep safe, ricochet up a hill and start a hill fort. Construct a wooden fence around the hill and build all your roundhouses inside. Some ditches outside the fence will make it safer. And don't forget to bring some farm animals – you'll need to eat.

FIGHTING SPIRIT

The Celts were always fighting each other, and as they migrated across Europe they came into conflict with the Romans, too. Warriors were the heroes of the Celtic world. Every role has got its down sides though – as a warrior, your sword, made of soft iron, is a bit bendy. You'll just have to stop fighting to straighten it every now and then.

DUNG DWELLING

Now you've settled, build a house. Celtic roundhouses had a low, circular outer wall made of poles with bendy hazel sticks woven between them. The roof was made of reeds attached to a tall, central pole, and the walls were plastered with mud and animal dung (poo). Mmm, fragrant.

METAL MANIA

Chances are you'll have a great career as a metalworker. The Celts were wizards at turning gold, silver, iron, and bronze into decorative and useful items, especially objects to use in warfare. A twisted metal neckband, or torc, might be all a warrior wore in battle. Must have been a bit nippy!

YOU'D BETTER BELIEVE IT

As a Celt, you'll have hundreds of gods to choose from. Nature played a big part – different features in the landscape had different gods, such as Cocidius, who was a forest god. Celtic priests called druids performed outdoor religious rituals. Cernunnos here is the god of plenty, so take 50 bonus points.

AND YOU'RE OFF!

The Celts spread out across Europe from southern Germany and Austria. By about 200 BCE, they had settled as far afield as Scotland and Poland to the north, Ukraine and Turkey in the east, Spain in the west, and Italy in the south. So put your coin in the slot and get the ball rolling!

10 POINTS WHEN LIT

50   50   50   50   50

Buddhism

Buddhism is one of the main belief systems in India and many eastern countries. It began with the life and teachings of Buddha, who lived in India sometime between 600 and 400 BCE. Buddhism is a religion, but it does not teach belief in a god. Instead, it teaches followers how to navigate a path through life so their soul can reach nirvana (perfect peace).

Buddha's life

Siddharta Gautama was born to a wealthy family near the River Ganges in India, but gave up his comfortable life after witnessing hardship in the world. He wanted to find out how to escape the suffering caused by disease and death. After a period of meditation (focused thought) he received enlightenment and became a Buddha, or "awakened one".

Before Buddhism

Before Buddhism, the main religion in south Asia around 600 BCE, involved many different gods and goddesses, Hinduism, involved sacrifices. Some people wanted a more elaborate approach. Buddhism and less elaborate approach. Buddhism and some of its rituals, and because of this, but some of its personal part because reincarnation, are similar to arose in part as reincarnation, are similar to ideas, such as in Hindu holy texts. those found in Hindu holy texts.

The Spread of Buddhism

in the 3rd century BCE, the Indian emperor Ashoka the Great encouraged the foundation of Buddhist monasteries, Buddhism began to spread throughout central Asia and China. Today, branches of the religion in different areas have different beliefs.

Buddhist teaching

After he achieved enlightenment, Buddha began to teach others how they might do the same. He set out the Four Noble Truths, which recognize the suffering in the world, and an Eightfold Path, often represented by a wheel, by which people should live their lives in order to escape suffering.

Realms and reincarnation

Reincarnation is the idea that the soul moves from one being to another after death. There are six realms of being that a soul can inhabit – hell beings, ghosts, animals, humans, demigods, and gods – and a being's actions determine which realm it is born into in the next life. Gods and demigods have the most comfortable lives, but the human realm is considered the most fortunate because its inhabitants can break out of the cycle of reincarnation by reaching enlightenment and nirvana.

Early followers

After Buddha's death, his disciples gathered together to agree the main points of his teaching. They spread his teachings and set up monasteries and temples. In the century following his death, Buddha's ideas spread throughout northern India.

WASSUP HOMIES! I'M DARIUS THE GREAT, KING OF PERSIA. LET ME SHOW YOU MY NEW CRIB,

PERSEPOLIS!

PERSIA CHANNEL CRIBS

WHEN I WAS CROWNED IN 522 BCE I WANTED A NEW HOOD TO HANG IN AND SOMEWHERE TO STASH MY BLING, SO I GOT ME A CAPITAL CITY. IT'S PRETTY CHILLED HERE IN THE DESERT, BUT THE SPOT WAS PICKED BY COUSIN CYRUS. HE WAS KING BEFORE ME, AND I RECKON I'VE INHERITED ALL HIS BOSS QUALITIES.

So, I'm gonna show you around. The city is cut from the side of a mountain. I had state-of-the-art underground sewers put in. There are palaces, plazas, and columned halls that show visitors how awesome us Persians are. Check it.

This right here is my throne hall. Representatives from across the Empire come here to hang out. We get dudes from all over – India, Babylon, you name it. I just conquered Egypt, which is pretty fly. I've got my sights on Greece, but that's turning out a bit trickier. They keep revolting. I'm like, chillax, man!

This is me and my son Xerxes. When I'm gone, all this will be his. At the moment he's off punishing the Greeks – the cities we control revolted so he's gone to give them hell. To be honest, I don't fancy his chances much. That King Leonidas of Sparta is quite a cool customer...

Throne hall

Back in the day, MY main man Cyrus the Great took over the lands of the Medes – these guys from Iran who had a huge empire. Then he took over Turkey and Babylon. That was way back when. He died in 529 BCE. Now I rule Asia Minor. We had these reliefs done of some Medes. You gotta keep it real.

The Medes massive

When the army is on parade they march through this ornate gate. The crowds go crazy for them. MY army is drawn from all our conquered peoples. It's the backbone of the Empire and of course the army has a huge presence in the palace. Whatever.

Awesome gate

The Apadana Palace is the best. It can fit 10,000 people in – it's a totally sick place for a party! People from all over the Empire helped build it. We're a harmonious Empire like that. We let people keep their old religions, improved the roads so they can get around, and minted some bling coins.

Family guy

Apadana Palace

DON'T MISS IT!
FRIDAY 8PM

ALEXANDER – he's great!

Greetings from the Alex the Great official fansite, bringing you all the very latest news from the campaign trail. It was a crying shame when Philip of Macedonia met a suspicious end in 336 BCE, but our teen sensation Alex was ready and waiting to take the throne. Taught by famous Greek philosopher Aristotle, he was leading major military campaigns and conquering new lands before you could say "Alex rocks". Just check out his latest adventures…

Join Team Alexander!
Click here to sign up
for email updates

NEWSROOM

323 BCE ALEXANDER TAKEN ILL

Those close to Alexander are concerned at his sudden illness. The conqueror ignored bad omens to march on Babylon, then drank heavily at a banquet. He fell ill with a fever soon after. Alex says he feels like he's "been hit in the liver with an arrow." Here's hoping he'll pull through, but it's not looking good.

324 BCE HEPHAESTION IS DEAD

The death of his beloved companion Hephaestion has hit Alexander hard. The pair had been best buddies since boyhood, and Hephaestion accompanied the hero on all his campaigns. Alex is said to be utterly inconsolable at the loss of his friend.

333 BCE ALEX CUTS GORDIAN KNOT

Ever the man of action, Alex has ended 100 years of speculation at a stroke by slicing though the Gordian Knot. The fabled knot in Phrygia had confounded all comers. Legend told that the person who untangled it would rule all Asia. Some feel Alex cheated, but it looks like he is on his way to fulfilling the prophesy!

PRESS RELEASE ARCHIVE

331 BCE ALEXANDER LEADS HIS CAMPAIGN TO GAUGAMELA

Hot on the heels of the 333 BCE victory at Issus, Alexander's troops have once more clashed with the army of Persian king Darius III, this time on a plain near the town of Gaugamela. Darius was humiliated, fleeing the battlefield without his treasure. Our Macedonian boys massacred the Persians then went in hot pursuit of Darius. He burned bridges as he ran, but it was futile – Alex followed him all the way to Babylon. Rumour says Darius is hoping the luxurious living in Babylon will soften and weaken our boys – but they can take it!

CLICK HERE FOR MORE PRESS RELEASES

HOME   EVENTS   CONTACT US   CAMPAIGN   VIDEOS   STORE

ALEXANDER TV

| ⏩ ⏹ ▶ ⏪ | The taming of Bucephalus | 45:31mins |

At last, the historic tape of the young Alexander taming Bucephalus has been restored. Alex's dad, Philip of Macedonia, bet him he couldn't conquer the spirited stallion, but Alex had spotted the horse was afraid of his own shadow. He simply turned Bucephalus towards the Sun to win the debt. Genius!

MORE VIDEOS

BATTLE OF ISSUS
Thrilling action footage shows how Alex's troops, though outnumbered two to one, routed Darius's Persians at Issus in 333 BCE.

ALEX IS A GOD
On a visit to the shrine of Egyptian god Ammon at Siwa, Libya, the oracle declares Alexander to be the son of Zeus, king of the Greek gods. Awesome!

CAMPAIGN TRAIL

Asia Minor   334 BCE
Alex begins his dedicated battle against the Persians by crossing the Hellespont – a narrow strait between Greece and Asia Minor.

Syria   333 BCE
After defeating Darius at Issus, Alex moves through Syria taking one city after another. He's unstoppable!

Tyre, Gaza, and Egypt   332 BCE
Fresh from sieges at the cities of Tyre and Gaza, Alex frees Egypt from Persian rule and founds a new city – Alexandria.

Gaugamela   331 BCE
Marching from Egypt, the Macedonians meet Darius's men at Gaugamela. Darius is defeated and after fleeing is murdered by one of his own officials.

Persia   330 BCE
After a drunken row, Alex kills one of his most trusted commanders, Cleitus. Four days of remorse end with sacrifices.

Punjab   326 BCE
Alex invades the Punjab. He makes an alliance with Porus, the defeated ruler, and founds a city called Bucephala in honour of his beloved Bucephalus.

FOLLOW ALEXANDER'S CAMPAIGN

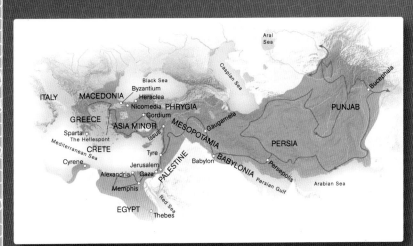

For hundreds of years, the great Persian Empire of the Achaemenids stretched across Asia Minor from the Mediterranean Sea into Pakistan. Alexander and his army conquered it in just 10 years, adding it to other Macedonian conquests in Europe and North Africa to make a vast empire. Our campaign trail map shows Alex's territory in orange, with arrows indicating the direction of his travels.

Alexander has brought Greek culture to the countries he conquered and put in place his own governing officials, but our noble hero graciously allows local traditions to continue alongside them. He's a diamond.

THE MAYA

The centrepiece of our fabulous fiesta celebrating the cool cultures of Mesoamerica (Central America) is a piñata filled with surprises. Bash it open to release a cascade of knowledge stretching back to 1800 BCE about the Olmecs, Zapotecs, and Maya. The best-known are the Maya, whose heyday began about 200 CE. They developed city-states with ornately carved temples, towering pyramids, and huge palaces. How smashing!

DON'T LOSE YOUR HEAD

Many Mesoamerican cultures had a ballgame played with a heavy rubber ball. Players had to bounce the ball off the walls of a long, narrow court, and score by passing the ball through a hoop. The price of losing was more than just hurt pride – the captain of the losing team was sometimes beheaded as a sacrifice.

BIG HEAD

The Olmec people had an advanced civilization in south Mexico until they mysteriously disappeared about 350 BCE. The Maya inherited elements of their culture from the Olmecs, including the ballgame. Olmec art features massive stone heads, the largest of which are a whopping 3 m (9 ft) tall.

STEP UP

Mayan pyramids had steep, stepped sides, made of layers of stone, which led up to a temple. Some of these stepped pyramids took hundreds of years to build. Outside the temple, priests would make ritual human sacrifices to the many Mayan gods.

BUSTLING METROPOLIS

In 300 CE, Teotihuacán (now in north Mexico) was the largest city in Central America – bigger than any city in Europe. Like many Mesoamerican cities it was built on a grid pattern. Little is known about the people who built the city.

BLOOD SACRIFICE

The Maya sacrificed adults and children to their gods. The Olmecs, and others, offered their own blood, piercing themselves with spikes.

ZAPOTEC BELIEF

The Zapotec people of south Mexico (100–900 CE) believed that their ancestors emerged from the earth or changed from trees and jaguars into people. This ornate pottery urn is from the Zapotec capital, Monte Alban, a city built on an artificially levelled mountain.

RECTANGULAR READ

The Maya recorded their history, astronomy, and beliefs on long, folded manuscripts called codices, made of fig-tree bark. The glyphs – picture writing – were written in coloured inks using a porcupine quill. Each character was roughly rectangular.

69

QIN SHI HUANG (259–210 BCE)

Emperor who unified the warring states of China loses his fight for immortality

QIN SHI HUANG, the emperor who was obsessed with finding the elixir of life, has died at the age of 49. Under Qin's firm hand, China has been transformed from a group of seven warring states into the largest empire the world has ever seen. Reports that Qin in fact died two months ago whilst on a tour of his empire, and that the imperial litter returned to the capital flanked by wagons of fish to disguise the smell of his decaying corpse, have been dismissed as "codswallop" by officials.

From boy-king to supreme emperor

The late Emperor was born Ying Zheng, in Qin state, northwest China, and became king of Qin in 246 BCE at the age of 13. At 21 he came of age and took full power, employing a combination of espionage, bribery, and ruthless military leadership to bring the other six states under his control. In 221 BCE, he declared himself Qin Shi Huang, or "First Sovereign Emperor", of a united China. Characteristically confident, he predicted that the new Qin Dynasty would "rule for 10,000 generations".

Under Qin's firm hand, China has been transformed from seven warring states into the largest empire the world has ever seen

One China

The Emperor put in place standard units of weights and measures, as well as a common currency and written language. He built new roads and canals to ease the movement of troops and goods, and demolished fortifications separating states. However, those critics brave enough to speak out against the Emperor suggest that thousands of peasants, scholars, and soldiers died due to the appalling working conditions on his building projects.

Qin Shi Huang in his prime

Qin's tomb is guarded by an army of terracotta soldiers

The burning of books and burying of scholars was a low point in Qin's reign

A committed legalist

Qin Shi Huang will be remembered as a keen proponent of legalism, a form of government that recognizes that people are not naturally virtuous. Strict laws and severe punishments were put in place, aimed at enhancing the power of the state and emperor. Qin's harsher acts include burning books of no practical use and the alleged burying alive of 460 scholars.

The quest for eternal life

The Emperor feared death and became obsessed with finding the secret of immortality. His recent demise proves that this was one venture that was ultimately doomed. The Emperor's body will be sealed inside an elaborate mausoleum running with rivers of mercury, guarded by an army of 7,500 terracotta warriors, and booby-trapped against tomb raiders.

We've been at sea for days, and still no sight of land! Although rowing has been a bit tricky, what with not having any arms. Look at all this water... The Pacific is a big place! Makes you realize how brave the Polynesians must have been. Their ancestors came from Papua New Guinea and settled on islands as far away as Tonga and Samoa. Then about 300 BCE the Polynesians set out to sail vast distances over open ocean and settle on 1,000 small islands.

Papua New Guinea

Hawaii

Tonga and Samoa

The Polynesians travelled 3,200 km (2,000 miles)

Easter Island

New Zealand

In the end they found New Zealand, many arriving around 900–1,000 years ago. Waves of Polynesian settlers set up home on the North Island, becoming the Maori people. As their numbers grew, the different tribes began to squabble, and some moved onto the South Island.

If they'd carved him a few tonnes lighter we might've got somewhere by now...

If they'd used boats like ours they wouldn't have got very far! Their boats were much better — they had two hulls joined together with a platform, stabilizing floats called outriggers, and sails for when there was a wind. These boats could carry 100 people and their animals, and go thousands of kilometres without landing. The Polynesians navigated by the tides, winds, currents, stars — and even the flight patterns of birds.

The Polynesians made stick charts to map the tides and currents, with cowrie shells marking the islands

I wish I were at home right now... We Moai have got the run of the place! The Easter Islanders chopped down all the island's trees to use as rollers to get us from the quarries to our positions on the coast. With no trees, there was no wood left to build fishing boats and the settlers ended up starving.

The Moai were built about 1300 – there are 887 on the island, many still in the quarries where they were carved

How do you think they're getting on?

Tangaroa, the Polynesian god of the sea, is found in the beliefs of many Pacific islands

Once the Polynesians settled on an island, they lived quite an isolated existence. So the Polynesian cultures were all different, but there were some similarities — the same gods for example. As for us, no one knows what on earth we were for.

73

Jesus was born in Bethlehem, Palestine, in about 4 BCE. The story of his life forms the New Testament of the Bible, the central text of Christianity, which was written during the first 100 years after his death. According to the Bible, Jesus was born to a virgin mother, named Mary. He performed miracles during his life, which his followers and later Christians took as evidence that he was the son of God. He gathered a band of disciples (followers), with 12 main disciples who were later called apostles, and travelled around Galilee, Israel, teaching and converting people to his faith. He taught using parables – stories with an embedded meaning – rather than through intellectual debate. His message that God loves the poor, and that anyone can be saved through showing love towards God and fellow human beings, was popular with the common people. However, the ruling Romans and Jewish elders saw Jesus as a challenge to their authority. The local Roman leader Pilate had Jesus executed by crucifixion. Christ's followers claimed that he returned from the dead after three days, then ascended to heaven.

The birth of Christianity
The Christian religion stems from the life and acts of Jesus Christ, who lived
The life and death of Christ

Christianity first flourished in Jerusalem and Antioch but it quickly spread around the Mediterranean, carried by apostles and other converts. Soon after Christ's death, the apostle Peter preached the first sermon and converted 3,000 people to the new faith. He ended his life as the first bishop of Rome, or pope, and is considered the founder of the Christian Church.

Origins of the Church

2,000 years ago in Palestine, when it was part of the Roman Empire. Christianity is rooted in Judaism.

Spreading the faith

Life was not easy for the early Christians. The Romans and Jews resented the threat to their own beliefs. At times the Roman authorites actively persecuted Christians – condemning those who refused to give up their faith to crucifixion, or pitting them against gladiators and wild animals in the arena in fights they were doomed to lose. Christians were forced to worship in secret, but their faith spread quickly and there were Christians throughout the Roman Empire within 200 years of Christ's death. The Christians brought a comforting message, and exciting stories of martyrdom and saints attracted ever more followers. Between 303 and 306, Roman emperor Diocletian ordered the burning of churches and holy texts, and the arrest and torture of Christians. Persecution ended in 311, and under Constantine, the first Christian emperor, religious freedom was granted throughout the Empire in 313. Christianity became the official religion of Rome in 380.

CAT FIGHT! (OR...

UNDER NEW MANAGEMENT

Since the late 2nd century, Germanic tribes from northern Europe had been stirring up trouble for the Roman Empire. As Roman rule weakened, the tribes grew in strength and ganged together. In 378, the Goths killed the emperor Valens in battle, and went on to sack Rome in 410. Peace was restored, but the attacks continued. Could it be last orders for the Roman Empire?

Quintus, it's good to see you. A familiar face is very welcome – this place isn't what it used to be. It's crawling with Goths, Visigoths, Huns, and Vandals. They don't have any respect! Twice their kind have sacked this city, tearing through the place like a load of hooligans. Young people today!

The last time, in 455, it was carnage. And forcing the Emperor to abdicate in 476 – I ask you! You'd expect better – that Odoacer was a Roman general, after all! It was a sad day when he deposed Romulus Augustus. Bring back the emperors, I say!

Nonsense, Vibius, they're all as bad as each other. If I were a younger man I'd box their ears! Romulus Augustus may have been the so-called "last Western Roman emperor" but really he was little more than a puppet – a mere boy!

Don't you remember how his father Orestes kicked out Emperor Julius Nepos? He persuaded Odoacer and his barbarian tribes to revolt, then when Julius Nepos fled, Orestes stuck his son Romulus on the throne and called him emperor. But Orestes didn't keep his promises to the barbarians, so Odoacer killed him, kicked his son out, and declared himself king of Italy. Not emperor, mind you – king. That was back in 476, was it? How time flies!

We should move east, Quintus, old man – they still have an empire there. It's going from strength to strength, even expanding! And they say the Eastern Roman Emperor will restore the Empire here one day...

You're dreaming, old timer! They've got their own problems. Why do you think they roped in Theoderic the Ostrogoth to get rid of Odoacer? It was because Odoacer was starting to look like a threat to the Eastern Roman Empire.

Hundreds of Native North American tribes (**p110**), all with different customs and ways of life, thrive across North America.

Barbarian kingdoms (**p84**) rule in Europe. Charlemagne, king of the Franks, unites many of these kingdoms in the late 700s and early 800s (**p86**), extending his Empire across western Europe. The feudal system (**p90**) evolves as the system of government. Knights (**p92**) grow wealthy from serving their lords. Europe is also dominated by the increasingly powerful Catholic Church (**p94**). From the late 11th century, trade and commerce flourishes in Europe (**p112**), leading to the rise of a new merchant class.

The Aztecs (**p106**) dominate Central America.

In 1337, England and France begin a conflict that will last for 116 years (**p114**). Fighting is stalled in the 1340s, when the Black Death (**p116**) hits Europe. This terrible plague wipes out up to a third of the continent's population.

On the western coast of South America, Inca civilization (**p108**) reaches its height.

The middle bit

It's fighting talk with Viking raiders, jousting knights, and Mongol warriors making their mark in this time of wars, plagues, and… more wars. Deadly!

During the Middle Ages (aka the "Dark Ages") many advances of the Greek and Roman civilizations are lost and Europe is divided into feuding barbarian kingdoms. But around the rest of the world, the lights are on. The Aztecs and Incas dominate Central and South America, and the Khmers reign supreme over southeast Asia. Back in Europe, a feudal system puts kings on top, supported by warrior knights. The Christian Church grows rich and powerful, while a new religion – Islam – emerges in the east. Expanded trade routes aid the spread of new beliefs.

Take me back to the years 400–1399

Vikings (**p88**) from Scandinavia raid and trade their way across Europe, reaching as far afield as Greenland, North America, and the Byzantine Empire in their longboats.

The eastern part of the Roman Empire survives the decline of the western part and becomes the Byzantine Empire (**p80**), with its capital at Constantinople.

Under the leadership of Genghis Khan, the fearsome Mongol warriors (**p104**) sweep across Asia, amassing an empire that stretches from India and Russia to China and North Korea.

When the Pope (head of the Catholic Church) calls for a holy war to reclaim Palestine from Muslim rule, knights from all over Europe join the Crusades (**p96**).

In China, the Tang and Sung dynasties preside over a golden age of arts and literature (**p100**).

Followers of the prophet Muhammad (**p82**) spread Islam across the Arabian Peninsula in the 7th century.

Regional kingdoms rule India (**p102**).

The Khmers (**p98**) reign over southeast Asia.

A mighty empire rules southern Africa, with its monumental stone capital at Great Zimbabwe (**p118**).

Going up ▶▶

Surcoats: By wearing a long tunic called a surcoat, knights could protect their armour from overheating in the sun or rusting in the rain.

Books: Beautifully decorated and laboriously written out by hand, books are a serious luxury – except in China where they've invented block printing.

Human sacrifices: Head to the Aztec and Inca empires for a full-on gorefest. The Aztecs will sacrifice thousands at once.

Bald patches: Medieval monks cut hair from their scalps to leave a large, bare circle at the back. Known as a tonsure, it is a sign of their commitment to the Church. Good look!

Paper money: Rest of the world take note – the Sung Dynasty in China came up with the ingenious notion of paper money. No more bartering goods for them.

Going down ◀◀

Rats: The flea-infested rodents spread the Black Death plague far and wide, killing thousands.

Religious tolerance: A series of Crusades pitted Christians against Muslims for control of Palestine.

Roman numerals: No more using letters as numbers. The numbers we use today were first developed in India in around 500, adopted by Arabs in the 800s, who passed them on to Europe in the 900s.

BYZANTINE EMPIRE

In 324, a new capital for the Roman Empire was established at Constantinople, in modern-day Turkey. Soon after, the Empire was divided into east and west. While the western part of the Empire collapsed against barbarian invaders, the Eastern Roman Empire endured for another 1,100 years. Its citizens called themselves Romans, but they became known as the Byzantines, after the original name of the town where Constantinople was founded.

DEEPLY DEVOUT

With Rome in decline, Constantinople became the richest and most influential centre of Christianity. The Byzantine Church did not recognize the authority of the pope, and took on a distinct form of worship from Roman Catholicism, involving different rituals and ceremonies.

ARCHITECTURE

Constantinople was a rich city, with great churches and glittering mosaic decorations. The Byzantines are famous for having worked out how to build huge circular domes on square bases. They can be seen on hundreds of churches, including the great Hagia Sophia, which was built during the reign of Justinian.

EMPEROR JUSTINIAN

The Empire reached its height under Justinian, who became emperor in 527. He recovered territory that had been lost, and during his reign the Empire stretched right across Spain, Italy, Greece, and North Africa to Persia.

THE END

By 1081, a succession of weak emperors had left the Empire in pieces. Constantinople was looted by Christian soldiers from the west in 1204, and the city never recovered. The end finally came in 1453, when it was captured by the Ottoman Turks and renamed Istanbul.

ICONS

In Byzantine Christianity, religious icons (images of Jesus, the saints, and other Christian figures) were worshipped and prayed to. In the 8th century, Emperor Leo III banned them, believing the creation of such images to be blasphemous (disrespectful to God).

EMPEROR CONSTANTINE

Constantine was the emperor who moved his capital from Rome to Byzantium and named it after himself. He was the first Christian Roman emperor and allowed Christians to worship freely. During the reign of Theodosius I (379–395) Christianity became the official Roman religion.

THE BIRTH OF ISLAM

Early in the 7th century a religious movement was born in Arabia. The man who revealed this new religion was called Muhammad.

Muhammad was born in the city of Mecca (in modern-day Saudi Arabia) in 570 CE. He grew up a thoughtful man, and used to visit a cave outside the city where he could meditate. One night he saw an angel who revealed some holy verses to him and instructed him to preach a new faith based on the one true God, Allah. Muhammad became a prophet, or messenger of God, and began teaching in Mecca. He gave the new religion the name Islam, which means "submission and obedience to the will of God".

The people of Mecca became uneasy about the new religion and early converts were persecuted. Muhammad was forced to flee with his friend Abu Bakr. They went to a city called Medina, where Muhammad was treated with respect. He soon gathered a large army behind him, and in 630 he re-entered Mecca as undisputed leader.

Muhammad died of a fever in 632. There was much controversy over who should succeed him – should the new leader be elected or hereditary? Muslims eventually split into two groups, called Sunni and Shia. To this day, the dispute has not been settled. Sunnis believe that the Prophet intended Abu Bakr to become the new leader, while Shias think that only Muhammad's descendents should be eligible. Within 100 years of Muhammad's death, countries as far apart as Spain and India were ruled by Muslims. Muhammad's visions and teachings were gathered in a book, the Qur'an, which Muslims follow as the word of God.

Some Muslims use prayer beads, or misbaha, to help them recite verses from the Qur'an.

Islamic art often uses calligraphy (beautiful writing) – this example spells out Muhammad's name in Arabic.

Islamic styles of art and architecture developed, with artists producing outstanding textiles, metalwork, and ceramics, such as this floor tile.

BARBARIAN BEAT 'EM UP

Ready to take your chances against some of the scariest figures in medieval history? Well grab your consoles, gamers, because this hack 'n' slash will take you back to the Dark Ages. In the 4th and 5th centuries, barbarian peoples from the east migrated across Asia to Europe. They laid waste to the remains of the Western Roman Empire and then set about trying to waste each other. Their name comes from the Latin "barbarus", meaning uncivilized, and their fierce, warlike nature earned them a fearsome reputation. Ready to play? First select your fighter...

ALARIC THE GOTH

The Goths were a Germanic people, who split into the Visigoths (western Goths) and Ostrogoths (eastern Goths) in the 5th century. Between them, they ruled southwest France, Spain, and parts of Greece and Italy. In 410, led by Alaric, the Visigoths invaded Italy and actually managed to capture Rome. A disaster for the Western Roman Empire. Good Goth!

GOTH

75:50

THEODELINDA, LOMBARD PRINCESS

The Lombards from northern Europe plundered Italy at the end of the 6th century. They established a kingdom there that lasted 200 years, until Charlemagne, a Frankish king, ended their rule. Theodelinda was a Lombard ruler who encouraged the spread of Christianity – a good choice if you prefer a strategy game.

CLOVIS THE FRANK

Late arrivals on the scene, the Franks became a force to be reckoned with. They started in northern Germany. Then, in about 490, they converted to Christianity and fought their way south, under an ambitious king, Clovis. They beat the Visigoths and took over France.

GAISERIC THE VANDAL

In 429 the Vandals seized the Roman city of Carthage on the North African coast and established a stronghold there. In 455, led by Gaiseric, they sacked Rome itself and went on to rule the Mediterranean Sea. Not to be messed with, but not averse to doing a bit of messing – their unique style gave us the modern word "vandalism".

ATTILA THE HUN

If you're a newbie, steer clear of these most barbaric of barbarians. The Huns were a fierce nomadic tribe who invaded Europe in the 4th century. They came out of the steppes (grasslands) of central Asia and spread to Germany. Under the leadership of Attila, the Huns attacked the Eastern and Western Roman empires and clashed with the Goths. But they fizzled out after Attila's death in 453.

HUN

CERDIC THE ANGLO SAXON

Originally known as the Angles, Saxons, and Jutes in northern Germany, they attacked the old Roman province of Britain in the 5th and 6th centuries. They took over most of Britain, dividing it up into small kingdoms. Cerdic ruled Wessex, one of these kingdoms, in the 6th century.

CHARLEMAGNE
AS HE IS CROWNED HOLY ROMAN EMPEROR

...ristmas Day was particularly special this year ...use of the remarkable honour bestowed upon ..., Charlemagne by Pope Leo III. Charlemagne, ... in 742 and made sole king of the Franks at ...ge of 29, has had a meteoric rise to celebrity. ...aught up with the the newly crowned Holy ...an Emperor for an exclusive interview.

...gratulations Charles. May I call you Charles?
...s cut to the chase. We've just witnessed a
...ning moment. Everyone will be dying to know,
...t were you wearing for this grand occasion?
...ally wasn't a grand occasion. I didn't even know

it was going to happen. So I was wearing my usual simple garb. Just a woollen tunic.

Lovely. And is that coat made of otter skin?
Er… Perhaps we can talk about my achievements? I am, after all, the first Holy Roman Emperor.

Quite. Tell us, then, how did it happen?
I'd come to visit Rome and was kneeling at the altar of St Peter, deep in prayer, when Pope Leo surprised me by seizing a golden crown and placing it upon my head. He then announced my new status as Holy Roman Emperor.

How do you feel about that then? It does suggest

that if he can give you the title, Pope Leo is more powerful than you.
Let me just say that this is the first time in history that a pope has bowed to an earthly king. And by this action, Pope Leo has showed his support of the west and rejection of the eastern Byzantine Empire. This is very welcome.

Was the Pope wearing anything special to mark the occasion? No? OK, moving on, can you tell us what you regard as your major achievement?
There have been so many! I started out as king of the Franks, and now I'm the undisputed leader of

western Europe. I've conquered the various Germanic tribes in northern Europe and fought hard against the Sorbs, Avars, and Slavs from the east.

And gained enormous treasure and riches…
Which I used to build churches and monasteries, and a new capital in Aachen.

So it's war, then, that has given you the greatest sense of pride?
Not war for war's sake. The spread of Christianity, that's my main aim. And I'm very loyal to the pope – for example, in 773 I defeated those barbarian invaders in northern Italy, the Lombards, at Pope Leo's request.

This spread of Christianity that you mention – in 772 you began a series of bloodthirsty wars with the Saxons to the north of your kingdom. In 782 they launched a surprise attack, and you responded by beheading 4,500 Saxon prisoners during a single day.
They were pagans.

Still, it seems a bit harsh…
I gave them the option of choosing between Christianity and death. They chose death. I was determined to turn barbarism into civilization. It has taken me nearly 30 years, but I think I've succeeded.

Indeed, you've been described as "tireless". You've brought order to Europe and united the barbarian kingdoms of western Europe. Charlemagne means "Charles the Great", doesn't it?
Yes, but I'm a simple man, with moderate tastes. I don't like to show off.

To what do you owe your military successes?
Organization! You have to plan ahead. Before a campaign I tell my counts, princes, and bishops how many men they need to bring, what arms they should carry, and what to put in the supply wagons. And I make sure we march swiftly.

But you didn't always win, did you?
I had 53 campaigns, and led nearly all of them. Only a few didn't go as planned. Back in 778, I led my army to Spain to battle with the Saracens. The Basques of northern Spain pounced on us in the Pyrenees as we returned.

Ah yes, they killed your best knight, the legendary Count Roland. He was a favourite pin-up of ours. Now, moving on from war…
Must we? My war record is unparalleled.

Can we discuss your family? There was a bit of argy-bargy with King Offa of England, wasn't there, over marriage to your daughter Bertha?
That was a few years ago. I proposed that my son marry one of Offa's daughters. He countered this with a request that his son Ecgfrith marry Bertha. I was incensed.

Why was that?
It implied that Offa was my equal, but it's all in the past. King Offa is my dearest brother.

You've survived family rebellion. Pepin, your eldest son, plotted to kill you.
He was disappointed when I told him he would not succeed to my title. I spoilt him perhaps, and expected too much…

Why was he called Pepin the Hunchback?
Are you serious?

It's just that most of our readers won't have seen a picture…
Its good that there are readers. When I came to the throne most people were illiterate. It was appalling! I've welcomed hundreds of foreign scholars to court and have started several schools. I've regulated agriculture, established a government, and encouraged better morals. And don't forget industry and finance. We have a stable currency! I've even taxed the nobles. We've built new roads and waterways, and developed a system of poor relief. And I'm a great patron of the arts.

Yes, they are calling it the Carolingian Renaissance.
That's very flattering. My family name means a great deal to me.

Well, thank you, King Charlemagne. That's a good place to finish. On behalf of *Heated* magazine, we wish you many more years of happy leadership.

INTERVIEW: HILDEGARD PENPUSHER
PHOTOS: LOUIS THE ILLUMINATOR

Charlemagne did not receive a fee for this interview but requested that a donation of his new currency, the "pound", be given to the Carolingian Arts Council.

"It wasn't a grand occasion – I didn't even know it was going to happen. So I was just wearing my usual simple garb"

Pepin the Hunchback, Charlemagne's eldest son, is illegitimate and had to be exiled after plotting to kill his father and his family back in 792. "He never got over being disinherited," admits the King.

Charlemagne's reign has been marked by near-constant warfare in his battle for supremacy in Europe (the pink area of this map shows how far his empire extends).
By establishing a central government and spreading Christianity, it is thought Charlemagne has paved the way for a modern Europe.

Danes
Anglo-Saxon Kingdoms
Saxons   Slavs
Aachen   Sorbs
Avars
Lombards
Rome
Muslim Empire

The King is a big fan of books, despite struggling to read himself. Literary men of every nationality are welcomed at his court, and every cathedral and monastery has been urged to establish schools so that people can learn to read and write.

Jobs • Property • Events • Travel

Since the 8th century, the Vikings have been raiding and trading across Europe. The *Viking Times* reaches more Vikings than any competitor – from wild warriors to skilled craftsmen, Scandinavians to Greenlanders and the Rus from Kiev, explorers to homemakers. Call now to place an ad.

Jobs

Boat builders needed

Knowledge of the latest technology, especially keels, is essential

■ Openings available for axe-wielding types who like living life at the sharp end.

■ You will spend an age expertly crafting a beautifully balanced ship designed to strike terror into the enemy, only to see it taken over by burly oarsmen who might smash it against the Irish coast.

■ Failing this, it might be used as part of a burial and never seen again.

For more information, visit **Dragon Designs***, our workshop on the seafront*

Do you have a head for figures and a body for strenuous travel?

Do you know the difference between glass and pottery? Would you recognize a spice if you sneezed on it?

Then this is the job for you!

Travel across Europe and Asia, trading our Viking honey, wool, fur, iron, and tin for wine, silk, and silver. We have orders coming in for British wheat, so don't delay, join up today.

King Trader

Bringing you the finest goods the Viking world has to offer

Excellent salary and benefits

Berserkers

This is not a position for the faint-hearted. A longship captain requires 10 men to leap to the front of his ship when it nears the enemy coastline, jump over the side waving swords about, and basically go crazy. Battle-whooping training and bearskin outfit provided. An ability to scare children a must. Good lookers need not apply.

Warning!
Beserkers are known to get so worked up, they jump too soon and drown in deep water. A good sense of timing is therefore an advantage.

GO CRAZY!
Shouting and shield-biting auditions take place a week on Tuesday

Erik the Red seeks raiders

Have you got strong arms, a love of fish, and a burning ambition to get filthy rich? Good at running, with a complete lack of conscience?

■ The Viking raider needs to be keen to see the known world, a confident sailor, and, more importantly, not scared of the Saxons. If you're a bit handy and fancy an adventure, take to the waves in one of Erik's longboats. Riches await in the monasteries on England's coastline.

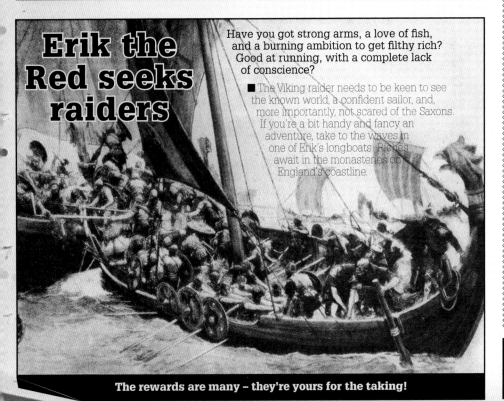

The rewards are many – they're yours for the taking!

Weaveking
urgently seaks weavers

If you're super skilled with an eye for fashion, here's a great way to supplement your income.

Weaveking supplies colourful cloaks, trousers, and tunics for both sexes, as well as cloth for blankets and sails. We have looms ready and waiting for you to get weaving!

All looms are the latest in technology: vertical, well-maintained, and fully fitted with heavy stone rings to keep the up-and-down (warp) threads straight and tight.

Our fabulous bright dyes are taken from traditional, all-natural plant ingredients.

Staff discounts and flexible hours!

For sale

The ideal gift for every occasion

A timeless, classic design

Keepsake

Lovingly modelled on a brooch seen in the British Isles. The silver pin and ring are inlaid with gold. This marvellous status symbol is very useful as a clasp for a cloak.

BJÖRN'S JEWELLERY

Since 749 CE

15 Gokstad Street, Thorsheim

THE VIKING CHRONICLE

COMPLETE Viking History FOR ONLY 39

pieces of hack-silver

This comprehensive history of the Viking peoples explains how they ventured out of their Scandinavian homelands of Norway, Sweden, and Denmark in the 9th century, and terrorized the coasts of northern Europe with their raids on monasteries and small communities.

The Chronicle explains how they settled in the lands they raided, colonizing Greenland, Iceland, Russia, France, Britain, Ireland, and Newfoundland. It explores how these Norse warriors also turned their hand to farming. There are informative chapters on their trade all over Europe and Asia, and as far afield as the Byzantine Empire.

"Packed with interesting facts. Better than a saga any day" – **Erik the Ready**

NorBook co.

Wanted

Bric-a-brac

Good prices paid for the genuine article

Have you got the latest in looted booty? We're seeking relics carefully prised from the hands of grovelling monks. Particularly interested in bishops' crosses from Ireland and gold from the 793 raid on Lindisfarne.

ALL MONASTERY TREASURES CONSIDERED

Property

Icelandic turf house

1,250.00

On the market at a fantastic price. The fortress-like structure has thick turf walls, floors of compacted earth and charcoal, and interior walls lined by raised sleeping benches. It also boasts attached toilets. Tired of living in a big, open-plan longhouse? Then this is a must-see property.

Longhouse

7,999.00

Viking Fort Properties is thrilled to offer an established longhouse consisting of one 20-m- (65-ft-) long room with rounded corners. Built of stone and timber it has a newly replaced thatched roof. No stairs. Some modernization required. Ideal for communal living: cooking, eating, storytelling.

Events

"The Most Fun You Can Have" Promotions brings you the feast to end all feasts. As much elk and wild boar as you can eat. New season berries. Harry the Harpist will play your requests. The king's own poet, back by popular demand, will perform his latest ode.

Dancing on Ice! Grab your furs, sharpen those animal bones, strap them to the bottom of your boots, and get skating. Large gathering of ice skaters to meet on the lake. Warm mead provided.

Skiing Do you worry that your sons will not be able to hunt for meat in the winter? Unsure about their cross-country endurance? We're offering a one-off ski session to hone those essential skiing skills. Archery practised, too. Any meat caught can be taken home.

Travel

Wish you were here?

Take a holiday with a difference. Come and see the famous Norse Men of northern France.* Relax in the sun. Take home some wine. Worried about foreign food and strange languages? Our Viking settlers have been there since the 9th century so you'll feel right at home.

LONGBOAT TOURS

*Or see our other great package deals to Russia, Constantinople, and China.

GREENLAND

HAVE YOU GOT THE NERVE?

Legendary adventurer Erik the Red seeks intrepid explorers to begin a new life in Greenland, discovered by the Vikings in 870. Beautiful surroundings and superb hunting opportunities. Possibility of violent storms during the crossing.

Daring discoverers must be ready to set sail about 985. All interested parties to meet at Erik's mother's longhouse.

club arctic

Deaths

Rollo (860–932) It is with great sadness that we report the death of Rollo the Walker. Named for the fact that he was so large, no horse could carry him, Rollo will be remembered as the founder of Normandy, land of the Norse Men. Converted to Christianity but never forgot his pagan roots.

Leif the Lucky (970–1020), son of Erik the Red, has finally been unlucky and died. Leif grew up in Greenland but visited Norway around 999 where he converted to Christianity. Returning to Greenland he was blown off course and reached North America, becoming the first European to reach the New World. What a Viking!

Feudal Europe

Medieval Europe was a dangerous and violent place. In western and northern Europe, a system called feudalism evolved to help people protect themselves. This system was like a tree of loyalty, with the king at the top. The king would give land to his lords, and in return each lord would vow to protect the king by providing armies for him. The lord passed on some of his land to his knights so that they would join his private army. At the bottom of the tree were the serfs (slaves) who worked the land.

Knight

The nobleman has given me some land and in return I have to protect him, his family, and the king. I'm quite wealthy, but never have time to enjoy it because I'm always off fighting!

Woman

Whinge, whinge, whinge. You should try being a medieval woman! I have to obey my husband or I get beaten. I have no rights. I got married at 12, and will work myself to an early grave.

King

I am right at the top of the tree. The royal court is the centre of the kingdom and I have huge power to rule over my subjects. But it's a bit wobbly up here. There's always someone after my throne, that's why I need soldiers to fight for me!

Lord

As a nobleman, I'm sitting pretty. I've vowed to serve my king, and in return he has given me land and a fine manor house. I lend him my knights when he needs it, but the fact I've got an army makes the king nervous, so he's always trying to keep me happy.

Serf

He's lucky he's not a serf! The lord has allotted me some land, but I have to pay him rent *and* work on his land as well as my own. It's difficult enough to grow enough food to feed my family! I am tired, poor, hungry, and live in a squalid little cottage.

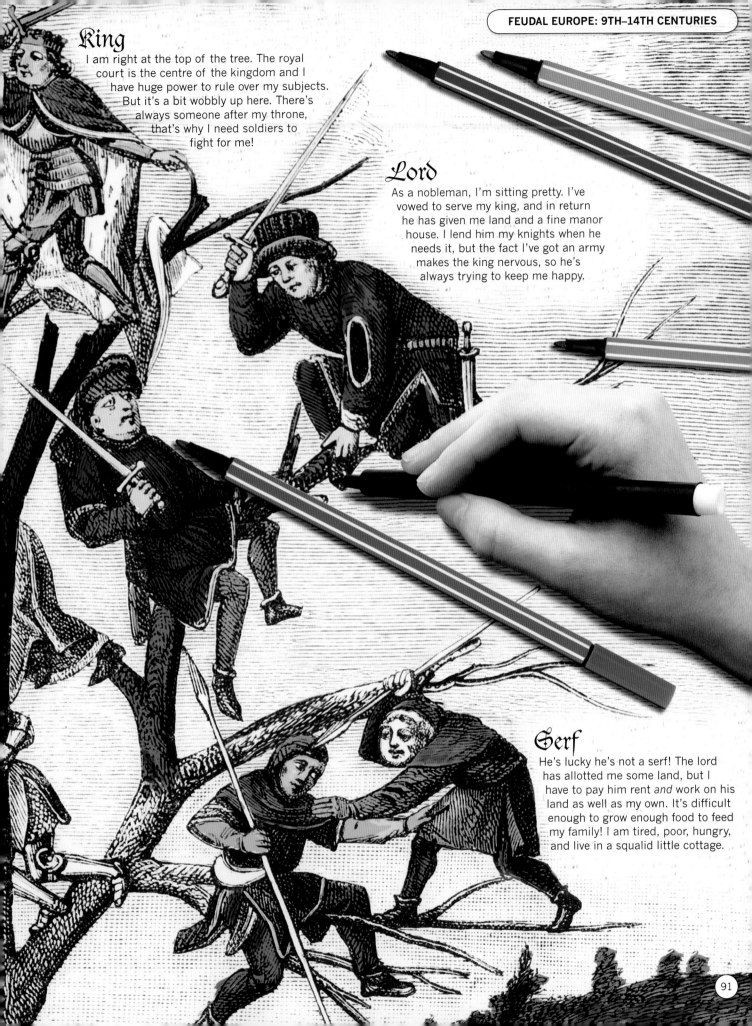

ULRICH VON LICHTENSTEIN

This week we meet a knight who has been making quite a splash at the summer's jousting tournaments – the lance-wielding poet from Lichtenstein, Sir Ulrich.

Ulrich became a page at age eight

Q: How would you describe yourself, my lord?
A: Above all, as an expert warrior. I know how to ride, and use a lance and sword. Guys like me, we're the backbone of the army. But it's not all about war. Yes, I'm a rough fighting man, but I also write poems, dance, and I enjoy jousting. Not wishing to blow my own trumpet, but you could say I'm a bit of a hit with the ladies, too, if you know what I mean...

Q: Yes, you claim to joust for the honour of a noblewoman. You've also recently been spotted touring dressed as Venus, the goddess of love...
A: I just feel a lot more comfy in a dress.

Q: OK, well moving on... How did you become a knight?

> *"There can be nothing more important to a knight than fighting for the honour of a lady"*

A: It takes a combination of things really – money, a noble birth, and of course years of training. At first I was a page. I served food, ran errands, that type of thing. When I was 17, I swore allegiance to the king and proved myself on the battlefield. I spend about 40 days a year fighting, but that leaves plenty of time for chillin' in my castle!

Ulrich's book of autobiographical poetry, Frauendienst: Service of the Lady, *is available from all good bookshops, priced two groats.*

Unbeaten: Ulrich claims he's never lost a joust.

ULRICH VON LICHTENSTEIN
Frauendienst

Top chivalry tips
Chivalry is the code of conduct all knights should follow. Knights are expected to be bold in battle, but also sporting and fair.

1. **Protect the weak, poor, and defenceless**
2. **Fear God and defend the Christian faith**
3. **Respect women**
4. **Tell the truth at all times**

Get the look
"It's an expensive outfit and you'll need a squire to help put it on."
Ulrich's armour is made of metal – metal plates and interlocking links called mail – and is very heavy. Underneath, he wears a shirt lined with satin and trousers called hose.

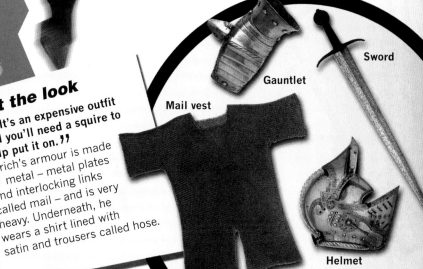

Sword

Gauntlet

Mail vest

Helmet

CASTLE PROFILE:

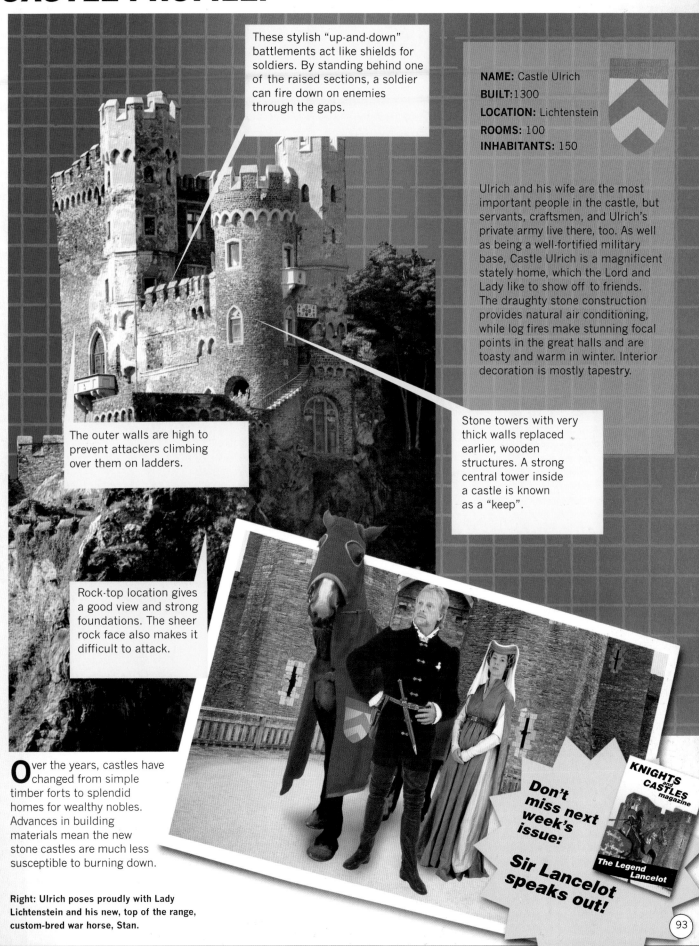

These stylish "up-and-down" battlements act like shields for soldiers. By standing behind one of the raised sections, a soldier can fire down on enemies through the gaps.

NAME: Castle Ulrich
BUILT: 1300
LOCATION: Lichtenstein
ROOMS: 100
INHABITANTS: 150

Ulrich and his wife are the most important people in the castle, but servants, craftsmen, and Ulrich's private army live there, too. As well as being a well-fortified military base, Castle Ulrich is a magnificent stately home, which the Lord and Lady like to show off to friends. The draughty stone construction provides natural air conditioning, while log fires make stunning focal points in the great halls and are toasty and warm in winter. Interior decoration is mostly tapestry.

The outer walls are high to prevent attackers climbing over them on ladders.

Stone towers with very thick walls replaced earlier, wooden structures. A strong central tower inside a castle is known as a "keep".

Rock-top location gives a good view and strong foundations. The sheer rock face also makes it difficult to attack.

Over the years, castles have changed from simple timber forts to splendid homes for wealthy nobles. Advances in building materials mean the new stone castles are much less susceptible to burning down.

Right: Ulrich poses proudly with Lady Lichtenstein and his new, top of the range, custom-bred war horse, Stan.

Don't miss next week's issue:

KNIGHTS and **CASTLES** magazine

The Legend Lancelot

Sir Lancelot speaks out!

Christian Europe

In medieval Europe, nearly everything was influenced by religion and the Christian Church was an important part of people's lives. People believed that if they did not go to church they would burn in hell. Most Christians were Roman Catholic. This made the Catholic Church, and the pope, its head, very powerful.

HIGHWAY TO HEAVEN

Roman Catholic Christians believe that after death a person's soul has to wait in an unpleasant place called purgatory before reaching heaven or hell. Medieval preachers were forever warning people of the horrors of purgatory and hell. Failing to go to church every week might mean not getting a place in heaven.

LOSING THE LATIN

Not all Christians were Catholic. The Eastern Orthodox Church split from Rome in 1054. The Orthodox camp included the Greek and Russian Churches and developed its own style. Orthodox worship involved many rituals and the use of religious images called icons, and moved away from using Latin for services.

BUILT TO INSPIRE

Designed to be spectacular monuments to God, cathedrals could take centuries to build. They were a focus of stunning art and architecture, and a sign of the wealth of the Church in Europe. Most cathedrals were built in the shape of a cross in a "Gothic" style, with pointed arches and tall spires.

A LOT AT STAKE

Anyone who was suspected of disagreeing with the Church's teachings was called a heretic and burnt at the stake. Some were Christians who worshipped God in a different way. Others were people accused of having contact with the devil, such as witches. Careless talk could cause hot bother!

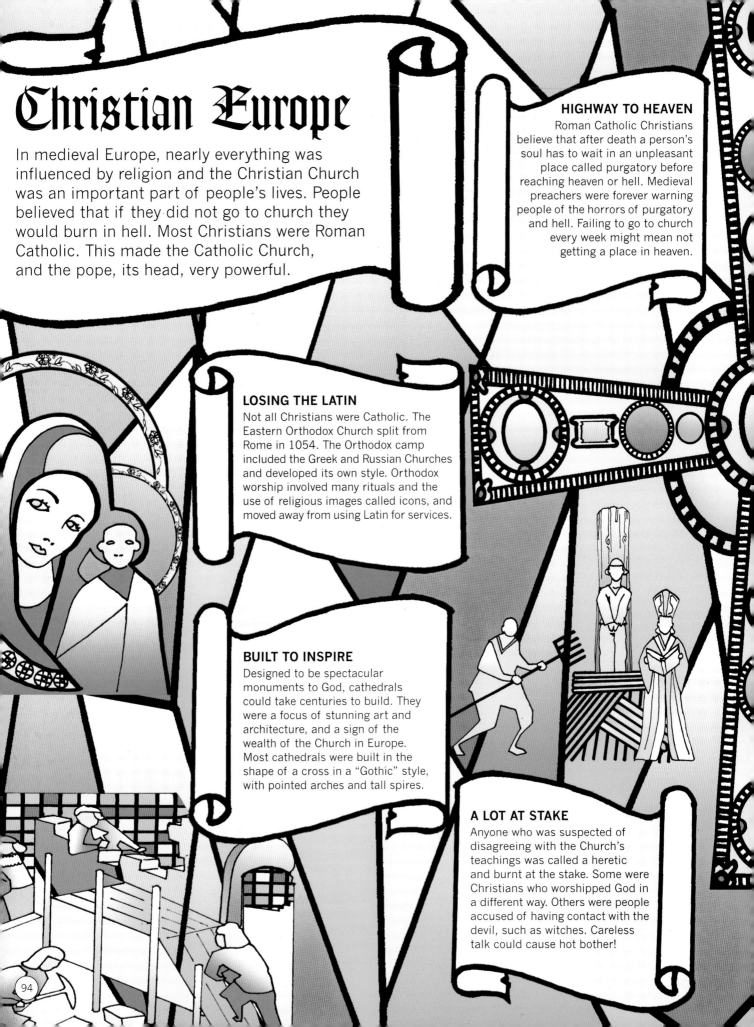

GOOD HABITS

Monasteries sprung up across Christian Europe. Life for the monks who lived in them was very strict. They wore robes called habits and had the back of their heads tonsured (shaved bald). As well as going to church, monks attended prayers seven times a day and worked hard farming monastery lands, doing the laundry, or tending to the sick.

BOOKED UP

Monasteries were the centres of knowledge, and many ran schools and libraries. Monks produced beautiful illuminated manuscripts. Pages of parchment (material made from animal skin) were written on and decorated, then bound into books.

TROUBLE AT THE TOP

For much of the medieval period there was a power tussle between the pope (the head of the Church) and kings (the heads of states). In 1076 Pope Gregory VII even claimed the right to dismiss emperors and kings. Powerful kings often ignored a pope's wishes, and this could lead to them being excommunicated (cast out from the Church).

CHANGING PLACES

In 1305, Pope Clement V decided to live in Avignon, France, instead of Rome. Seven (French) popes later, papal power returned to Rome – but not for long. A schism (split) resulted in two popes – one in Rome and one in Avignon – until Rome won out in 1417.

Spotlight on the Crusades

The Crusades were a series of wars between Christians and Muslims for control of the Holy Land (Palestine), an area important to both religions. In the late 11th century, Muslim Turks from central Asia invaded Palestine and began attacking Christians on pilgrimages to holy sites. In response, the Pope called for a "crusade", or holy war, to win the area back. There were nine major Crusades in all, over a period spanning 200 years, but by the end of the 13th century most of the Holy Land remained in Muslim hands.

Pope Urban II

In 1095, I called on all Christians to attack the Muslims who ruled Jerusalem, and recover the city and the rest of the Holy Land. I assured them that anyone who died fighting would go straight to heaven. The First Crusade succeeded in taking Jerusalem in 1099, but it was lost again to Saladin in 1187.

Peter the hermit

Europeans from all walks of life answered the Pope's appeal, including me, a humble preacher. In 1096, I inspired thousands of peasants to go with me to the Holy Land. This became known as the "People's Crusade", but it ended in disaster when we crusaders were slaughtered by the Turks before reaching the Holy Land.

Richard I

I'm King Richard I of England, a legendary soldier. I won fame on the Third Crusade (1189–1192), earning the nickname "Lionheart". I also earned a reputation for cruelty, after I had 2,700 Muslim captives slaughtered in front of their leader Saladin.

Saladin

My name's Saladin. I'm a Muslim sultan and a leading opponent of the Crusades. I defeated the Crusader armies at the Battle of Hattin in 1187, recapturing the cities of Jerusalem and Acre. My conduct won me a high reputation for chivalry, even among my Christian enemies.

Soldier Monk

I come from an order of Christian monks called the Knights Templar. Like all members, I took a vow of poverty, but am also a trained soldier. Our main purpose is to protect pilgrims going to the Holy Land. You can recognize us by our distinctive white tunics with a red cross. We were among the most skilled fighters in the Crusades.

LEVEL 1:
KHMER
EMPIRE

YOUR MISSION: *To help the Apsara find hidden gems in the vast Khmer Empire. First, you will have to locate modern Cambodia, Laos, and Thailand, and go back in time to between 802 and 1431, when the Khmer Empire controlled a large area of southeast Asia. In a race against time, you must explore the Khmer capital city of Angkor (in modern-day Cambodia). But beware — you may get lost in one of its thousand ancient temples.*

BOOST YOUR ENERGY: Gain extra lives by stocking up on supplies. The Khmers were an agricultural people, who lived mostly on rice and soup. They cooked in earthen pots and served their food in tiny bowls, using ladle sticks made of coconut shells. Collect some bowls of rice; they will come in useful.

BACK   PLAY   PAUSE

KING JAYAVARMAN

To get to the next level, you'll have to battle with Jayavarman (1181–1220). The most forceful of Khmer kings, he expanded the Empire and built hundreds of monuments, vast waterworks, roads, and hospitals. He broke with 400 years of Hindu tradition and made Buddhism the state religion. Be careful – he's a brilliant soldier.

MEDITATION STOP:

At first, the Khmers worshipped Hindu gods, but gradually the religion shifted to Buddhism. Go to the Bayon Temple in Angkor Thom, within the huge Angkor temple complex, and find all the gigantic Buddhist statues. Stop here to meditate and restore your health.

ENERGY LEVEL

LOCATOR MAP:

You'll need this map to track your location through Angkor Wat. It is the biggest temple at Angkor and the largest religious monument in the whole world. Built as a royal temple by King Suryavarman II in the 12th century, the walls are covered with battle scenes carved in stone. Tip: watch out for snakes while swimming across the moat!

THE APSARA

The graceful figures of the Apsara are found on the walls of the temples at Angkor. These mythological women were said to perform Hindu dances at the royal court. They represent the height of artistic achievement, when music, poetry, sculpture, and elaborate buildings flourished. Take time to learn the Apsara hand movements to progress through the game.

LEVEL SELECTION:

Work your way through some of the other empires in southeast Asia.

LEVEL 2: CHAMPA EMPIRE

Set in the mountains of south Vietnam, level two will pit your wits against the kingdom of the Chams. The Chams prospered between 921 and 1471, and were enemies of the Khmers.

LEVEL 3: SRIVIJAYA EMPIRE

Moving to the island of Sumatra, you'll find yourself in Palembang. This sea port was at the heart of the Srivijayan civilization (740–1402), which controlled an area of Indonesia.

LEVEL 4: DAI VIET EMPIRE

You'll need all the energy points you've gathered so far to take on the might of the Dai Viet Empire, which ruled north Vietnam from 1010 to1527.

TANG AND SUNG CHINA

Many ruling families have come and gone in China's long history. The Tang (618–907) made China one of the most powerful regions in the world. Buddhism flourished, and printing and pottery entered a golden age. All good things come to an end though – a spell of government corruption and in-fighting and bang went the Tang. The Sung Dynasty (960–1279) really struck a chord. It reunited China and presided over a period of great wealth and cultural achievement. But then the Mongols invaded and things went off key…

THE SILK ROAD
Trade routes known as the Silk Road linked China with other central Asian kingdoms. These important routes were expanded and secured by the Tang. This brought great wealth and saw the rise of the merchant classes.

BUDDHISM
All religions were permitted in Tang China, but it was Buddhism that became the most important part of Chinese culture. Many statues and jade treasures depicting Buddha were created, and stunning shrines and temples were built.

MONEY MATTERS
One of the most important innovations of the Sung was the widespread use of money. The copper and silver coins made it easier to do business, and foreign trade accelerated. Goods were traded as far afield as Africa and the Middle East.

ARTS AND LEISURE
The Tang infused China with creative energy. Silverwork was perfected, furnishings transformed, poetry became popular, and new musical instruments were introduced, such as the stringed pipa. Leisure time was encouraged and the upper classes enjoyed hunting, archery, cock fighting, and playing polo on horseback.

SPREADING THE WORD

By carving into wooden blocks and printing on paper, the written word was made accessible to a larger audience. Calligraphy (fancy writing) flourished and the Tang era became a golden age of literature.

FULL-ON FARMING

Rice was grown on stepped terraces on the sides of hills. Although rice was the main crop, farmers also grew cotton, which was used to made clothing. Improved tools increased agricultural efficiency and production – essential for feeding and clothing the growing urban populations.

MIND THE MONGOLS!

During the last 50 years of the Sung Dynasty there were sustained attacks by Mongol warriors from the north. The Empire could not survive and, in 1279, the Sung fell to Mongol leader Kublai Khan, grandson of the fearsome Genghis.

CITY LIVING

Sung China saw an explosion of urban populations. Cities became centres of trade and industry. Teahouses, wine shops, and parks popped up everywhere to meet the demands of the city dwellers. Festivals thrilled with fireworks and puppet shows.

PERFECT PORCELAIN

Chinese porcelain was first manufactured in the 7th century, a thousand years before the method to produce it was discovered in Europe. Sung porcelain was famous for its purity of colour. Kilns were built near ports and vast quantities were exported.

NDIA: What's On

Switch on to some of the regional kingdoms of medieval India. These empires were named after their ruling dynasties (royal families). Their boundaries changed as the various dynasties came into conflict with one another. Over the centuries, groups of outsiders were absorbed into Indian society and became part of the fabric. With the growth of trade, great temple building, and an explosion of poetry, drama, music, and dance, this colourful era of India's past is a visual feast.

CHOICE — PICK OF THE DAY

Chalukyan Architecture
Channel 2, times vary

Temple architecture blending the styles of northern and southern India is the legacy of the Chalukya Dynasty. The new style is known as "Vesara", a Sanskrit word meaning mule (a hybrid animal). The rock-cut temples of Pattadakal (pictured), built around 725, demonstrates the Chalukya style.

The Chola Arts Show
Channel 3, 1000s CE

The magnificent bronzes of Hindu gods that adorned the Chola temples were dressed up and carried outside to take part in processions and festivals.

CHANNEL 1
Harsha Dynasty (northern regions)

400 CE

Golden Oldies
Drama based on the last days of the Gupta Empire. Often described as the golden age, when art blossomed. Younger viewers may be disturbed by scenes of violence as the Huns invade in 455, and India is split into small kingdoms.

The Ajanta caves (2nd century BCE) depicting Buddhist religious art were added to during the Gupta period.

606–647 CE

In Praise of Harsha!
A biopic of Emperor Harsha, who ruled northern India 606–647, uniting several small republics. Crowned at just 16 years old, he was a tolerant ruler, supporting Buddhism, Hinduism, and Jainism. In 641, he sent a mission to China, establishing the first diplomatic relations between India and China.

650 CE

Decline and Fall
A compelling drama chronicling the decline of Harsha's kingdom after his death. His empire swiftly broke up into smaller states.

 **Letters**

"I loved the programmes dedicated to the Gupta Empire, which aired 320–467 CE. So much fabulous art and literature, not to mention the wonderful palaces and temples! How amazing that their physicians excelled in bone setting and skin grafting. What a surprise that the 'Arab' numerical system actually originated here — and the decimal system. Incredible! More shows like this, please!"
Mr Kalidasa, Bengal

CHANNEL 2
Chalukya Dynasty (southern regions)

550–750 CE

Meet The Chalukyas
This dynasty emerged to rule much of southern India between 550 and 750. They had a strong army and navy, and an efficient system of government that divided the Empire into provinces, each split into smaller districts. Overseas trade boomed.

550–750 CE

Spotlight on Religion
Most Chalukyan temples were dedicated to Hindu gods, such as Shiva and Vishnu, but some followed the Jain faith. Buddhism was in decline.

973–1189 CE

Never Say No More Chalukyas
After a period of decline, the Chalukyas rule again between 973 and 1189. This docudrama shows how they clashed with the Cholas and defended their kingdom against invasion by Turks and Arabs.

The art of the Chalukyas, including this 12th-century sculpture of a female dancer, features in Never Say No More Chalukyas.

Times vary

Chalukyan Architecture*
This spotlight on the unique building style of the Chalukya Dynasty includes the magnificent Cave Temples, built in 600, and temples in the town of Pattadakal.
CHOICE *See Pick of the day.*

1189 CE

Chalukyas: The End
Tracing the end of the Empire in 1189 when other dynasties took over. Wars between the Chalukyas and Cholas during the 12th century led to the collapse. Although the Cholas won, these wars sapped their strength and they also began their decline.

CHANNEL 3
Chola Dynasty (southern regions)

800s CE

The Rise of the Cholas
This film about the rise of the Cholas – the most powerful empire in the south of India from the 9th to 13th centuries – focuses on the Chola rulers as great patrons of the arts.

The valley of the Kaveri River, Karnataka, southern India, was the heartland of the Chola Empire and features in the film.

985–1044 CE

Ready, Steady, Rule!
Following the lives of the greatest Chola kings, Rajaraja and his son Rajendra. Their vigorous maritime policy secured trade routes and expanded the Empire to include parts of the Maldives and Sri Lanka.

1044 CE

Chola V Chalukya
Documentary on Rajendra Chola's death in battle with old foe the Chalukyas. After this, his successors let things slide, as the two empires carry out revenge attacks on each other.

1000s CE

The Chola Arts Show*
Award-winning series based on the flourishing Chola arts scene. Following episodes on poetry, drama, dance, and Chidambaram (the Chola capital city), today's show looks at their stunning bronzes of Hindu gods.
See Pick of the day.

CHOICE

Times vary

Temple Tours
A look around the stunning temples of southern India built by the Cholas, with a special focus on Rajaraja's Brihadisvara Temple. Crowned by a 13-storey pyramidal tower (*vimana*), the temple boasts many murals and sculptures of the god Shiva.

CHANNEL 4
Pala Dynasty (northern regions)

700s CE

Hello Palas!
A round-up of the Pala Dynasty, which ruled Bihar and Bengal India from the 8th to 12th centuries. All the kings' names ended in "Pala", which means "protector".

750 CE

The Pala Show
This week's focus is the dynasty's founder, Gopala (750–770), a military leader who was elected king (probably unique in medieval India). He extended his control over all Bengal. His successor, Dharmapala, made the Palas the dominant power in northern and eastern India.

A statue of Dharmapala outside the 9th-century Buddhist temple at Prambanan, Java, Indonesia – a Pala colony.

860 CE

Great Pala Buildings
The Palas were big supporters of Buddhism and built many temples, as well as the famous universities of Nalanda and Vikramshila. Before the Palas, Buddhism was in decline and Buddhists were often persecuted. Scholars from the Pala Empire are responsible for the spread of Buddhism to Tibet.

1200 CE

Hot Topics
Today's question to the panel: why did the Pala Empire disintegrate after 860? Was it down to the invasion of the Cholas in 1023, or was the rising power of the Sena Dynasty in the mid-12th century the deciding factor? Experts share their views.

CHANNEL 5
Invaders (all regions)

711 CE

Conquest of Sindh
Following the fall of Sindh, in modern-day Pakistan, to the invader Mohammed bin Qasim in 711, this topical debate examines why India came to be invaded so frequently. The panel asks whether following religions opposed to war, such as Buddhism and Jainism, weakened India's resistance to invaders.

Times vary

Big Isn't Always Best
A feature on Indian war elephants. These were no match for nimble invaders on horseback. It is reported that the Chalukyas made their elephants drunk before battle. This caused a few hiccups.

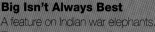
Indian elephants were good at trampling the enemy.

1001 CE

Khyber Pass!
A thrilling crime caper showing how Arab armies swept down the Khyber Pass and hit like a storm in 1001. They raided every year for about 26 years, leaving decimated cities and a nervy population in their wake.

1024 CE

The Muslims Are Coming!
This breathless thriller begins in 1008, with Turkish leader Mahmud defeating a mighty Indian army outside Peshawar. See part two next week, when later Muslim invaders lay the foundation of a permanent Islamic state ruled by a sultan.

WAVES OF EASTERN INVADERS THREATEN

INVASION OF

★★

INTRODUCING THE EASTERN NOMADS

On the vast, wind-swept steppe of 13th-century China, the Mongols are a group of fragmented, nomadic tribes – at war with themselves. But in a time of war, one man's vision will lead them to greatness. Through a combination of military mastery and excellent organizational skills, Genghis Khan leads them to kill and conquer. The plot is full of gore and mayhem, but the Empire will ultimately bring order and stability, and promote trade and cultural exchange.

"...GENGHIS DELIVERS AN OUTSTANDING RULE. UNSTOPPABLE!"
★★★★
THE MONGOL TIMES

"The mounted archers are a tour-de-force… They ride in, fire a volley of arrows, and disappear. Thoroughly demoralizing for the enemy!"

ARCHERY NOW MAGAZINE

NOW SHOWING AT A CINEMA NEAR YOU

THE FABRIC OF EUROPEAN CIVILIZATION
THE MONGOLS

★★

"THE HEART-THUMPING THRILL-RIDE OF THE YEAR"
★★★★
THE NOMADIC HERALD

STARRING GENGHIS KHAN

In his most convincing performance to date, Genghis Khan stars as the Mongol leader. Born Temüjin in what is now Mongolia, he is just a scared young boy of nine when his father is assassinated. But Temüjin grows up to become a supreme soldier who unites the Mongol tribes and leads them out of Mongolia to take on the world. In 1206 he becomes Genghis Khan ("Universal Ruler") and at his death in 1227 the Mongol Empire stretches right across Asia.

A FINE SUPPORTING CAST BRINGS REALISM TO THE BATTLE SCENES

The Mongol warriors are unmatched for speed and mobility. Admire their long bows, sabres, and arrows, and gasp as they throw flaming naphtha (tar). The armour of leather and iron has been lovingly recreated by the costume department. Brilliant military tactics and forward planning also on show.

WARNING! PLOT CONTAINS SCENES OF BLOOD AND VIOLENCE

The Mongols massacre those in their way and level cities to the ground. After Genghis Khan's death they tear through Asia to rule China, Korea, Russia, and eastern Europe, becoming the largest empire the world has ever seen. But the Islamic nations fight back, and they are repulsed in Palestine in 1260.

COMING SOON: MONGOLS, THE NEXT GENERATION

The eagerly awaited sequel will follow the grandsons of Genghis Khan as they continue his quest for world domination. Mangu Khan rules more of the planet than any before or since. Kublai Khan declares himself emperor of China in 1271. Hulegu Khan founds the Ilkhanate Dynasty, centred in Persia.

"IT IS NOT SUFFICIENT THAT I SUCCEED. ALL OTHERS MUST FAIL" ★ GENGHIS KHAN

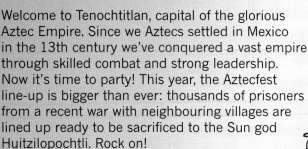

WELCOME TO AZTECFEST!

Welcome to Tenochtitlan, capital of the glorious Aztec Empire. Since we Aztecs settled in Mexico in the 13th century we've conquered a vast empire through skilled combat and strong leadership. Now it's time to party! This year, the Aztecfest line-up is bigger than ever: thousands of prisoners from a recent war with neighbouring villages are lined up ready to be sacrificed to the Sun god Huitzilopochtli. Rock on!

BLEEDIN' HEART STAGE

On the main stage, humans will be sacrificed to please the gods, who require human blood as nourishment. Witness some of the best abdomen opening ever performed! Still beating hearts to be torn from victims and burned as an offering to Huitzilopochtli.

FAMILY TENT

While the gore fest takes place on the Bleedin' Heart stage, the family tent provides all you need to keep the little ones entertained: team games, the popular board game *patolli*, and craft activities, such as making rattles and conch-shell trumpets.

MARSHALS

Marshals will ensure that this is a well-ordered and safe festival. Misbehaving children will be held over a fire of burning chillies. Drunkenness is banned except for the over 70s. Warriors, please leave your *macuahuitl* (war clubs) at home.

SIDE SHOWS

Head to the side shows for drumming, flute-playing, singing, and prayers to honour the gods.

WATERWAY TRIPS

Our canals are the envy of Central America. Take a canoe tour to see temples and other glorious sites.

HAIR SALON

Warriors who have taken their first prisoner in battle can get a special haircut to mark the occasion. Cut off the long boyish locks and become a man!

CLOTHES STALLS

Shop for a fine array of goods including skirts, tunics, cotton garments, necklaces, lip-plugs (piercings), and bracelets.

ABSOLUTELY THE BIGGEST AND BEST AZTEC FESTIVAL OF HUMAN SACRIFICE: THREE DAYS OF NON-STOP SLAYING, FLAYING, AND HEART-GOUGING

FIRST-AID TENT

Powerful herbal medicine will be on hand in the first-aid tent: spider bites treated with the root of rabbit fern tree; broken skulls washed with urine; coughs treated with chilli and salt. It's kill or cure!

BATHING AREA

If you've got festival feet or have fallen over in the blood, take a steam bath. Not only are they good for hygiene, they will also drive out evil spirits. Slaves are on hand to pour water over heated stones – the steam will cure many illnesses!

CRAFT STALLS

See the latest in Aztec plasterwork, stonework, weaving, and pottery. Buy a fan made out of bird feathers, or some dyed cloth.

FOOD STALLS

Something for everyone. Cocoa beans, chilli peppers, and the hottest food in the land are on offer. Spicy stews and sauces are also ready to be slurped. Check out our festival menu:

Hot chocolate sweetened with honey and flavoured with vanilla

Cactus wine fermented for months (strongly alcoholic)

Freshly caught fish and fish eggs

Dog meat in a spicy sauce

The best tortillas in the land: made from flour and baked on a hot stone. Choose from pepper, chilli, and avocado fillings

Gruel (porridge) - a local favourite. Wild sage or amaranth seed flavour

Lizards seasoned with chillies

Roasted turtle flesh

PLEASE NOTE:

All stall holders use the latest in numbers – counting in twenties. For payment they will accept exotic goods, such as colourful feathers, puma skins, cocoa beans, and gold dust. No credit cards or money accepted, as they haven't been invented yet.

VISIT THE INCA EMPIRE

If you're looking for a holiday with a difference then look no more. The Incas will offer you a warm welcome, and are always happy to share their proud history. Since the 12th century they have ruled from their capital, Cuzco, in the Andes Mountains of South America. Inca ruler Pachacuti began rapid expansion of their territory from 1438, establishing four provinces each with its own governor. Formidable soldiers, the Incas are also known for their peaceful exploits – growing crops and building vast monuments, roads, and bridges.

Gold figurine of Inca deity

SIGHTS AT A GLANCE

Historic sites

1 Cuzco

2 Machu Picchu

3 Tiwanaku

GETTING AROUND

Inca territory stretches thousands of kilometres along the western coast of South America. The Incas have a great road network linking the capital to the rest of the Empire. However, they don't know about the wheel, so you'll have to travel on foot. If you're lucky, you might get hold of a llama to carry your suitcases.

KEY DATES

1100s: Incas begin as a tribe in the area around Cuzco

1438: Beginning of Inca expansion throughout the Andes, modern-day Peru and Ecuador

c1450: City of Machu Picchu built

1500s: Empire declines when Europeans arrive

Cuzco

The Inca capital city in southern Peru

The Incas believe that Cuzco is the sacred home of their gods. The head of state, the Sapa Inca, lives here and is treated like a living god. His every need is tended to. Even when the Sapa Inca dies, his attendants continue to tend to his embalmed body.

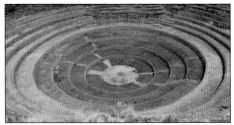

These circular terraces near Cuzco were probably used for agriculture

You'll be expected to take your shoes off when visiting his palace to show respect. And watch it girls: if the Sapa Inca takes a liking to you, he might take you as one of his many wives.

Machu Picchu

"City in the clouds", which offers a unique hiking experience

Don't be put off by the 3,000 stone steps or the dizzying heights of this stunning Inca city – it is definitely a star sight (see facing page). Built in the Andes Mountains at an altitude of 2,429 m (7,970 ft), it is completely self-contained on a ridge between two mountain peaks and boasts palaces, temples, and houses. The hike to reach it can take several days, but there are plenty of settlements along the way where you can rest.

Outside the city walls you'll find hillsides covered with terraced fields

Tiwanaku **3**

A place of wonder for the Incas – you'll be blown away

By the shores of Lake Titicaca, the highest lake in the world, rose the city of Tiwanaku.

Legend has it that Tiwanaku was built overnight by a race of giants

It was established about 400 BCE by the Tiwanaku people, who reached their peak around 700 CE. When the Incas conquered it in 1470, Tiwanaku was already a city in ruins. However, the Incas were so impressed with its massive buildings that they copied them in Cuzco. A visit to the ruins makes a great day out.

Machu Picchu

This famous mountain city was constructed in about 1450, at the height of the Inca Empire. The Incas do not believe in quarrying rock from the living Earth, so the entire city was built of rock cut from loose boulders. Machu Picchu is a holiday home for the Sapa Inca, and doubles as a religious retreat. The Incas worship many gods, and believe that rivers and trees have their own *waca*, or spirit. Prayer is important to ensure good harvests. Human sacrifice is rare, but may take place during hard times.

★ **Skilled architecture**
The buildings were constructed without using mortar. Instead, builders carved the blocks in such a way that they slotted together.

MORE TO EXPLORE

Also to see at Machu Picchu:

• Simple one-room houses
• Storerooms for food
• Dungeons
• Soldiers' barracks
• Burial caves
• Palace buildings

★ **Sacred plaza**
This plaza is used for religious ceremonies and is surrounded by the most important buildings in Machu Picchu.

Terraces are farmed to provide food for the inhabitants

For hotels and restaurants in this region, see the directory on page 315

★ **Temple of the Sun**
This round building is used to worship the Sun god Inti. When the sunlight of the winter solstice enters through the central window, it falls directly on the ceremonial stone.

Practical Information

Great delicacies

You'll be familiar with some of the Inca foods: potatoes, corn, porridge. Guinea pig makes a tasty treat. The best food, including baked fish, birds, and bananas, is to be found in the royal palaces.

Inca staple foods

Potatoes

Popcorn

Cocoa leaves

Pumpkin

Pineapple

Transport

Getting around the Inca Empire is easy. The Incas have built excellent roads, and strong rope bridges to cross gorges. If you find yourself at one of the many lakes, why not take a canoe trip?

Communication

The imperial messenger service is a group of highly trained runners known as *chasquis*, who between them can cover distances of 240 km (150 miles) a day. You might not be able to understand their messsages

though. Instead of writing, Incas record information in collections of knotted and coloured strings called *quipas*. Each *quipu* is made from llama or alpaca hair and might contain hundreds or even thousands of threads.

An Inca *quipu*: we think this one is a shopping list

TRAVELLERS' TIPS

Exhausting climbs and thin mountain air might make you ill. Inca doctors are experts at treating ailments using plants.

Don't break the law – you might be stoned or clubbed to death, or imprisoned in a snake-filled chamber.

Make sure you're not picked as a sacrifice. Animals are normally used, but in a crisis, only a child sacrifice will do.

Avoid the "teen test" – a rite of passage for boys that involves spending nights out in the cold and having your earlobes split.

Native North Americans

The original people of North America were the Native Americans. Hundreds of nations, each with a different way of life, stretched right across the continent. The Native North Americans are sometimes referred to as "Indians", a mistake that stuck when the first Europeans arrived in the 15th century and wrongly thought they had reached India.

CARIBOU HUNTERS
In the far north of Canada, Native Americans hunted caribou, beavers, moose, and bears.

SPIRIT DOLL
The different Native American peoples had a wide range of religious beliefs. Their religions were often closely tied to the natural world, and the belief that many spirits ruled their lives. The Hopi used kachina (spirit) dolls like this one to teach children about their gods.

NORTHWEST FISHERMEN
On the northwest Pacific coast, tribes including the Chinook and Snake made dugout canoes from tree trunks and lived off the fish they caught.

PLAINS TRIBES
Nomadic tribes, such as the Cherokee and the Dakota (or Sioux) lived on the vast plains and moved about following huge herds of buffalo.

CALIFORNIA TRIBES
Tribes such as the Mohave and Pomo were separated from other tribes by deserts and mountains. Seeds (especially acorns) made up a major part of their diet.

SHARING THE WEALTH
Although they traded extensively, many Native Americans did not believe in accumulating wealth. The tribes of the northwest held parties called potlatches, where the host would give away lots of his possessions. By being generous, he increased his status and power.

FARMERS AND HERDERS
The tribes that lived in the hot and dry lands of modern Arizona and New Mexico farmed the land using river water to irrigate their crops. They included the Hopi and Pueblo.

SELF SERVICE

To the Plains Indians, the buffalo was a walking supermarket. It provided all kinds of food – even the bone marrow and nose gristle were made into culinary delights. Hair was made into rope, horns became cups, teeth were used for jewellery, and hides made dresses and robes. Waste not, want not...

ESKIMOS

Also known as Inuit, Eskimo tribes still live in this vast icy region spanning 5,630 km (3,500 miles). Eskimo means "eater of raw meat".

STATUS SYMBOL

Many Native Americans wore clothes that had a deep symbolic meaning. The war bonnet (headdress), worn by Plains tribes, was made from eagle feathers and attached to a leather skullcap. Each feather told a story of the wearer's exploits in battle, so the more feathers in the cap, the braver the warrior.

EASTERN WOODLAND INDIANS

The Native Americans in the forests on the east of the continent were hunter-gatherers. They included the Algonquian, Iroquois, Mohawk, and Shawnee – warlike tribes who were often in conflict with one another.

HOME FROM HOME

Tribes that lived on the plains did not build houses, they lived in tepees. These dwellings, made of buffalo skins thrown over poles, suited their nomadic way of life, because tepees could be dismantled and reassembled easily. They were warm in winter, cool in summer.

Bakers Guild*

Join our guild –
we always look after our poor

If you're a baker, you'll have to join our guild to get on in life. We control wages and prices, and make sure produce is good quality. Our accomplished bakers train their apprentices until they too become masters in the art. And if you're ill or have an accident, a payment from the common box will tide you over.

Other guilds available for other crafts.

Bank of Italy

Brand new gold coins

Great rates on loans

Loaned money to many important rulers

With trade booming, you might need a loan to help you get in on the act. Rich Italian families can help. They have set up the first banks to lend out money. New accounting methods will help keep track of your cash. Worried about losing your ship and its cargo at sea? No problem – they've invented insurance. Just pay an insurance premium and you'll be compensated for any losses.

Medieval Mall

Don't drive on by! Visit the medieval mall, where trade is booming. Time was, people grew their own food and bartered (exchanged goods) for anything else they needed. Now a growing population is demanding the latest new goods from abroad, like lemons and sugar, and the nobles want nice possessions to show off to their friends. We are busy importing and exporting goods to meet demand. Before, towns were small and only built to defend their inhabitants in case of attack. Now, towns are bustling places of craft and commerce. Skilled workmen have gathered together in guilds, international banking has been established, and merchants are everywhere.

Cloth fairs in Flanders
The finest cloth in northern Europe

A trade fair like this only comes around once a year! Flanders (an area spanning parts of modern Belgium and Netherlands) is at the forefront of the modern textile industry. The three cities of Ghent, Bruges, and Ypres have workshops turning wool into the finest cloth. Their annual trade fairs are huge! Tapestries and stockings a speciality.

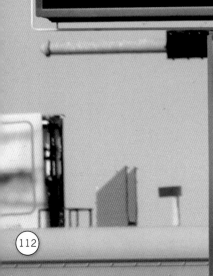

Self Help

CONFUSED ABOUT THE NEW COINS? OUR CRASH COURSE IN CURRENCY WILL HELP YOU TELL YOUR DUCATS FROM YOUR FLORINS.

There are so many different coins being used in Europe, it can be hard to keep up. Learn about the different designs, weights, and inscriptions, and you'll soon be laughing all the way to the bank. This is a one-off course, as in years to come currency in Europe will be standardized to make trading easier.

Evening   Classes

Apprentices wanted

Are you a teenager looking for a career? Master craftsmen have apprenticeships for hard workers who can keep trade secrets. You'll have to work for free for up to nine years, but in return your master will provide food, shelter, clothing, and training. Call in at the job centre for more info.

jobcentre

ARE YOU A MERCHANT FEELING UNLOVED?

Have you been called a parasite or a sinner? For too long, merchants have been discriminated against and called "usurers" – those who don't make anything but get rich off those who do. Well listen up, because times are changing and we merchants are on our way to the top! Join our support group to meet like-minded individuals.

Handsome hanse town

The German merchants of the Hanseatic League are proud to announce the arrival of another great Hanse town, with trademark red-brick buildings and central market place. The League is an alliance of more than 70 trading towns across Europe, set up in the 13th century to protect members' interests.

THE HUNDRED YEARS' WAR
and sixteen!

I'm Sir Piers, an English knight. We're off to war with the French, and this is my scrapbook of events. Let's hope I get home safe and sound!

50 groats to anyone who can hit a bullseye!

On the way to Crécy, French soldiers mooned the English archers, but lived to regret it...

1346, BATTLE OF CRÉCY

We landed in Normandy with 10,000 men and were chased all the way to Crécy. There, we took our position on a hill, with the French spread out on the plain below us. They outnumbered us four to one, but we had our longbows. When showered with arrows, they ran away.

Don't worry, I reckon we'll be home by Christmas.

1356, BATTLE OF POITIERS

King Edward's son, Edward the Black Prince, led us into battle. What a guy! Outnumbered again, but the French attack was a disaster. We won, took King John of France hostage, and demanded a huge fee for his release.

Developed in the 1200s, the longbow revolutionized land warfare. It could pierce armour and be reloaded quickly.

1415, BATTLE OF AGINCOURT

They're saying this battle is going to go down in history. Again we were outmanned — not only that, but this time we were tired, sick, and starving, too. It looked hopeless. When we met the French it had been raining for days. The battlefield got churned up and the mud soon came up to our knees. Horses sank up to their bellies! Still our longbowmen won the day. Quite a brilliant victory for Henry V, if I do say so myself.

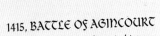

Knight-cap anyone?

After the battle of Agincourt, Henry V threw a feast for his senior commanders, waited on by captured French knights.

La Vienne Rivière

WHY WERE THEY FIGHTING?

At the beginning of the 14th century, England ruled more than half of France. The French wanted this territory back. But Edward III of England believed himself to be the true heir to the French throne because he was the grandson of Philip IV and nephew of three previous French kings, and he was willing to fight for what he thought was his. This struggle between England and France became known as the Hundred Years' War and was the longest war in recorded history. It lasted, with interruptions, 116 years, through the reigns of five English kings and five French kings.

1420, VICTORY IN SIGHT?

It's not a good time to be French at the moment. Charles VI is clearly mad, and his son is useless. The French are so weak that they've agreed to take our King's son as their monarch once Charles VI pops his clogs. Which is good, because I'm getting a bit too old for this mullarkey.

KINGS OF ENGLAND

Edward III (1327-1377)
Richard II (1377-1399)
Henry IV (1399-1413)
Henry V (1413-1422)
Henry VI (1422-1462, 1470-1471)

KINGS OF FRANCE

Philip VI (1293-1350)
John II (1350-1364)
Charles V (1364-1380)
Charles VI (1380-1422)
Charles VII (1422-1461)

Henry VI's reign was marked by a series of struggles over the English crown that has become known as the Wars of the Roses. He was ousted from the throne, then briefly reinstated, only to end up being executed in the Tower of London.

1431, JOAN OF ARC

Just when we thought it was all over, some country maiden showed up in battle gear, claiming heavenly voices told her to drive the English out of France. She's really whipped the French up into a nationalist fervour. Their army started winning for a change, and then this Joan of Arc character crowns Charles VII king of France at Rheims Cathedral. By the time we burned her at the stake, the damage had already been done.

The Battle of Castillon, won by the French, was the first battle in history where use of the cannon decided the victor.

1453, BATTLE OF CASTILLON

The tide has turned. The French have become a unified nation and they're pretty determined to kick the English out. Our King, Henry VI, is just a child and to top it all we've run out of cash. Charles VII turned out to be a good leader after all and we got a bit of a kicking by his army at Castillon. Is that it now? Can I go home?

That lasted a bit longer than I thought it would...

Finally, after 116 years, the last major battle had been fought. The war was over, though no one realized it at the time.

THE BLACK DEATH

IN THE 1340S, A DREADFUL DISEASE SPREAD ACROSS THE WORLD, TRAVELLING ALONG TRADE ROUTES CARRIED BY THE FLEAS ON RATS. KNOWN AS THE BLACK DEATH, OR PLAGUE, IT WIPED OUT A THIRD OF EUROPE'S POPULATION IN THE SPACE OF JUST FOUR YEARS.

> CAN WE STOP NOW, FATHER? I'M SO HUNGRY. IT'S AGES SINCE WE LAST ATE.

> WE'RE ALL HUNGRY, JOHN. THESE ARE HARD TIMES. THE PRIEST SAYS THAT MENACE IS STALKING THE LAND AND WE HAVE TO PRAY.

> NOW STOP YOUR MOANING AND HELP ME WITH THESE LOGS.

AN ENGLISH VILLAGE, 1348. A SHORTAGE OF FOOD AND MANY WARS IN EUROPE HAVE WEAKENED THE POPULATION.

TWENTY-FIVE YEARS EARLIER...

IN THE FOOTHILLS OF THE HIMALAYAS, A TERRIBLE FORCE OF DESTRUCTION STIRRED. A MYSTERIOUS DISEASE, CAUSED BY THE BACTERIUM *YERSINA PESTIS*, WAS BEING CARRIED BY FLEAS IN THE FUR OF BLACK RATS.

> DOCTOR, WHAT'S HAPPENING TO ME?

> IT'S THE SICKNESS. I'M SORRY, MY FRIEND, THERE'S LITTLE I CAN DO.

THIS DISEASE WAS THE BUBONIC PLAGUE. RATS, DISTURBED BY EARTHQUAKES AND FLOODS, WERE FORCED OUT OF THEIR HOLES AND MADE CONTACT WITH HUMAN BEINGS. THE FLEAS JUMPED FROM THE RATS TO BITE HUMAN FLESH, PASSING ON THE DEADLY GERMS. THE PLAGUE STRUCK ASIA FIRST.

> PEPPER! FINEST ALMONDS! SAFFRON!

BY 1347, THE PLAGUE WAS SPREADING RAPIDLY ACROSS EUROPE.

> IN THE SHIPS CARRYING GOODS TO MEDITERRANEAN PORTS, PLAGUE-BEARING RATS SCRATCHED BELOW DECKS AND SNIFFED THE SALTY SEA AIR.

LURED BY SILK AND SPICES, MEN VENTURED DOWN NEW TRADE ROUTES AND TOOK THE PLAGUE WITH THEM. IT SWEPT ALONG THE SILK ROAD TO STRIKE THE BYZANTINE EMPIRE.

IN 1348, IT HIT ENGLAND. RATS FLOURISHED IN THE FILTH OF MEDIEVAL VILLAGES.

> WRETCHED FLEAS!!!

THERE'S TALK OF THE SICKNESS IN THE NEXT VILLAGE. THEY'RE SAYING FOUL AIR HAS CAUSED IT, SO I'VE PUT SWEET-SMELLING LAUREL AROUND THE HOUSE TO WARD IT OFF. AND YOU ARE NOT TO BATHE, JOHN. IT LETS THE SICKNESS IN. GOD HELP US ALL!

NO ONE KNEW WHAT CAUSED THE DISEASE. PRIESTS SAID IT WAS A PUNISHMENT FROM GOD FOR HUMAN SINS.

WE ARE SUFFERING HEAVEN'S REVENGE! WE WILL KNOW THE WRATH OF GOD

...AND YOU WILL BE NEXT. YOU AND YOUR IDLE FRIENDS. THAT'S WHAT YOU GET FOR NOT GOING TO CHURCH!

AS THE DISEASE SPREAD, FAMILIES SPLIT UP. BROTHER ABANDONED BROTHER. PARENTS REFUSED TO TEND TO THEIR CHILDREN.

HELP ME JOAN, I'VE NOWHERE ELSE TO GO.

BE GONE. YOU'RE NOT WELCOME HERE.

BUT YOU'RE THE ONLY FRIEND I HAVE LEFT!

PEOPLE DID ALL SORTS OF STRANGE THINGS TO STOP THE DISEASE FROM SPREADING.

HEY! GIVE HIM BACK – THAT'S MY CAT!

NOT ANY MORE HE'S NOT. ALL CATS ARE BEING SLAUGHTERED. THEY ARE SPAWN OF THE DEVIL AND SPREAD DISEASE. NOW GO TELL YOUR PA TO COME AND HELP WITH THE BONFIRES. THEY'RE THE ONLY THING THAT'S GETTING RID OF THE STENCH AROUND HERE.

I'M NOT GOING ANYWHERE, SON. AND YOU'RE BETTER OFF STAYING AWAY FROM FOLK, TOO.

BESIDES... I DON'T FEEL SO GOOD.

I'LL SEND JOHN OUT TO FETCH THE WISE WOMAN.

THE SYMPTOMS WERE GRUESOME: FEVER, PURPLE BLOTCHES ON THE SKIN, COUGHING UP BLOOD, AND SWELLINGS IN THE NECK, ARMPITS, AND GROIN. FIVE DAYS AFTER THE ONSET, THE VICTIM WOULD USUALLY DIE.

I'LL LAY LEECHES ON HIM TO SUCK THE EVIL OUT, BUT FEW HAVE SURVIVED THIS TERRIBLE CURSE. HE'LL NEED ALL OUR PRAYERS.

PEOPLE TRIED TO PROTECT THEMSELVES WITH NICE SMELLING HERBS, OR BY SOUNDING CHURCH BELLS AND FIRING CANNONS. SOME OF THE CURES WERE EQUALLY STRANGE.

THREE DAYS LATER...

BRING DOWN YOUR DEAD! BRING DOWN YOUR DEAD!

WHERE ARE YOU TAKING MY FATHER?

JOHN'S FATHER WAS JUST ONE OF ABOUT 25 MILLION PEOPLE WHO DIED OF THE PLAGUE, OR BLACK DEATH AS IT CAME TO BE KNOWN.

SPARE US SOME FOOD, BOY.

WE'RE STARVING. I'VE NOT EATEN A PROPER MEAL FOR WEEKS.

THERE'S NO FOOD TO BE HAD. THE MARKETS HAVE CLOSED. IT'S THE END OF THE WORLD!

JOHN WOOD, AGED 10

THE BUBONIC PLAGUE CONTINUED TO WREAK HAVOC FOR MANY YEARS. IT DIDN'T FULLY DISAPPEAR FROM EUROPE UNTIL THE END OF THE 1700S.

TO THE PLAGUE PITS – THE CEMETERIES ARE ALL FULL UP.

GREAT ZIMBABWE

In the 12th century, the ancestors of the modern-day Shona people established a mighty empire in southern Africa. It was called Monomotapa, and its capital city, Great Zimbabwe, was built around a citadel of stone. In the 14th century, with 10,000 inhabitants, Great Zimbabwe grew rich from a roaring trade in ivory and gold. Today, all that remains of this ancient empire are the spectacular stone ruins of its capital.

HOUSES OF STONE

The most impressive of the remains is a large oval-shaped enclosure. Known as the *Imba Huru* (Great Enclosure), it is believed to have housed around 300 people, including the royal family. Its huge stone walls gave the king privacy and kept him apart from the commoners outside.

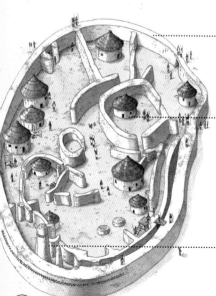

The outer walls were 11 m (36 ft) high, and an estimated 1 million blocks were used in their construction

The huts in the Great Enclosure housed only the most important people; the rest of the population lived in small mud huts set close together some distance away

The purpose of this conical tower remains a mystery, but it may represent a grain bin – a symbol of good harvests

WALLS WITHOUT MORTAR

The stonework at Great Zimbabwe is remarkable for its precision. Granite blocks were taken from the surrounding hills and set down in layers.

The blocks were cut and shaped so carefully that no mortar was needed to hold them together. The outer walls are up to 5 m (16 ft) thick.

GOLDEN ERA

The rich Mali Empire dominated West Africa in the 1300s. Its most famous ruler, Mansa Musa, was so wealthy that when he travelled to Mecca in 1324, he took more than 60,000 attendants with him and gave away so much gold that the price of gold fell in the countries he visited.

Wolof
Ghana
Songhay
Mali
Kanem–Bornu
Yoruba
Ethiopia
Buganda
Congo
Kilwa
Monomotapa

AFRICAN KINGDOMS

Many kingdoms thrived in Africa at the same time as Monomotapa. The city-state of Kilwa grew on the east coast, while the empires of Ghana and Mali rose to power in the west. The development of long-distance trade meant that African gold and salt were transported all over the world and African kingdoms grew rich. Contact with Muslim Arab traders introduced Islam to much of Africa.

STONE THE CROWS

Several soapstone birds were discovered at the site. They look like birds of prey, but with human features. Thought to represent the spirits of former kings, the Zimbabwe birds were adopted as a national symbol of modern-day Zimbabwe. One appears on the country's national flag.

RACIST RESPONSE

The first European to visit Great Zimbabwe was German explorer Karl Mauch, in 1871. He refused to believe that such an impressive monument could have been the handiwork of Africans, and suggested it was built by Phoenician or Israelite settlers.

Many Europeans, including the Spanish, Dutch, French, and especially the English, establish colonies in North America (**p154**).

The Spanish invade the Aztec capital, Tenochtitlan, in 1510 and conquer it in 1521 (**p136**).

The Dutch win independence from Spanish rule following an 80-year war (**p144**).

During the reign of Elizabeth I (**p132**) in England, a promising playwright named William Shakespeare takes his plays to the stage.

While Louis XIV (**p152**) is king of France, the country shines with many political, military, and cultural achievements.

Genoese explorer Christopher Columbus arrives in the Caribbean, mistaking it for Asia (**p124**).

The Spanish, with hearts set on finding gold and riches, wage war with the Incas in Peru in 1527 and vanquish them (**p136**).

EXPLORING AND REFORMING

Exploration is the name of the game, opening up the world as a global marketplace. Religious and political reforms ruffle the feathers of the old ruling order.

With Europeans making the most of improved navigational tools and ships, and with Asian rulers heading up mighty naval fleets, an age of exploration evolves, and peoples all over the world unite (or fight). At the same time, a period of religious struggle explodes in Europe as the Reformation takes hold. The period also gives birth to the Renaissance – a revival in learning and the arts that leads to a whole new world of ideas.

Take me back to the years 1400–1699

The Ottoman Empire (**p134**) goes from strength to strength, with a colossal seaforce and formidable army invading and expanding its territories.

Russian territory is won back from the Mongols, and the state of Russia is expanded and stabilized by Ivan III (**p140**), who declares himself "Tsar of all the Russians".

The royal households of Europe (**p122**) go through dramatic modifications as the role of the monarchy changes, brought about by the upheaval of the Reformation (**p138**) and subsequent religious wars (**p142**).

The first circumnavigation of the globe is achieved by a fleet initially headed by Portuguese explorer Ferdinand Magellan (**p124**).

Persia (now Iran) is unified under Shi'-ite Muslim leaders the Safavids (**p148**).

The Ming Dynasty (**p128**) encourages the opening up of China, with the voyages of Zheng He.

The shogunate leaders Oda Nobunaga and Toyotomi Hideyoshi succeed in unifying Japan, bringing stability (**p150**).

The city of Florence patronizes many artists and writers, beginning the Renaissance (**p130**).

The Mughals (**p146**), an Islamic dynasty, dominate India. They make their mark with an array of magnificent buildings and set up important trading networks.

The Spice Islands became the world's source of spices – an extremely valuable commodity in the 15th and 16th centuries, literally worth their weight in gold (**p126**).

GOING UP ▶▶

Navigational tools: The compass, astrolabe, and backstaff are in common use by European sailors.

Scurvy: With increasing numbers of sailors taking to the seas to travel further afield in this age of exploration, so this vitamin-C deficiency disease causes many to perish.

New foods: Spice routes are established between Europe and Asia, and foodstuffs native to the Americas are introduced into the European diet.

The arts: A great period in art and architecture with takes off in Europe at the same time so-called Renaissance. At the "golden ages" occur throughout empires. eastern empires.

The Byzantine Empire: This once powerful empire comes to an end with the Ottoman conquest of its capital city, Constantinople.

Religious tolerance: As the Reformation spreads across Europe, Catholics and Protestants clash. Islamic dynasties seek unity in their empires by imposing particular beliefs.

GOING DOWN ▼▼

HAPPY FAMILIES

Europe's royal rulers were used to calling the shots, with dynamic dynasties passing the power down through the generations. When people started questioning the role of the Church in the 16th century, doubts also emerged about the rights of royals to rule absolutely. The cards were on the table. The royal flush turned to mush and monarchs were destined to become mere symbols of their nations. Here are some of the wildest cards in the royal family decks.

TUDORS

This royal dynasty ruled England for 118 years, from the late 15th century to the 16th century. Although there were only five Tudor monarchs, they brought stability to the country after the rocky times of a bitter civil war, gave England a new state religion, and, in Henry VIII and Elizabeth I, a winning pair of the most charismatic leaders in history.

ELIZABETH I
1533–1603
Quick-witted and bright, she made her country a force to be reckoned with throughout the world.

TUDOR

HENRY VIII
1491–1547
Founder of the Church of England, this hard-working king was fun-loving and married six times

TUDOR

JAMES I
1394–1437
STEWART
One of Scotland's ablest kings, he was kidnapped by the English, then assassinated by the Scots disputing his right to the throne.

JAMES VI AND I
1566–1625
STEWART
The first king of all Britain as James VI of Scotland and James I of England, he survived an attempt to blow up the Houses of Parliament.

STEWART

In 1371, the throne of Scotland passed from the Bruce family to the Stewarts, who took the surname from their ancestors' job title, "High Steward of Scotland". When Elizabeth I died without children, she chose James Stewart to succeed her as king of England and Ireland. The quick-thinking Stewarts hastily rebranded themselves with the English spelling of "Stuart".

LOUIS XI
1423–1483
VALOIS
Nicknamed the "Universal Spider" after the web of intrigue he wove around his reign, his love of scheming made him many enemies.

LOUIS XII
1462–1515
VALOIS
A popular king, nicknamed the "Father of his People", Louis cut taxes and reformed the French government and courts.

We love Louis XII

Louis

CHARLES VI
1368–1422
VALOIS
Called "the Beloved" and later "the Mad", Charles battled frequent bouts of mental illness, which affected much of his reign.

FRANÇOIS I
1494–1547
VALOIS
A leading patron of the arts, this Renaissance king encouraged artists like Leonardo da Vinci to come work in France, and lavished money on the Louvre palace.

VALOIS

Kings of France between 1328 and 1589, the Valois monarchs were a series of complex and interesting characters who ruled during the turbulent times of the Hundred Years' War with England, in conflict over the French throne. After the war they began to restore their royal power and established the sole right of the king to wage war and levy taxes to pay for them. Not surprisingly, few civilians sang "Long live the King" during those times.

HABSBURG

This amazing Austrian dynasty ruled across Europe for 600 years, from Germany, Spain, the Netherlands, and parts of Italy to the Holy Roman Empire. The first to make it big was Count Rudolf von Habsburg – a superb politician who knew just how to weasel his way into or out of any situation. As Holy Roman Emperor he "discovered" documents that "proved" all Habsburgs were royal from birth. It was crazy but it worked – the family were continuous crown-wearers until World War I.

PHILIP II
1527–1598
HABSBURG
The Spanish Empire went global during Philip's reign, through exploration across both the Atlantic and Pacific oceans.

CHARLES V
1500–1558
HABSBURG
Under the motto Plus Ultra (Further Beyond), he ruled the Holy Roman Empire, and united the Austrians with Spain.

MAXIMILIAN I
1459–1519
HABSBURG
His shrewd choice of an heiress bride spread Habsburg rule to the Netherlands, and then to Spain through his son's marriage.

SAVOY

From Scotland to Sicily, the Savoy family made a string of advantageous marriages that gave them access to every important royal household in Europe. With small beginnings in the Italian region that gave them their name, the Savoys eventually ruled the entire kingdom of Italy until the end of World War II, and were one of the longest surviving dynasties in Europe.

VICTOR AMADEUS II
1666–1732
SAVOY
He streamlined his government and, to remove French influence, broke alliances with France.

HUMBERT I
c980–1048
SAVOY
The first Count of Savoy, his nickname, "the Whitehanded", may well refer to his open-palmed generosity.

EMMANUEL PHILIBERT
1528–1580
SAVOY
Called "the Ironhead", he started his rule with very little money, but managed to regain territories and make the family wealthy again.

BOURBON

The Bourbon kings ruled France from the 16th to 18th centuries. Under their watch France became the greatest power in Europe, but the Bourbons also saw the end of the monarchy in France. First, they annoyed people so much as to incite a revolution (oops), and then, unwilling to learn from their mistakes, they refused to rule by the very constitution they granted after being restored to the throne.

HENRI IV
1553–1610
BOURBON
The first Bourbon king, he ruled during fraught times of religious civil wars, economic chaos, and the threat from the Spanish Habsburgs.

PHILIP V
1683–1746
BOURBON
HOLA
He founded the Bourbon Dynasty in Spain, but a dispute over this Frenchman's claim to the throne led to a war that saw Spain's Empire decline.

LOUIS XVIII
1755–1824
BOURBON
His country welcomed him back to the throne after Napoleon's defeat at Waterloo. Louis gave France a constitution, but also curbed civil liberties.

MEDICI

The fantastically wealthy Medici family were often counted on for a loan by other royal houses when their coffers were running low. Who said money isn't power? The family yielded a succession of colourful dukes, popes, soldiers, scholars, and patrons of the arts. Their name screamed "Renaissance" in Italy and they influenced European politics for some 300 years, often pulling strings from behind the scenes rather than serving in a public office.

COSIMO THE ELDER
1389–1464
MEDICI
He made a fortune through trade and banking, and, as the first Medici head of state, ruled Florence.

LEO AND CLEMENT
1475–1521
1478–1534
MEDICI
This pair of 16th-century Medici popes held political power in both Rome and Florence, sharing diplomatic skills and a patronage of Renaissance artists.

COSIMO I
1519–1574
MEDICI
An excellent administrator, a bright idea of his was to put all the government offices in one building. He eventually brought most of Tuscany under Medici control.

123

WORLD CRUISES

Fancy the adventure of a lifetime? Choose from one of the featured all-inclusive cruises for the best offers around. With grand improvements in navigational tools and more seaworthy ships, the 15th century is definitely the time to explore whatever there is of the world outside Europe. Headed by the Spanish and Portuguese, embark on one of three extraordinary voyages of discovery. We may not know exactly what's out there, but hopefully you'll bring back some great souvenirs!

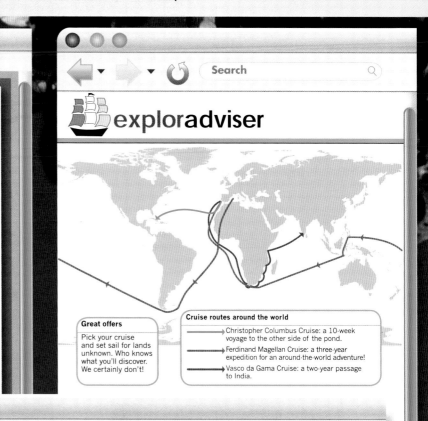

exploradviser

Great offers

Pick your cruise and set sail for lands unknown. Who knows what you'll discover. We certainly don't!

Cruise routes around the world

- Christopher Columbus Cruise: a 10-week voyage to the other side of the pond.
- Ferdinand Magellan Cruise: a three-year expedition for an around-the-world adventure!
- Vasco da Gama Cruise: a two-year passage to India.

Search　Exploring the New World

exploradviser

| ROUTE MAP | **VOYAGE 1** | VOYAGE 2 | VOYAGE 3 |

CHRISTOPHER COLUMBUS CRUISE

DEPARTURE: 3 AUGUST 1492 FROM PALOS DE LA FRONTERA, SPAIN
ARRIVAL: 12 October 1492 in Asia (that's the plan, anyway).
DESCRIPTION: With genius Genoese Chris Columbus at the helm, we'll set sail across the Atlantic Ocean in a history-making trip to exotic Asia (well, the Caribbean actually).

TRANSPORT
Take residence on one of a trio of super-seaworthy ships: the *Santa Maria* (your flagship), the speedy caravel *Pinta*, or the *Nina* (the Captain's favourite).

▼ Highlights

Fancy a taste of something spicy? Why not book yourself on this history-making journey across the Atlantic to Asia (we think) – celebrated land of exotic spices and legendary riches. Join Christopher Columbus and his crew as they go where no Europeans have gone before, if you completely ignore the Vikings.

Fabulous beaches are a must-see

Errm, an embarrassed swan…?

Don't get too close to these…

Checklist: Super Souvenirs!

- **Pineapple:** looks like a pinecone with hair
- **Potatoes:** for chips with every meal
- **Corn:** when it pops, you can't stop eating it

exploradviser traveller reviews

What to expect:
Sail-blazing adventure in uncharted waters, possibly sailing right off the edge of the Earth.

Recommended for:
People who don't believe in sea monsters; jaded travellers seeking a holiday with a difference.

FANTASTIC TRIP! ★★★★
Rodrigo de Triana, Spain
The journey across was a little rough. I did wish I'd brought some extra cloth to towel dry when we hit stormy weather, as the cabin facilities were minimal. Still, Chris Co offered a reward for the first person to spot land, and that lucky lookout was me! Amazing times.

PARADISE FOUND ★★★★
Sanchez de Segovia, Spain
I was on business to keep an eye on Queen Isabella's investment. Business trips are usually a chore, but not this one. To think, we made it to Asia… although it does seem a bit odd that we got there so quickly and our mileage was a little off. Still, it was on expenses, so mustn't grumble.

TOO CRAMPED ★★
A Sardine, Spain
Call me a small oily fish, but this cruise was way overbooked. You could barely find a place to sleep at night. And get this: we were also carrying 28 horses, three mules, plus sheep, goats, cattle, and chickens. It was a zoo on board, I tell you. I won't travel with that clown Columbus again.

HATED THE CAPTAIN ★
Holden A Grudge, Spain
This was a working holiday for me – and how I worked! Pumping bilge, cleaning the deck, and all for the "reward" of one meal of bug-infested biscuits a day. And then that tenacious dude Columbus dumps some of us in the middle of nowhere and kidnaps a bunch of natives to show off back home. Two words. Never. Again.

Done

Search: Trips to India

 **exploradviser**

ROUTE MAP | VOYAGE 1 | VOYAGE 2 | VOYAGE 3

VASCO DA GAMA VOYAGE
DEPARTURE: 8 JULY 1497 FROM LOVELY LISBON, PORTUGAL
ARRIVAL: May 1498, depending on the monsoon winds!
DESCRIPTION: Journey to the Indian subcontinent, rich land of spice and pepper, with Vasco da Gama, a Portuguese captain really worth his salt.

TRANSPORT
Sail under the captain on the *Sao Gabriel*, or come aboard the *Sao Rafael* or the *Berrio*. Top tip: stash your bags on the supply ship.

▼ Highlights
Set sail with da Gama and crew around the African continent, taking in the Cape of Good Hope at its very tip before winding our way up the eastern African shores. Note: we might not linger in some of the less welcoming spots. A 23-day trip (if the winds are right) then takes us to glorious India.

Sunset and scurvy on the beach

 Must-haves...

● Barter trinkets from home for this African salt cellar!

 exploradviser traveller reviews

What to expect:
Quite a lot of open ocean; fascinating encounters with other cultures (sort of).

Recommended for:
Non-landlubbers; people anxious to boost their sea-miles account, a lot.

UNFRIENDLY LOCALS ★★
Paulo da Gama, Portugal
I don't like to diss my own brother, but his advance planning was awful. The trade goods he brought along to barter with were rubbish. You could get better stuff free with a kid's meal. In most places, we were laughed out of town. We were the first Europeans these people encountered. You'd think we'd get a little more respect!

TAKE SEASICKNESS PILLS ★★
Gil Green, Portugal
OMG, 9,500 km (6,000 miles) of open ocean between here and the Cape of Good Hope? I feel woozy all over again. And the monsoon winds on the way back from India; that 23-day trip took 132! I wanted my friends to be green with envy over my adventures. Instead, I was green with sea-sickness. Ugh.

DON'T FORGET X
 ASTROLABE
PACK AN ASTROLABE... YOU NEVER KNOW WHEN YOU MIGHT NEED TO NAVIGATE YOUR WAY HOME

HELLO SAILOR! GOT A TASTE FOR EXPLORATION? BRUSH UP YOUR SKILLS AT HENRY THE NAVIGATOR'S SAILING SCHOOL

Search: Sailing around the world

exploradviser

ROUTE MAP | VOYAGE 1 | VOYAGE 2 | VOYAGE 3

FERDINAND MAGELLAN TRIP
DEPARTURE: 10 AUGUST 1519, FROM THE PORT OF SEVILLE
ARRIVAL: 6 September 1522... in Spain again!
DESCRIPTION: This is not just a holiday. It's a circumnavigation! Let's just hope what goes around really does come around.

TRANSPORT
A fabulous fleet of five ships: the flagship *Trinidad*, *San Antonio*, *Concepcion*, *Victoria*, and *Santiago*. And 270 sailing companions.

▼ Highlights
Book now for this unbelievable journey to right back where you started from. Yes, sail across the Atlantic to the very tip of South America, cross a strait named after our very own captain, take in the Spice Islands before a crew change in the Philippines and, with a rich cargo of spices, head for home.

Waters so calm they called it "Pacific"

FRESH WATER SPECIAL DEAL

exploradviser traveller reviews

What to expect:
The unexpected! Water, water everywhere, but not a drop to drink.

Recommended for:
People who enjoy eating sawdust and leather; people whose lives go around in circles.

MUTINY AT SEA ★
Juan Awayout, Spain
OK, I may only have agreed to this voyage to get out of jail (few Spanish sailors would work for a Portuguese captain), but when Magellan couldn't find a way through South America, mutiny broke out, and the instigators were hanged! Not my idea of fun.

CAPTAIN KILLED ★
Juan Sebastian Elcano, Spain
First our drinking water went all slimy, then we had to eat rats and ship bits to stay alive. And talk about a warm welcome in the Philippines: shot at by natives with crossbows! The captain was hit by a poisoned arrow and died. How we managed to carry on, I just don't know.

YOUR EXTRA LUGGAGE SPACE NOW!
Stock up on mace, nutmeg, and cloves (but make sure to leave room for the actual crew and other cargo, please).

Done

☙ Black pepper ❧
Tiny, dried fruits (called peppercorns) from the pepper plant, which is mainly found in India, are ground into black pepper.

☙ Cloves ❧
This extremely strong spice is from scented, dried flower buds of a tree native to the Spice Islands in Indonesia.

☙ Mace ❧
This is the fragrant, lace-like covering of the nutmeg seed, which is dried and has a more delicate flavour.

Cash crops
Spices were so valuable in Europe that they could be used as currency. A sackful of spice might have paid the bills, or even bought you some land. Spices were literally worth their weight in gold.

Banda Islands (nutmeg and mace)

India (black pepper)

Philippine Islands

Hormuz

Malacca

Maluku Islands (cloves)

Afonso de Albuquerque A Portuguese naval general, Afonso captured important trading ports including Malacca in 1511 and Hormuz in 1515. His goal was total Portuguese control of the Islamic spice trade.

António de Abreu After travelling with Afonso to Malacca, António led an expedition to the Banda Islands, which for centuries was the world's only source of nutmeg and mace.

Miguel Lopez de Legazpi After starting a new life in New Spain (Mexico), Miguel set up the first Spanish colony in the Philippines in 1565. It became an important trading port.

Cornelius de Houtman This Dutch explorer led a disaster-prone voyage to Indonesia in 1595, but the Dutch traders who followed would soon control the spice trade.

Trade and trade alike
The Arabs had the spice market cornered for centuries. With all the middlemen and mark-ups along the traditional trade routes, spices were often incredibly costly by the time they got to Europe. The Portuguese and Spanish were the first Europeans to look for ways of getting spices directly. They sent explorers to find new routes to the east. In 1602, the Dutch founded the East India Company – a group of merchants who banded together and reaped huge profits from establishing total domination of the spice trade. Unlike their goods, they weren't always sugar and spice and all things nice. Anyone objecting to their business practices could soon end up dead!

Nutmeg
The seed of an evergreen tree native to the Banda Islands in Indonesia, nutmeg is sweet tasting.

WORLD OF SPICE

The role of spices in the 15th and 16th centuries is nothing to be sneezed at. Not only were they essential to flavour bland (or slightly off) food, spices were also key ingredients in medicine and magic. As such, they were highly prized goods, and European explorers sailed the globe in search of new routes to the spice-rich islands of south and east Asia.

THE DUTCH EAST INDIA COMPANY'S GUIDE
TO TONICS, ELIXIRS, AND CURE-ALLS OF ALL KINDS

CHAPTER 1

Ever wonder what to do with all those spices on your spice rack? Check out these potion ideas for ridding yourself of some of life's little annoyances. Hopefully you'll find them recipes for success.

A run-of-the-mill ingredient: black pepper

This spicy hot seasoning was loved by the Ancient Romans and remains a staple of the poshest of European tables. They say the wealth of a man can be measured by the contents of his pepper pot, so don't let your neighbours catch you running low on pepper. These dimpled little berries also have many medicinal and household uses for you to spice up your life:

Feeling a tad gassy? Enjoy pepper as a carminative (a substance that prevents the formation of excess intestinal gas). Your friends will thank you for it, too.

To stimulate your circulation and to give digestion a helping hand, sprinkle away!

Piperine (the spicy compound in pepper) repels some insects, so strew a little pepper in your garden to keep the spiders and bugs at bay.

Are you all a-croak? Gargle a pinch of pepper mixed with cider vinegar and warm water to soothe a sore throat.

Follow the scent: cloves

These aromatic little flower buds are quite strong, so a little will go a long way. They are delicious with Indian food (try a clove with your rice) and their unmistakable scent adds a spicy tang to incense. You'll find countless ways to use cloves in your home potions, so although we say a little goes a long way, stock up aplenty. From the DEIC/VOC.

Suffering from a sore tooth? Apply a little clove oil to the gum around the relevant gnasher to soothe away the pain.

Are mosquitoes bugging you? Try cloves as a natural repellent.

The ancient Chinese used cloves to treat hiccups, so next time a bout of hiccups strikes, take a leaf out of their book and try this reliable remedy.

A time-tested African remedy for upset stomachs and digestive dismay is clove steeped in water to make a tea. Time then for a cuppa!

No first-aid kit is complete without eugenol. This compound not only gives cloves a wonderful aroma, but is both an anaesthetic and antiseptic.

Nutty stuff: nutmeg

This little egg-shaped seed is delicious in both sweet and savoury dishes. We Dutch adore it, especially in vegetable dishes. You should also keep plenty of nutmeg to hand for the following elixirs. You'd be nuts not to.

With useful breath-freshening properties, nutmeg oil is an important ingredient of toothpaste and mouthwash.

Nutmeg oil is used as the base for many perfumes. You'll smell just fabulous.

To cure an upset stomach, place a few drops of nutmeg oil on a sugar cube or a spoonful of honey and swallow.

Don't even think about mixing up a batch of home-made cough syrup without nutmeg.

A real delicacy: mace

Make a place for mace on your spice rack. This deep, brick-orange spice has a similar, but more delicate, flavour than nutmeg. Mace is found in all kinds of food from curries to ketchup. But it's absolutely wizard as a potion ingredient.

If you're constantly running to the loo, run for the mace. It contains a compound that puts a stop to diarrhoea.

Can't sleep at night? Mace has been used as a cure for insomnia.

Need to get in Granny's good books? If her joints are creaky with rheumatism, a little mace oil can ease the pain.

Are you feeling down in the mouth? Mace can soothe mouth ulcers and make you smile again.

MING DYNASTY

Founded in 1368, the Ming Dynasty restored rule of China to the native people, and reconquered much of its territory. Under the Ming, the Chinese experienced an economic and creative boom. Chinese cities expanded quickly and education, along with the arts and literature, flourished. Chinese ships explored the world's sea routes. By the 16th century, China had built itself a massive, million-man army, and was protected by an equally impressive barrier wall. As the century drew to a close, however, a series of incompetent rulers and economic problems weakened the dynasty, opening the door once again to foreign invasion.

一 A DYNASTY IS BORN

Born a dirt-poor peasant, Zhu Yuanzhang, seized control of Nanjing from the Mongols with his rebel army. He proclaimed himself the emperor of a new dynasty in 1368, taking the name Hongwu ("Mightily Martial"). After driving the Mongols out of China and beyond, Hongwu sacked all his advisers to single-handedly take control.

二 THINGS FORBIDDEN

In 1402, Hongwu's son Yongle (whose name means "Perpetually Jubilant") seized the throne. He moved the capital to Beijing, employing 200,000 men to rebuild its mud-and-straw city walls with brick and stone. Within them he ordered the construction of the Forbidden City – a palace that no one could enter without permission.

三 GRAND WORKS

Between 1411 and 1415, Yongle commissioned yet another major construction work: the renovation of the Grand Canal – the world's longest artificial river. The canal, at about 1,790 km (1,112 miles) long, was a lifeline for Beijing, providing a vital link to other cities in the Empire, as well as a means for the government to communicate with more far-flung places.

四 VOYAGING AFAR

Yongle (who we should perhaps rename "Perpetually Busy") also built a massive navy and fleet of treasure ships. The fleet's commander, Zheng He, made seven voyages to southeast Asia, India, Arabia, and the east coast of Africa. The fleet returned laden with tributes from foreign rulers, including rare spices and exotic animals, such as giraffes.

五 MING BLING

Chinese artistry bloomed during the Ming Dynasty. The beautiful cobalt-blue glazed porcelain, which became known as Ming china, was perfected by artisans in Jingdezhen and became an instant collector's item in Europe. Luxurious silks were created in Hangzhou for export, and Chinese novels were printed in a more accessible language for the masses.

六 ALL WALLED IN

In 1449, Yongle's young and inexperienced successor, Zhengtong, was kidnapped during an attack by the Mongol-speaking Oriat army. He was released, but the shaken Mings decided to forget about offence and focus on defence. They strengthened the earthen Great Wall, built to defend the Empire in the Qin Dynasty, with brick and stone, and lengthened it to 2,414 km (1,500 miles).

RENAISSANCE

In the hundred years between 1450 and 1550, a resurgence of interest in the ancient world throughout the cities of Europe – especially those in Italy – led to an era known as the Renaissance. Meaning "rebirth", the name "renaissance" alludes to the way people cast a fresh eye over the works of the past for inspiration in the future. The artists, inventors, and writers of the Renaissance created an impressive collection of innovative works that astounded the world.

FRIENDS WITH MONEY

Money made the Renaissance go round, and there was a great deal of it to be made in the thriving cities. Rich kings, ambitious popes, and noble families such as the Medicis of Florence (that's Lorenzo de Medici, important patron of the arts, on the right) lavished money on art and architecture as a way to make themselves look more important.

IT'S A HUMAN THING

The European scholars who helped kick-start the Renaissance were known as Humanists. They studied long-forgotten classical texts in Greek and Latin (the language of educated Europe). So-called "Prince of the Humanists", Dutchman Erasmus revised and translated some of these ancient texts, making their ideas and principles accessible to others.

ART AND ASPIRATIONS

Renaissance painters and sculptors aspired to match the artistry of Ancient Greece and Rome, while also introducing more progressive styles and techniques into their work. Depicting people in a realistic way, using perspective, light, and shadow to make subjects appear fuller and more lifelike, was an artistic innovation that came into fruition with the Renaissance. It can be seen in Botticelli's famous Birth of Venus, which was created for Lorenzo Medici's villa.

HOT OFF THE PRESS

In 1455, German craftsman Johannes Gutenberg printed the Bible on his printing press. This key development in book-making meant that texts no longer had to be laboriously copied out by hand, making them much cheaper and easier to produce, and allowing information to be exchanged much more quickly than ever before.

BUILDING ON IDEAS

The Ancient Greeks and Romans discovered a special ratio – the Golden Ratio – which they used to build perfectly proportioned structures. Renaissance architects revisited such ancient techniques to create their own beautiful buildings. Churches were no longer built in the shape of a cross, but were designed around circles – the shape considered most perfect by the ancients. Circular domes topped many key buildings, including the iconic cathedral in Florence.

TIME FOR A GOOD BOOK

The printing press immediately put its stamp on history, reproducing the inspired words and ideas that were bursting forth from leading Renaissance writers and philosophers – such as Dante, Erasmus, and Machiavelli. At this time authors also began writing in their own languages rather than in Latin, making their works much more accessible to the masses rather than the sole preserve of scholars.

DRAWING IT OUT

Perhaps the ultimate Renaissance man, known today mainly for his paintings, was Leonardo da Vinci, a genius inventor, scientist, naturalist, mathematician, writer, and human anatomist. His notebooks – some 13,000 pages of notes and drawings – include everything from amazingly inventive ideas to grocery lists. He, too, looked back to the ancients, and fused their findings with his own observations. His drawing of the Vitruvian man is one such classic example, based on the ancient writings of Roman architect Vitruvius on ideal human proportions.

The Tudors

In the words of Mr William Shakespeare, playwright extraordinaire, all the world's a stage, and all the men and women merely players. Come, then, and cast thine eyes upon some of the biggest players in English history: the House of Tudor. Perhaps thou hast heard of them? Well lend us your ears, dear audience, as we reveal all – of magnificent exploits, dastardly dealings, and triumphs at home and abroad.

ACT 2: ARTHUR OF TUDOR

In 1501, Henry VII's son Arthur makes a diplomatic marriage to Catherine of Aragon, but dies just a year after they wed.

As eldest son of Hen and Liz,
raised was I to be king,
With the finest education and
a princess to wear my ring.
Yet just one year upon the throne
and I die of consumption.
My brother, he will seize it all,
at least, that's my assumption.

ACT 3 SCENE 1: HENRY VIII

Upon Henry VII's death, in 1509, his second son Henry VIII becomes king… six wives later, his state and Church reforms are well underway.

O Arthur, bro, I will take the throne.
I shall have Catherine, too.
Though if an heir she cannot give,
five others shall say "I do".
A reformed England I shall create,
the government I will also fix.
So remember me, please, for
these good deeds, and not just for
the chicks.

ACT 1: HENRY VII

At the end of the Wars of the Roses, which saw the Houses of York and Lancaster fight for the crown of England, Henry VII's Tudor clan (on the Lancastrian side) beats Richard III's Yorkists.

The glorious house of Tudor, it all begins with me.
I sealed my fate at Bosworth Field where I claimed victory.
I wed thy lovely Lizzie York to keep her family sweet;
Red rose of Lancaster, white rose of York, as the Tudor Rose they meet.

ACT 3 SCENE 2: PRIEST

Henry VIII breaks from Rome and the Catholic Church.

I used to be a happy priest,
Life in the Church was easy.
We'd stacks of cash, to say the least,
But then along came Henry Sleazy.
He wanted a split from his first wife
But the Pope, he sayeth no.
So the King, he said "go get a life",
And took all of our dough.

ACT 3 SCENE 3: THOMAS CROMWELL

Under Henry's orders, Thomas – the King's chief minister – takes the Church's wealth for the Crown.

The boss has his own Church now
And what he says, I do.
So this, o' Priest, is your farewell bow,
It's time for something new.
I'll have your money and your goods,
All for King Henry's glory.
Get out of town, now, understood?
Here endeth the Catholic story.

ACT 4: EDWARD VI

Henry VIII's son Edward inherits the throne in 1547, aged nine. His advisers insist that England continues under Henry's legacy as a Protestant country.

I'm just a little weedy kid,
I barely dent the throne.
They tell me I should make England
a no-Catholic zone.
I'll do just what they ask me,
but I'm feeling rather rough.
My sister Mary's next in line;
she's Catholic, strangely enough.

ACT 5: BLOODY MARY

After Edward dies in 1553, his Catholic sister comes to power. She marries Prince Philip II of Spain, despite opposition from her advisers.

I'm the very first queen of England and
although I love you dearly,
If you meddle with my wedding plans,
you're toast – I mean that sincerely.
I'll tie the knot with Spanish Phil and
then get rid of heathens;
I'll burn thine Protestants at the stake;
be gone, ye Church of England.

SHAKESPEARE (1564–1616)

Parting is such sweet sorrow,
but we must leave the Tudors be.
Enough, in fact, about them all,
let's have a cheer for me!

(Curtain)

ACT 6 SCENE 1: ELIZABETH I

After Mary's death, Elizabeth is crowned queen in 1558. Catholic rebels plot against her after she proclaims England to be Protestant once more, but her reign is long and glorious.

I'm married to my country,
and it shall rise to glory,
Returning England to the top
will be my true life story.
My father's faith returneth,
despite scheming cousin Mary,
I'll lock her up for eighteen years
as she doth make me wary.

ACT 6 SCENE 2: MARY QUEEN OF SCOTS

Elizabeth's Catholic cousin is a worrying threat for Elizabeth.

My cousin, with all due respect, should not
be on the throne,
For I have a claim to that very spot, and it
should be mine alone.
She can lock me up in prision and then
throw away the key,
But she'll have to cut my head off to see
the end of me.

ACT 6 SCENE 3: SIR FRANCIS DRAKE

In 1588, the English navy, led by Francis Drake, defeats the Spanish Armada — an important victory for Queen Elizabeth.

My queen entrusts her ships
to me, as leader of the fleet,
One midnight on the open
waves the Spanish we did meet.
They said they were invincible
and none could ever beat them,
But know you this, oh one and
all, we did of course defeat 'em.

AUDIENCE

Elizabeth I never married and had no heir. Upon her death in 1603, her Scottish cousin James Stuart took over.

"All is well that ends well," as yonder bard
hath written.
But life is not a rose bed, lest not from where
we're sittin'. (*Aside*: well, standing)
The rich grew ever richer while we poor
did feel the sting.
So farewell to ye Tudors, long live the
Stuart king!

MURAD I

The third ruler of the Empire, Murad I (c1326–1389), extended Ottoman rule with important inroads into Europe. Under his rule Byzantium and Bulgaria became vassals ("servants" of the Empire). In 1389 the Serbian army challenged Murad at Kosovo. The Serbs were soundly defeated, but one of their number assassinated Murad in his tent.

Ottoman Empire

Spanning three continents at its height, the Ottoman Empire was one of the most powerful Islamic states in history. It began in 1301 under the leadership of Osman I – a brave tribal warrior whose ancestors would rule in an unbroken family line all the way up until 1922. Some of their key moves are revealed here.

SELIM I THE GRIM

Selim I (1465–1520) seized power by dethroning his father, Bayezid II, and killing all of his brothers and nephews. Then his thoughts turned to the powerful Safavid Empire. In 1514 Selim's army crushed Shah Ismail's at the Battle of Chaldiran in Iran. Later victories brought Syria, Palestine, and Egypt under Ottoman control, as well as the holy cities of Mecca and Medina – the most sacred sites of Islam.

MEHMED THE CONQUEROR

The seventh sultan in the Dynasty, 12-year-old Mehmed (1432–1481) became ruler after his father abdicated. But young Mehmed did not rule well, so his father came out of retirement. As sultan again following his father's death, Mehmed laid siege to Constantinople. The great city fell, and, with it, what remained of the Byzantine Empire. Mehmed rebuilt the city as the capital of his empire and of Islam.

BAYEZID I THE LIGHTNING BOLT

Murad's son Bayezid (1354–1403) was next in line. His bold blink-and-you'll-miss-it raids led to his nickname, the "Lightning-bolt". Bayezid continued to wage battles to extend Ottoman control, but his game was met with a check at the hands of fearsome Mongol warrior Tamerlane, who wiped out the Ottoman army and made Bayezid his prisoner. The Empire was in a precarious state.

SULEYMAN THE MAGNIFICENT

The Ottoman Empire reached its golden age during the rule of the 10th and longest-serving sultan, Suleyman the Magnificent (1494–1566). He encouraged the arts to thrive in his capital city, and important new conquests extended Ottoman power from Asia Minor (modern-day Turkey) to North Africa. The Ottoman fleet became the greatest sea power in the Mediterranean.

MEHMED IV THE HUNTER

The Ottomans faced some tough times after Selim's reign, and the sultans that followed did not rise to the challenge. When Mehmed IV (1642–1693) took the throne as a six-year-old boy, the tender-aged sultan gave most of his power to his trusted advisers. During the reign of Mehmed IV (nicknamed the Hunter due to his love of hunting, funnily enough), the Ottomans found their feet again.

AHMET III

Building relations with western Europe was important to Ahmet III (1673–1736). Also in his reign the first printing press arrived in Istanbul. Ottoman painters and poets contributed to a flowering of the arts, called the Tulip Era after the craze for tulips among the Ottoman elite. Tension between Russia and the Empire was also sprouting, though, and a series of conflicts saw the Empire begin to fragment.

SELIM II

Suleyman's son Selim II (1524–1574) was something short of magnificent. He had little interest in the Empire and was happy to hand over power to his ministers. They made a valuable treaty with the Holy Roman Empire in 1568, but a series of naval disasters nearly totalled the Ottoman fleet. Selim seemed to be leading the Empire down the drain when a slippery wet bath-house floor led to his death.

ABDUL HAMID II

Abdul Hamid II (1842–1918) issued the Empire's first constitution to appease those who wanted reform, but he more or less ignored it. When revolts broke out, Abdul persecuted thousands and the government became even more autocratic. In 1909 the rebels deposed Abdul. It was the beginning of the end of the Empire, which was manoeuvred into a checkmate position in 1922 during Mehmed VI's reign. Game over.

End of the Aztecs

The mighty Aztec Empire, 20 million people strong, thrives in Mexico. A Spanish adventurer is about to pay a call...

"Quetzalcoatl, our creator, I have seen the evidence with my own eyes."

"The Feathered Serpent's arrival is near. I will tell the Emperor."

The year is 1510 and a comet scorches a path across the inky black sky over the beautiful floating city of Tenochtitlan – the Aztec capital.

"Send an envoy at once to greet the newcomers. We must make our great god welcome, if he is among them..."

"It is done, Emperor Montezuma. They have weapons that shoot out fire and sparks."

"Their skin is pale, and their hair stops at their ears. And they ride funny-looking four-legged beasts."

Rumours spread about strange white men in floating buildings off the coast. These are the armies of Hernán Cortés, conquistador (conquerer).

Cortés marches into the Aztec capital, intent on plunder. His army is swelled with tribespeople weary of paying tributes to Emperor Montezuma, who now emerges from his beautiful litter. The leaders meet.

"I give you necklaces of gold and precious stones. It would please the gods if you would join us here in our beautiful city."

"Er, could you go ba[ck] to the bit about gold and precious stone[s]"

End of the Incas

Another Spanish conquistador, Francisco Pizarro, heard rumours of a glorious inland empire in Central America...

It's 1527, and somewhere off the coast of Ecuador...

"Mon dios above me, would you look at all this silver and gold? It is brighter than the very Sun. I must seize these people at once, and find the source of these treasures."

"I have an inca-ling there may be trouble ahead."

Meanwhile, in the powerful Inca stronghold of Peru, new ruler Atahualpa has heard word of a small army marching into his Empire.

"Who are these people? Collect slaves and prepare the gold cups of beer. We will offer them up to keep the peace. The Inca will prevail, just as the gods wish."

"It will be done."

The Spanish stormed into the Inca capital, led by Pizarro's fellow conquistador, Hernando de Soto, on strange four-legged animals called horses, never before seen by the Incas.

"Accept this drink of maize beer as is our custom. You will be quartered tonight in one of my royal apartments, and in the morning I shall meet with Pizarro."

"Those llamas are loco, man!"

"This may be the maize beer talking, but I don't think that's a llama."

"But I am the emperor, the chosen-one of the gods. You cannot imprison me. And my people grow weary of your demands for gold."

"Ah yes, where did you say you kept the gold again?"

Cortés and his men are led into fabulous apartments in the heart of the city, where they marvel at incredible sights... but the stories about human sacrifices are worrying them. Cortés decides to take Montezuma hostage.

The Aztecs respond by attacking the Spanish, cutting off escape routes from the city. The Spanish soon run out of food and water, forcing them to retreat, but Montezuma is killed.

"I will be back for your gold, but I will bide my time. Your city will be mine. Tenochtitlan is doomed. I will let Spanish guns do the talking."

the End

In 1521, Cortés, true to his word, returns to a broken city, now ravaged by smallpox, starvation, and siege. The once mighty Empire of the Sun succumbs to the Spanish.

"For us to know you are civilized and worthy of our good will, renounce your gods, as per the message in the Bible, and follow Christianity."

"This book does not speak to me."

"Guards! Open fire! The savages reject our faith."

The next day, the leaders meet in the town square. Pizarro calls for a priest and demands the Inca convert to Christianity immediately. Or else.

An imprisoned Atahualpa, now understanding that the Spanish are actually after gold, offers to ransom himself for a roomful of gold and two of silver.

"Thanks for the gold, but you have plotted against me. You will undergo a trial!"

"Can you not just take the ransom and go back to wherever you came from?"

"You do not understand. We may go, but there will be more of us, thousands more. Your empire is no more, my friend. Let the trial begin!"

Emperor Atahualpa — considered a god by the Inca people — is found guilty and put to death. Before long, the Incas are vanquished.

"GUILTY AS CHARGED!"

the End

Reformation

From medieval times to the 16th century, the Catholic Church was the most powerful force in Europe. Few dared to openly criticize the Church and its leaders, but there were accusations of corruption and excessively lavish spending by Church officials. As money piled up in the Church coffers through the sale of indulgences (a payment made to the Church to wash away your sins), something had to give. The man who gave it to the Church was German priest and professor Martin Luther. His simple protest in 1517 led to a major shake-up in religion known as the Reformation. He'll take the story from here.

The rabble-rouser

As soon as I hammered home the last of my complaints, there was controversy. I wanted people to think about a new way of being a Christian, based on the Bible, in which God gives us the faith that saves us rather than our giving coins to the Church. Thanks to the newly invented printing press, my words spread across Europe. Guess what? I was excommunicated — that's kicked out of the Church — and I had to go into hiding disguised as a knight.

The reformer

Guten tag, kids. I am completely, totally, 100 per cent fed up with the Catholic Church. These Church officials are devoted to money and power, not the Bible. The very idea of swapping cash for forgiveness is appalling. So I said to myself, Martin, it's hammer time. You can't touch the Church like this. I wrote down all my complaints — 95 in total — and nailed them up here on the church door at Wittenberg.

The result

What a ruckus. I didn't set out to divide the Church — I only wanted reform. But there were plenty of people across northern Europe who agreed with me, founding a new Lutheran faith (catchy name, no?) based on my teachings. Some other chaps also worked on this whole Reformation thing (see my list above right). Of course, the Church fought back. They called it the Counter-Reformation, which is pretty naff if you ask me. They met up at Trent, Italy, three times between 1545 and 1563 to sort it all out. They spent a lot of dosh making the churches glitzier, and did a bang-up PR job so the pope was even holier than thou. They also told the clergy to behave. Boy, did I make things change — with just determination and a hammer and nails.

Reformed characters in Europe

Ulrich Zwingli (1484–1531)

This Swiss dude Ulrich didn't get all the way up to 95 complaints. He only had 67, back in 1523. Still, the city council in Zurich took them so seriously that they adopted them as official doctrine. Result! We had a couple of quibbles, yes, but this guy put the "reform" in the "Reformation".

John Calvin (1509–1564)

This French Calvin character experienced a sudden conversion to the reformed faith, like me. It was a dangerous time to do that, as the Catholic Church was hunting down non-believers and burning them at the stake. Heavy! In 1536 he moved to Geneva, Switzerland, where he played a major part in religious reform. He believed that people could have a direct relationship with God, rather than communicating through the Church.

Henry VIII (1491–1547)

So maybe this English guy's motives were not quite as pure as mine. When the Pope refused to give him a divorce, Henry broke from papal authority, remarried, and became leader of the newly formed Church of England.

Saint Ignatius Loyola (1491–1556)

Now, Iggy here was from Loyola in Spain, and he was loyol–a to the Catholic Church in a big way. He founded a religious order called the Jesuits and devoted his life to revitalizing the Church in the Counter–Reformation. You wouldn't have thought a guy like this was cut out to be a saint. In his early years, Iggy liked gambling and the ladies. He was destined for military stardom, but a cannonball shattered his leg. While he was recovering, he happened to read about the life of Christ, and he was hooked. Now that's a reformation for you.

A TERRIBLE TALE

Prince of Moscow, Ivan III (1440–1505), also known as Ivan the Great, laid the foundations for the creation of the Russian state. He invaded neighbouring territories, nearly tripling the size of his stronghold. His son, Vasili III, ruled after him from 1505 to 1533. But with no heir Vasili chucked his wife and married a Serbian princess... and then something terrible happened: the arrival of little Ivan IV, who became one of the most notorious rulers in Russian history. To put it mildly, he was no doll.

IVAN THE TSAR

In 1547, at age 16, Ivan was crowned tsar of all Russia, which let the boyars know he was intent on establishing a more bossy, or autocratic, leadership. The next month eligible girls from throughout Russia gathered in Moscow so that Ivan could look them over and select a bride. He chose Anastasia – a real doll and the first of his eight wives.

IVAN THE REFORMER

In the first summer of his reign as tsar, a devastating fire swept through Moscow, killing some 3,000 people and leaving the city in ruins. Young Ivan pledged to rebuild the city and reform the Church and state to benefit everyone. Ivan's government grew stronger and more stable, and military victories in 1552 and 1556 expanded Russian territory. During this time, Ivan also helped expand trade with Europe, and commissioned the building of the beautiful St Basil's cathedral.

IVAN THE VENGEFUL

When he was eight, Ivan's mother was poisoned and a power struggle broke out in the palace. In 1543, Ivan called the boyars to a meeting. He threw his dolls out of the pram and ripped into the boyars for neglecting him and the state. And, because actions speak louder than words, he chucked one of them into a pack of hungry hunting dogs. Suddenly, the boyars decided to let Ivan do whatever he wanted.

IVAN THE MISERABLE

Ivan was just three years old when his father died in 1533. Vasili had named Ivan as his heir, but only once he reached the age of 15. The boyars (members of the Russian aristocracy) seized control, helped by Ivan's mother, and poor little Ivan was ignored, appearing only at state ceremonies, when he would be dressed up and plonked on the throne to fool visitors. Not surprisingly Ivan was a bit of a misery guts and grew into a mixed-up kid who enjoyed torturing animals.

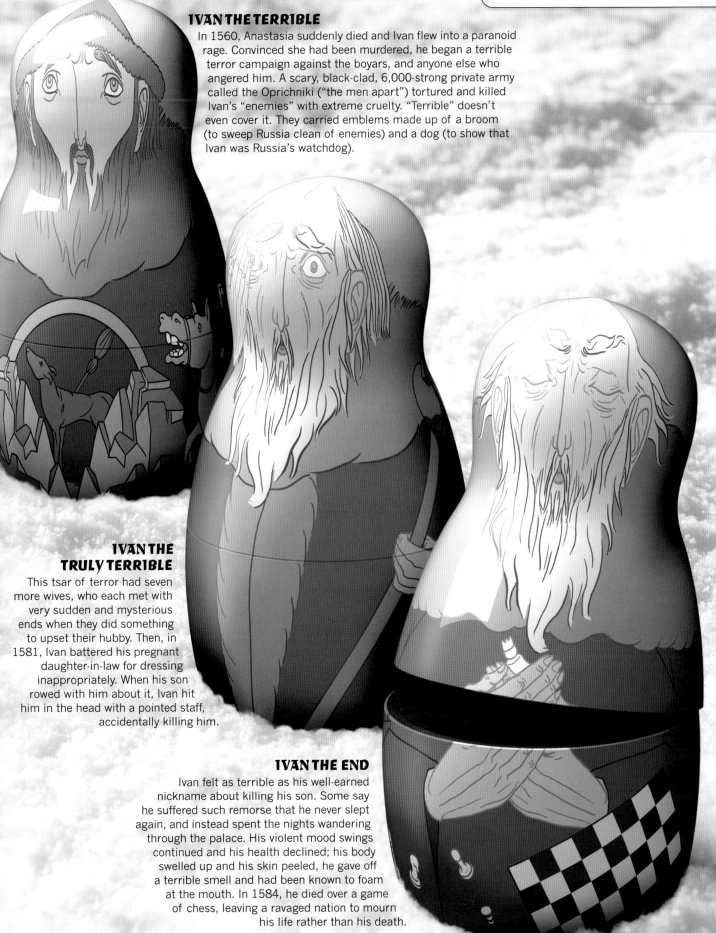

IVAN THE TERRIBLE

In 1560, Anastasia suddenly died and Ivan flew into a paranoid rage. Convinced she had been murdered, he began a terrible terror campaign against the boyars, and anyone else who angered him. A scary, black-clad, 6,000-strong private army called the Oprichniki ("the men apart") tortured and killed Ivan's "enemies" with extreme cruelty. "Terrible" doesn't even cover it. They carried emblems made up of a broom (to sweep Russia clean of enemies) and a dog (to show that Ivan was Russia's watchdog).

IVAN THE TRULY TERRIBLE

This tsar of terror had seven more wives, who each met with very sudden and mysterious ends when they did something to upset their hubby. Then, in 1581, Ivan battered his pregnant daughter-in-law for dressing inappropriately. When his son rowed with him about it, Ivan hit him in the head with a pointed staff, accidentally killing him.

IVAN THE END

Ivan felt as terrible as his well-earned nickname about killing his son. Some say he suffered such remorse that he never slept again, and instead spent the nights wandering through the palace. His violent mood swings continued and his health declined; his body swelled up and his skin peeled, he gave off a terrible smell and had been known to foam at the mouth. In 1584, he died over a game of chess, leaving a ravaged nation to mourn his life rather than his death.

Tug of religious war

The early years of the Reformation had been peaceful ones. But as change swept across Europe and people picked their sides, Catholics and Protestants alike were tugged into war. A series of violent clashes broke out, influenced by religious change and wrenching power struggles. For more than a century rival Christian groups battled it out. With all of Europe as the playing field, this was a game that could only end in tears.

Oh poo, not another war!

The Holy Roman Empire was a collection of states — some Catholic and some Protestant. The Treaty of Augsburg in 1555 had given the ruler of each state in the Empire the right to choose its religion. While this had calmed down tensions, things were still unsettled, and both Protestants and Catholics upped the ante by forming armies to defend their right to worship. In 1618, after Ferdinand II was elected king of Bohemia, he sent a missionary party to a castle in Prague to stop the building of Protestant churches. The Protestants responded by chucking them out the window. They survived, but by what means? The Catholics thanked the heavens and claimed they were carried to safety by angels, while the Protestants rubbished that story, saying instead that they simply landed on a pile of cushiony poo. Something stinks of prejudice.

Edict of Nantes

One of the earliest set of religious wars kicked off in France in 1562, between the Guises (a Catholic family of nobles) and two other noble families who supported the Huguenot (Protestant) cause. The King's mum, Catherine de Medici, played the rivals off against each other so that neither could take complete control, but this resulted in a number of bloody massacres. When Henry of Navarre, a Huguenot turned Catholic, took the throne, he understood only too well that the way to make peace was to show tolerance for both sides. In 1598, the Edict of Nantes ended the French war, granting Huguenots the same rights as Catholics.

Come on boys, put your backs into it!

I hope this war ends soon. I'm feeling a bit ropey

Oh no! I've got an itchy nose. Maybe if I just let go for a second…

CATHERINE DE MEDICI
Good day to you, peeps. I'm Catherine de Medici of France and I like to think of myself as everybody's friend, Catholic and Protestant – I'm not one to put all my eggs in one basket. You see, showing favouritism at times like these can get you into trouble right up to your frill-collared neck, so I prefer to pledge my allegiance to both sides and see what happens.

MAXIMILIAN, DUKE OF BAVARIA
I'm afraid I disagree with you, Catherine. I strongly believe in making a firm stand, which is why I gathered a group of German princes together in 1609 to form the Catholic League. With this union of Catholic states, we had an army of 30,000 men who were ready and willing to express their opposition to the Protestant Union.

HENRY OF NAVARRE
Well hello there. I took the throne and became king of France after my cousin Henry III was killed by a crazed monk. I know I'm pulling hard for the Catholics on this here rope now, but I was initially a Protestant. I swapped sides to become a Catholic, but a Catholic that was tolerant of Protestants. I just really, really wanted to bring peace to my country. So can we let go of this rope yet?

FERDINAND II
Let me introduce myself: I'm Holy Roman Emperor and king of Bohemia, and I have absolutely no time for non-Catholics in my kingdom. When I sent a couple of missionaries to Prague, I managed to aggravate the Protestants (one-up to me) and triggered the start of this raging war. So then I led a huge army in the subsequent battles against the Protestant uprising, and scored some key victories.

COUNT OF TILLY
I may be the Dutch commander, but I trained to be a monk, so you can just call me the "Monk in Armour". I became general of the Catholic League forces in 1610, and proceeded to win a series of pretty damn important victories against those pesky Bohemians during the run of the war. I don't like to blow my own trumpet (much), but I ruled.

Peace of Westphalia

As the motives for war moved away from religion (the Swedes, for example, were battling for Baltic Sea routes in northern Germany), a peace treaty in 1635 nearly, but not quite, brought the war to a close. But then France made an alliance with Sweden and declared war on Spain... Finally, after some seven million deaths, countless crushed villages, and the stripping of land bare by invading armies, the Thirty Years' War ended with the Peace of Westphalia — a treaty agreed to by members from both parties. Religious groups continued to spark against each other, but there was no more fire.

Battle of White Mountain

As a result of what had happened in Bohemia, the poo really hit the fan — a full-scale Thirty Years' War kicked off with the Battle of White Mountain in 1618. The Catholic League's army, under the command of the Count of Tilly, crushed the Bohemians in just a few hours. Protestants were forced to convert or leave. It was the end of Protestantism in Bohemia, but just the beginning of a more widespread war that would eventually rope in nearly every state in Europe. On one side of the fence were many of the German states of the Holy Roman Empire. On the other side, pulling against the Catholics, were German Protestants along with France, Sweden, Denmark, and England.

Give it some welly for the Protestants

Eeeuuuw. I think Frederick's just farted

Ow! You're stepping on my toe, Christian!

I wish I'd brought a cushion

GASPARD DE COLIGNY
Give it up for the Protestants! I'm a pretty well-known Huguenot leader, and am loud and proud about seeking tolerance for us Protestants. Yes, I have been called gobby in my time, although I think it was a bit much for the Guises (with a helping hand from Catherine de Medici) to try and silence me forever. Their assassination attempt failed, but still!

FREDERICK III
I'm leader of the Rhineland Palatinate state in Germany, and I grew more and more concerned after the tentative calm that the Treaty of Augsburg brought dissolved into conflict. That's why I founded the Protestant League. We are an armed alliance of Protestant states, loyal to the cause and willing to fight to protect our basic right to worship.

CHRISTIAN, PRINCE OF ANHALT
Yo! The name's Prince Christian and I rule over Anhalt in Germany... at least I did, until I was stripped of my land holdings and officially named an outlaw of the Holy Roman Empire. All because I led the Protestant troops in the Battle of White Mountain. We didn't even win! In fact, we were completely crushed by General Tilly and his Catholic army.

CHRISTIAN IV
As Protestant king of Denmark and Norway, I led the Danish foray into the Thirty Years' War. I'm a hands-on kinda guy, and prefer to get stuck in rather than simply bark out orders. I was proud to fight alongside my men against the troops of the Holy Roman Emperor, as well as those of the Catholic League. The Count of Tilly proved too great a force for us though, too.

GUSTAVUS, KING OF SWEDEN
I'm another Protestant king, this time of Sweden. I've heard tell that people sometimes refer to me as "the Great", but don't let that sway your opinion of me – too much... A real stickler for the Protestant cause, I tried my utmost to stop the Habsburgs from taking total control of the key Baltic sea routes, and I set up a stronghold in Germany to consolidate the Protestant position in the war.

A DUTCH MASTERCLASS

In 1556, the people of the Netherlands had a new king: Philip II, also ruler of Spain. He took the throne at a time of great unrest. Taxes were brutally high, people were none too keen on the Spanish soldiers garrisoned in their towns, and Protestantism was gaining support. Under Philip – who hadn't even bothered to learn the language of his subjects – things grew worse, and the people were driven to the edge of revolt. Could the Dutch underdogs defeat the mighty Spanish crown? Wooden shoe like to find out…

Be warned. You revolt, and I'll do something revolting!

EXHIBIT 1: DASTARDLY DUKE
The Duke of Alba, nicknamed the Butcher of Flanders, arrived in the Netherlands in 1567 with an army of 12,000 men and instructions from the King to do whatever needed doing to punish the Protestant rebels. He set up the Council of Troubles (known to the Dutch as the Council of Blood – can't imagine why) to put the troublemakers on trial. The council ordered the execution of some 6,000 Protestants. Alba's brutal acts were the final straw for the outraged Dutch.

I can be silent no longer!

EXHIBIT 2: WILLIAM THE SILENT
The leader of the revolt against the Spanish was William I of Orange. Nicknamed "the Silent" because of his discretion, he had actually served in the Spanish government. However, he grew angry with the treatment of Dutch Protestants and joined the rebels in attempting to overthrow the Spanish. He and his brother led an army to attack Spanish positions on land, while a group of rebel sailors known as the Sea Beggars fought at Spanish-held ports.

That will silence you for good, William.

EXHIBIT 3: FIGHT FOR INDEPENDENCE
In 1579, seven provinces in the north joined together in the Union of Utrecht, thus separating themselves from Spain. They chose Prince William of Orange to lead their Republic of the United Netherlands. However, following his refusal to appear at Alba's council, William was declared an outlaw and was ultimately assassinated by a supporter of the Spanish king. The war continued until 1648, when Spain officially recognized that the Republic was independent. It was time for the Dutch to bloom.

BUNCH OF TROUBLE
A tulip craze swept through Holland in 1636. People competed with each other to own the rarest, most unusual flowers, speculating huge sums of money on the tulip market. Here's how blooming crazy this era, known as Tulipmania, became: a single rare tulip bulb could command a price equal to 10 times the annual wage. But just a year later, the tulip market crashed. Anyone who'd invested all their money into tulips now faced a bouquet of bankruptcies.

EXHIBIT 4: GOLDEN AGE

The newly independent Holland emerged from the shadow of the revolt into a golden age of achievements in science, discovery, commerce, and especially art. Two remarkable painters, Rembrandt Harmenszoon van Rijn and Johannes Vermeer, painted, with a skilful use of light, portraits of ordinary people doing everyday things. Their works, often rich with symbols and hidden meanings, are amongst art's masterpieces.

Where are these etchings you promised to show me, Mr Vermeer?

EXHIBIT 5: APPLIANCE OF SCIENCE

Dutch scientists made many key discoveries during the golden age. One such brainiac was mathematician and astronomer Christiaan Huygens. He invented the pendulum clock and described the planet Saturn's rings. Anton van Leeuwenhoek, another clever so-and-so, made great improvements to the telescope, and used a microscope to study the human body, examining such intricacies as the structure of muscles.

Pearls are a girl's best friend.

Watch closely. I will show you only once!

I'd give my left arm to be as advanced in medicine as you Dutch. Oh… I just did.

EXHIBIT 6: PROSPEROUS TIMES

Built around a series of canals, the newly wealthy city of Amsterdam grew rapidly to become the leading financial centre of Europe in the mid-1650s. Ships sailed from its busy ports to the four corners of the world, and its atmosphere of tolerance following the struggle of the revolt attracted refugees from throughout the continent. By the mid-17th century, the Netherlands was the top maritime and commercial power in Europe. Things were good, you might say.

Mughal India

Mughal India, a dynasty over most In the 16th and 17th centuries ruled Indian of the Muslims in strong 100 million people were, but they of the Mughals majority, and respect. subcontinent The Hindu and positive a region with religious brought the government the encouraged emperors promoting of the The changes Mughal India, centralizing and Islam. Many as improving to education of culture just as colourful. faith, art, and culture were just as from the Dynasty's rulers were puppets of India. these traditional region of India.

BABUR (1483–1531) pretty bad apples With some the first With his family tree, the most on his emperor was most Mughal dreaded as a rotter likely core. In fact his northern to the empire, established in 1526, was a tolerant peaceful place, His first act was to ban cow killing, which consider him to Hindus who encouraged cows sacred and the promoted global trade and the arts. architecture, his son Humayun, Unfortunately Babur on the who was of a different stock throne, was a poor leader. and a poor leader.

JAHAN (1592–1666)

Emperor Jahan established a beautiful capital city at Delhi. He ruled there (the Red Fort) from the exquisitely built Lal Qil'ah famous ornamented – a tomb 1,000 architectural – than white the Taj Mahal. More the some for his wife. Where were the marble to workers the site, constructed elephants peanuts projects 20,000 Elephants for these large-scale wars don't work large-scale had to pay for the Jahan in, which To indulged taxes' unpopular. on top of the indulged which made him to raise him.

AURANGZEB (1618–1707)

The last great leader of the Mughals was Aurangzeb. After throwing his father in jail and killing his older brother to take the throne (he didn't have much family loyalty), Aurangzeb expanded the Empire to its greatest size, but he put a stop to religious tolerance and enforced Islamic law. He lost his grip on the people and the larger empire was too much to manage. Eventually the Empire went into decline, staggering on under new colonial puppet masters – France and Britain.

AKBAR (1542–1605)

Humayan's son Akbar was only 13 when he became ruler. He was a dab hand at architecture, the arts, inventing, and ... cheetah training. Naturally, Akbar expanded the Empire into central and western India, and promoted the policy of tolerance of all faiths (he even married a Hindu princess). Perhaps his only wooden headed move was creating a new religion with himself as the god. It didn't catch on, and when he died, so did the faith.

JAHANGIR (1569–1627)

The next emperor, Akbar's son Jahangir, ran a very tolerant empire. Although he declared Islam to be the state religion, he filled his court with members of other faiths. He also developed Urdu (a mix of Arabic script, Persian vocabulary, and Hindi grammar) as the official language. With an eye to the future and an impressive legacy, Jahangir invited Persia's top architects to begin work on the fabulous palaces and lush gardens for which the Mughals became famous.

PERSIA UNDER THE SAFAVIDS

In 1500, a 13-year-old boy set out to avenge the death of his father who was killed 12 years before. Young Ismail was no ordinary rebellious teenager; he and his band of warriors – the Safavids – were intent on taking control in Persia (modern-day Iran), conquering nearby lands, and spreading the Shia branch of Islam (many of their Muslim neighbours were Sunnis). Would Ismail succeed in pulling the rug from under his opponents to weave together the diverse tribes of Persia?

1500

1501: Ismail is declared shah (king), starting a new ruling dynasty – the Safavids

1508: The Safavids capture Baghdad, extending their rule to Iraq

1520

1514: The Ottomans defeat the Safavids, crushing hopes for expanding the Safavid Empire

1524: Shah Ismail dies and his eldest son, Tahmasp, becomes shah

1534: The Ottomans capture Baghdad from the Safavids

1540

1556: Qandahar is captured from the Mughals

1560

1576: Ismail II (son of Shah Tahmasp) is brought to power

1577: Shah Ismail II is poisoned and Mohammad Shah brought to power

1578: The Ottomans launch a major invasion of Iran

1580

1587: Shah Abbas I takes power

1598: The more centrally located Isfahan is made the new imperial city

1600

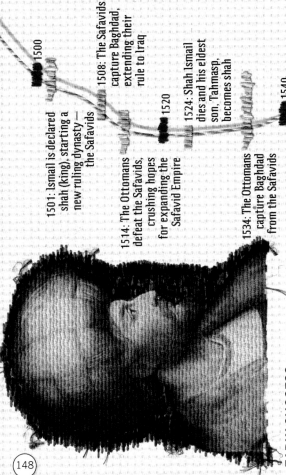

EARLY SUCCESS

Exiled after the death of his father, Ismail and his red-hat-wearing army secretly returned in 1499 and raided the city of Tabriz in Persia and made it their capital. A series of successful raids on the Uzbeks to the east and the Ottomans to the northwest put new territories under Ismail's control, and he was declared shah of Persia in 1501.

SPEND, SPEND, SPEND

The new shah set about putting Persia in order. At the top of his agenda was creating unity amongst the diverse residents of Persia by converting everyone to Shi'ism. He ignored the Sunnis at best and persecuted them at worst. He lavished money on building mosques and gave grants to religious schools. This spending policy was continued by the shahs who succeeded him and resulted in the fabulous Shah Mosque, begun in 1611.

THE SHAH'S STRUGGLES

The Safavids continued to battle with their old sparring partners, the Ottomans and the Uzbeks. Reports of Ismail's troops looting and destroying Sunni mosques and graves didn't go down well with the Ottomans in particular. In 1512 Sultan Selim responded by killing and exiling thousands of Shi'ites, followed up by an attack on the Safavids. In 1514 Selim's forces crushed the Safavids in Azerbaijan. It was said that Ismail never smiled again.

MAGIC CARPETS

Off the battlefield the Safavids were great supporters of the arts – Ismail even wrote a bit of poetry himself. Safavid architects built beautiful cities, and the fine metalwork and textiles, especially the gorgeous silks and beautifully woven Persian carpets, were highly sought after by European traders. The Safavids soon grew rich from these tradings. Of course, it didn't hurt business that they were smack bang in the middle of ancient trading routes.

HISTORY ON A PLATE

Safavid craftsmen and artists created a bounty of beautiful works, from porcelain pieces, such as this plate depicting the signs of the zodiac, to miniature paintings. Persian literature also became popular, especially in Anatolia and India. Sadly, though, the story did not end well for the Safavids. Just 300 years after its formation, the Empire fell to invaders.

1623: Shah Abbas I takes Baghdad from the Ottomans

1629: Shah Abbas I dies and his son, Shah Safi I, comes to power

1639: A truce with the Ottomans put an end to 100 years of sporadic conflict

1640

1642: Abbas II comes to power

1648: The Persians retake Qandahar

1660

1667: Shah Abbas II dies, and Safi II (Shah Soleyman) takes over, leading the Safavid Empire into decline

1680

1694: Shah Hussein takes power and the Empire continues to decline

1700

1720

1722: Afghan invaders capture Isfahan and kill Shah Hussein, ending the Safavid Dynasty

1740

A TOLERANT SHAH

The shahs that followed Ismail also had little to smile about. Skirmishes with the Ottomans continued, and the Dynasty's power diminished. In 1587 a new ruler, Abbas I, began to turn things around for the Safavids. He set up a permanent army and helped to open up Persia, encouraging trading and welcoming non-Muslims to his court. Time for the Safavids to crack a smile once more.

A GLORIOUS CITY

In 1598 Abbas chose the city of Isfahan as his capital. He filled it with monumental architecture – building schools, parks, a bazaar (market), and mosques such as Ali Qapu. People referred to this thriving city as Nisf-e-Jahan, meaning "half the world", from a Persian proverb that said seeing Isfahan was equal to seeing half the entire world.

149

SHOGUN SNIPPETS

What up? I'm Tokugawa Ieyasu, and I'm the super-cool shogun leader of Japan. With two other great warlords, I totally united Japan under one sword. Check out my stupendous purikura photo-booth pics in this scrapbook.

ME AS A SAMURAI WARRIOR

Here I am in my samurai uniform, with my trusty sword. (Are you loving the buffalo horns? LOL!) A samurai is top-class in both the military and society. We are brave, loyal, respectful, and awesomely skilled fighters, and we live our lives according to a code of honour. In the face of defeat, we are trained to commit hari kiri by slashing open our stomachs. That's why I prefer to win.

SUPER-SHARP SAMURAI SWORD!

ME AND NOBUNAGA

Teatime! This is me at tea with Oda Nobunaga (1534-1582), the first ruler to try to end the constant warfare between rival daimyo (warlords) in Japan. He united more than a third of the Japanese provinces, with the help of a few guns and iron-clad ships. But then in 1582, he stopped for a cuppa at a temple tea ceremony in Kyoto, and whoa! Out of nowhere one of his rivals appeared. Nobunaga did the hari kiri thing. It wasn't pleasant.

MORE TEA, NOBUNAGA?

ME AND HIDEYOSHI

The next great warlord was Toyotomi Hideyoshi (1537-1598). He was a little guy (and looked a bit like a monkey) but he had big plans. He basically carried on where his boss Nobunaga left off. He conducted "sword-hunting" raids to get weapons away from the peasants – probably a good move, seeing as his policy of maintaining a rigid class system locked the peasants into an eternity of poverty. All in all, Hideyoshi wanted to take over the world, so he kept raising taxes until they were crazy-high to help pay for it.

MONKEY SEE, MONKEY DO, HIDEYOSHI!

ME AS SHOGUN – RESULT!

Now my story: I served as a general under Nobunaga. My first wife and eldest son might have been plotting against that old man, so I killed them. Then, to earn extra points with Hideyoshi, I let that shogun adopt my other son. I even married his sister. In 1598, it all paid off. On his deathbed, Hideyoshi named his young son heir. As if! My time had come. I won a battle at Segikahara and took over most of Japan. Finally, in 1603...put your hands together for SHOGUN IEYASU. Woo!

I'm SHOGUN at last!

AT THE THEATRE

Time to celebrate! I'm never one to say no to the theatre (we samurai enjoy the performing arts as well as martial arts), especially Noh plays, where the performers wear awesome masks and only the upper classes can attend – no riff-raff. I didn't know it then, but Japan was about to enter a period known as the Great Peace. The country was united, but my government controlled nearly everything – from the clothes people wore to the way they drank tea. Outsiders stayed that way – outside.

Backstage at the theatre!

ME IN MY NEW PALACE

OMG, check this out. In 1590, I chose a small fishing village named Edo as my official residence. I ordered the construction of a fantastic castle, which became the heart of the city. The place was soon buzzing with craftspeople, merchants, restaurants, and shops. My samurai mates lived right next to me. Those were ace times for us at the top. Of course, there were loads of fancy stone castles built in Japan, but none as fantastic as mine.

MY NEW PALACE TOUCHES THE CLOUDS!

BIG BROTHER

Hmmm, let's take a little peekaboo at what's going on around here. Building this magnificent palace at Versailles was one of the best ideas ever. It may have taken a cast of thousands and a bottomless budget to create, but by making it the official seat of French government I can keep an eye on everyone. It's so me, so Louis XIV. You see, since I became king in 1643, I was determined to have absolute, hands-on rule over all of France. That's why I like to be called the "Sun King" – just as the planets revolve around the Sun, so should France revolve around me. Now what have we here...

PALACE CHAPEL

Who needs cathedrals when you have your very own chapel? I needed the full support of the Catholic Church to rule absolutely. So, in 1685, I revoked a law that allowed the Huguenots (that's what we called the French Protestants) to worship in France. Et voila! They left the country in droves, creating religious unity.

HALL OF MIRRORS

I needed to make Versailles pretty special if I was ever going to convince the government and nobility to make it a must-do project instead of a rather not, and I reckon I succeeded. Just look at this amazing ballroom, adorned with 17 huge mirrors. I throw the best parties ever! I even had Mozart come over to play.

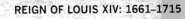

ALERT

CHECKLIST:

✗ Oh dear! A vile violation. Gentleman and ladies must not cross their legs in public.

✓ This is the proper way to stroll through the gardens, a female's hand on a gent's bent arm.

✓ No one must ever knock on my door. Instead, they must scratch it with their left pinky.

✓ These two are fighting over who gets to bring me my chamber pot. One is so amused by this sort of thing.

EMPTYING THE WAR CHEST

Now what is this chap up to? Ahh, he's counting out the soldier's pay. I'm afraid I'm constantly waging war in Europe. You see, each victory makes France more powerful and secure against invasion. That's good for yours truly, n'est ce pas? But it is a bit of a drag paying for it all. Thank goodness for taxes.

MAN IN THE IRON MASK

This is a most curious thing… In 1698, a mysterious prisoner was brought to the Bastille, wearing an iron mask that he never, ever removed. He died in 1703, but rumours about his identity lived on. Some people reckoned he might be a relation of mine and looked like me. What poppycock. I've never donned an iron mask in my life.

ETIQUETTE

I'm afraid I must insist on certain behaviour at my court. Good etiquette is, after all, essential in civilized society. Those who don't follow the rules are simply beneath contempt. If you want to rule absolutely, setting good standards is absolument the least you can do.

COLONIAL AMERICA

In the years after Christopher Columbus left the Americas, only the bravest adventurers returned to the New World. These Europeans were more interested in plundering riches than setting up colonies. Early attempts to colonize the Americas were hindered by natural disasters, starvation, disease, and enemy attacks. But by the early 1600s, the Spanish, Portugese, French, Dutch, and English had established New World colonies, mostly on the Atlantic coast.

ONE LUMP OR TWO?

The Europeans introduced domesticated animals, such as horses, cattle, goats, sheep, pigs, and chickens, to the New World. The Portuguese and Spanish set up plantations to grow crops, such as sugarcane, wheat, and rice. The native people were soon forced to work the land and enormous sugarcane plantations were up and running in Brazil.

UNWELCOME VISITORS

The Portuguese and Spanish were first to set up colonies in the lands of the Spanish-conquered Aztecs and Incas. They came for glory, gold, and silver, but brought with them disease. With no immunity to such illnesses as smallpox, measles, typhoid, cholera, and mumps, many native people died.

KEEP OUT
QUARANTINE

FURRY FRENCH

After Jacques Cartier's exploration of the Gulf of St Lawrence in 1535, his fellow French fur traders and fishermen followed him to the northeast. In 1608, the first French settlement was established on the site of present-day Québec. The colony grew to become a vast fur-trading outpost. French trappers travelled to the heart of America to hunt animals for their pelts.

GLITZY GOODS

The conquistadors of Spain came to the New World in search of gold and silver. They nabbed all the treasures they could find, but it was the discovery of a big stash of silver ore at Potosi (modern-day Bolivia) in 1545 that made Spain super rich. They put the locals to work mining silver and imported African slaves as helping hands.

FIRST EUROPEAN COLONIES

SAO VICENTE, BRAZIL – PORTUGUESE	1534
QUÉBEC, CANADA – FRENCH	1534
ST AUGUSTINE, FLORIDA – SPANISH	1565
ROANOKE ISLAND, VIRGINIA – ENGLISH	1585
NEW NETHERLAND (NEW YORK) – DUTCH	1625
NEW SWEDEN (DELAWARE) – SWEDISH	1638

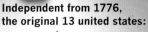

COMING SOON IN 1776:
COLONIAL AIRWAYS

Independent from 1776, the original 13 united states:

CONNECTICUT
MASSACHUSETTS
DELAWARE
GEORGIA
MARYLAND
NEW HAMPSHIRE
NEW JERSEY
NEW YORK
NORTH CAROLINA
PENNSYLVANIA
RHODE ISLAND
SOUTH CAROLINA
VIRGINIA

PUT THAT IN YOUR PIPE

In 1607, England established a colony at Jamestown. They came in search of gold, but found neither that nor food. A famine in 1609 nearly wiped out the colony. They might have gone under were it not for the export of a new cash crop: tobacco.

VOYAGE OF THE MAYFLOWER

Not all the colonists came to take things or make money. In 1620, a group of 102 Protestant men, women, and children set sail on the *Mayflower* for the New World to escape religious persecution. They were followed to present-day Massachusetts by another group of Protestant refugees, the Puritans.

GOING DUTCH

In 1625, the Dutch founded New Netherland in present-day New York. They hoped to set up a fur-trading post at New Amsterdam (Manhattan) and gave the Native Americans kettles and knives to secure the settlement. The rich lands along the Hudson River were divided up amongst the varying Europeans for farming.

155

All change

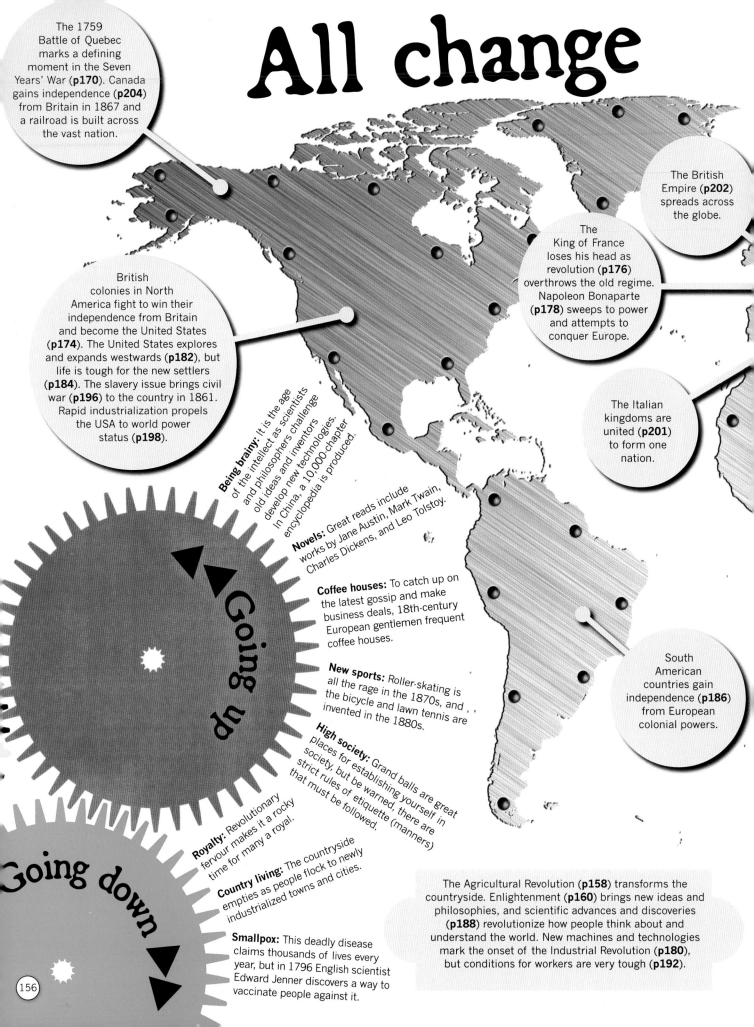

The 1759 Battle of Quebec marks a defining moment in the Seven Years' War (**p170**). Canada gains independence (**p204**) from Britain in 1867 and a railroad is built across the vast nation.

British colonies in North America fight to win their independence from Britain and become the United States (**p174**). The United States explores and expands westwards (**p182**), but life is tough for the new settlers (**p184**). The slavery issue brings civil war (**p196**) to the country in 1861. Rapid industrialization propels the USA to world power status (**p198**).

The British Empire (**p202**) spreads across the globe.

The King of France loses his head as revolution (**p176**) overthrows the old regime. Napoleon Bonaparte (**p178**) sweeps to power and attempts to conquer Europe.

The Italian kingdoms are united (**p201**) to form one nation.

South American countries gain independence (**p186**) from European colonial powers.

Being brainy: It is the age of the intellect as scientists and philosophers challenge old ideas and inventors develop new technologies. In China, a 10,000-chapter encyclopedia is produced.

Novels: Great reads include works by Jane Austin, Mark Twain, Charles Dickens, and Leo Tolstoy.

Coffee houses: To catch up on the latest gossip and make business deals, 18th-century European gentlemen frequent coffee houses.

New sports: Roller-skating is all the rage in the 1870s, and the bicycle and lawn tennis are invented in the 1880s.

High society: Grand balls are great places for establishing yourself in society, but be warned, there are strict rules of etiquette (manners) that must be followed.

Going up

Going down

Royalty: Revolutionary fervour makes it a rocky time for many a royal.

Country living: The countryside empties as people flock to newly industrialized towns and cities.

Smallpox: This deadly disease claims thousands of lives every year, but in 1796 English scientist Edward Jenner discovers a way to vaccinate people against it.

The Agricultural Revolution (**p158**) transforms the countryside. Enlightenment (**p160**) brings new ideas and philosophies, and scientific advances and discoveries (**p188**) revolutionize how people think about and understand the world. New machines and technologies mark the onset of the Industrial Revolution (**p180**), but conditions for workers are very tough (**p192**).

In this revolting period, revolutions sweep the globe. Some monarchs expand their empires, while others lose their heads.

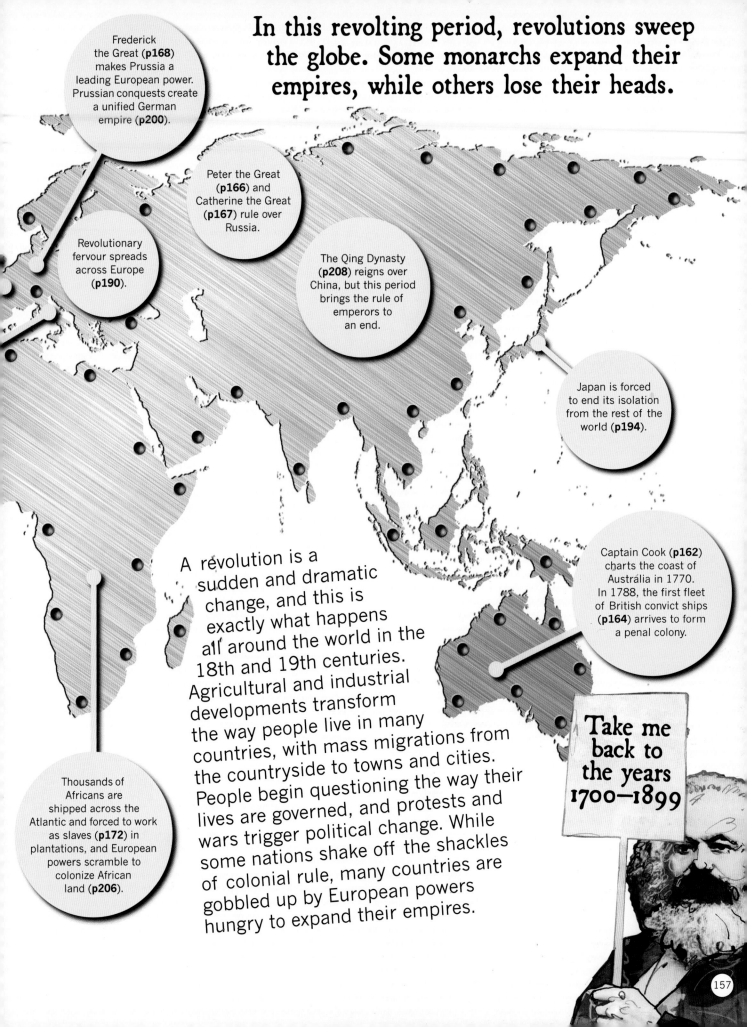

Frederick the Great (**p168**) makes Prussia a leading European power. Prussian conquests create a unified German empire (**p200**).

Peter the Great (**p166**) and Catherine the Great (**p167**) rule over Russia.

Revolutionary fervour spreads across Europe (**p190**).

The Qing Dynasty (**p208**) reigns over China, but this period brings the rule of emperors to an end.

Japan is forced to end its isolation from the rest of the world (**p194**).

Captain Cook (**p162**) charts the coast of Australia in 1770. In 1788, the first fleet of British convict ships (**p164**) arrives to form a penal colony.

Thousands of Africans are shipped across the Atlantic and forced to work as slaves (**p172**) in plantations, and European powers scramble to colonize African land (**p206**).

A revolution is a sudden and dramatic change, and this is exactly what happens all around the world in the 18th and 19th centuries. Agricultural and industrial developments transform the way people live in many countries, with mass migrations from the countryside to towns and cities. People begin questioning the way their lives are governed, and protests and wars trigger political change. While some nations shake off the shackles of colonial rule, many countries are gobbled up by European powers hungry to expand their empires.

Take me back to the years 1700—1899

AGRICULTURAL REVOLUTION

For centuries the countryside of northern Europe had not changed.
Fields were wide and open, with crops grown in long, narrow strips
that were left fallow (unplanted) every three years. There were few hedges
and no machines. During the 18th century, the landscape was transformed.
Farmers made sweeping changes so that they could produce enough food
to meet the demands of a rapidly expanding population.

SOWING MACHINE
Previously farmers sowed by hand,
scattering the seed far and wide, and most
was wasted. This seed drill machine invented
by Jethro Tull dropped seeds in straight lines
onto the ploughed land, which meant the farmer
could hoe between the rows of young crops
to stop the weeds from springing up.
How udderly fantastic!

STEAM POWER

Choo-choo! Shattering the calm of the countryside, farmers began to use steam-driven machines to pull ploughs, work threshing machines, and pump water. They were expensive and awkward to move, so horses still did most of the heavy work on the farm.

ROTATING CROPS

By growing peas and clover, which put goodness back into the soil, in rotation with other crops, farmers could raise a crop on the same piece of land year after year. Fields did not have to be left unplanted for a year to recover their fertility, and food production rose.

BIGGER BEASTS

Turnips were grown as a winter food for cattle, which were no longer killed in autumn, but could be kept indoors until spring and their manure (poo) used to fertilize the fields. Farmers also improved methods of breeding to produce bigger and healthier cows, sheep, and pigs. This really brought home the bacon.

CHANGING LANDSCAPE

Landowners enclosed the land for their own use, doing away with the open strip fields by growing hedges and erecting fences. New machinery meant that fewer people were needed to work on the farms, and rural poverty forced many to find work in towns and cities. Will they ever go baa-ck?

THE ENLIGHTENMENT

During the 18th century a number of thinkers, writers, and scientists began to ask questions. Why were people's ideas of the world dominated by what previous generations had thought? They believed that individuals should look at things for themselves and draw conclusions only from what they observed. Their ideas and discoveries helped to shape the modern world.

VOLTAIRE

My real name's François-Marie Arouet, but the world knows me as Voltaire the writer. I'm the bad boy of the class, always in trouble for my scathing put-downs.

I'm firmly on the side of tolerance and justice, though, and never hang back from telling people, even kings, when they're wrong.

BENJAMIN FRANKLIN

Hey there, I'm from America. I really love the way some of these guys I've met in Europe think and can't wait to introduce their ideas back home. For now, I'm working hard at my studies into electricity and am busy inventing the lightning conductor.

ISAAC NEWTON

I'd worked out the law of gravity (after an apple fell on my head!) and discovered the laws of motion before most of this lot were born. In fact, you could say it was my discoveries that began the Enlightenment.

DENIS DIDEROT

I've stuck my hand up because I know all the answers! I've edited a 28-volume *Encyclopedia* that has entries on almost everything. It's right up to the minute in its opinions and does away with a lot of stuffy old nonsense about religion. The French government thought its ideas were so dangerous they banned it. Blithering fools!

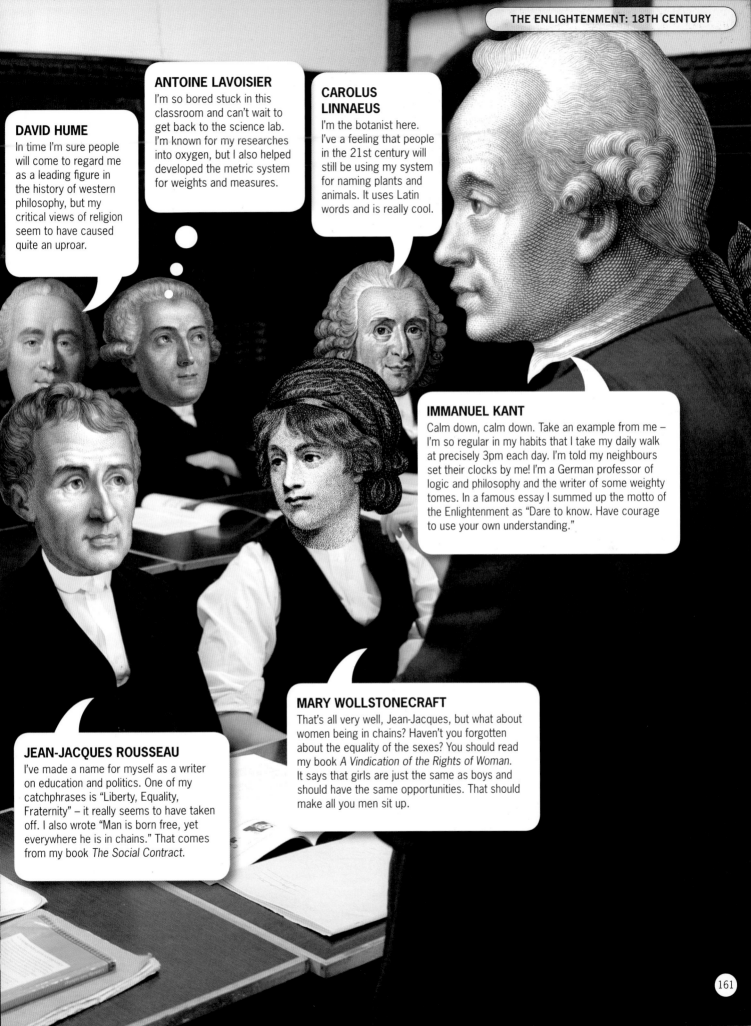

DAVID HUME

In time I'm sure people will come to regard me as a leading figure in the history of western philosophy, but my critical views of religion seem to have caused quite an uproar.

ANTOINE LAVOISIER

I'm so bored stuck in this classroom and can't wait to get back to the science lab. I'm known for my researches into oxygen, but I also helped developed the metric system for weights and measures.

CAROLUS LINNAEUS

I'm the botanist here. I've a feeling that people in the 21st century will still be using my system for naming plants and animals. It uses Latin words and is really cool.

IMMANUEL KANT

Calm down, calm down. Take an example from me – I'm so regular in my habits that I take my daily walk at precisely 3pm each day. I'm told my neighbours set their clocks by me! I'm a German professor of logic and philosophy and the writer of some weighty tomes. In a famous essay I summed up the motto of the Enlightenment as "Dare to know. Have courage to use your own understanding."

MARY WOLLSTONECRAFT

That's all very well, Jean-Jacques, but what about women being in chains? Haven't you forgotten about the equality of the sexes? You should read my book *A Vindication of the Rights of Woman*. It says that girls are just the same as boys and should have the same opportunities. That should make all you men sit up.

JEAN-JACQUES ROUSSEAU

I've made a name for myself as a writer on education and politics. One of my catchphrases is "Liberty, Equality, Fraternity" – it really seems to have taken off. I also wrote "Man is born free, yet everywhere he is in chains." That comes from my book *The Social Contract*.

The Endeavour

CAPTAIN COOK'S BLOG

My name's Cook, Captain James Cook, commanding HMS *Endeavour* on a voyage to the South Pacific. My instructions? To find new lands and claim them for Britain before the French get there. You can follow my progress on my ship's blog.

FIRST STOP TAHITI

It's taken eight months to get here from England and I haven't lost a single man from sickness. The pickled cabbage I've been giving the crew may taste and smell disgusting, but it's stopped them getting scurvy, a killer disease on board ship. We've brought lots of iron nails and knives with us for barter – would you believe the islanders of this tropical paradise still only have stone and shell tools? The scientists on board plan to build an observatory to view the eclipse that will take place in June, when the planet Venus passes in front of the Sun.

99 COMMENTS

Posted 13 April 1769

NATIVE UNREST

The Māori natives of this island (named New Zealand by Dutch explorer Abel Tasman when he passed this way a century ago) don't seem very friendly. They performed a fierce war dance with a lot of shouting and tried to stop us landing, so I ordered my men to open fire, killing four of them. I hope I can establish better relations soon as I intend to spend some months here exploring right around the coast.

101 COMMENTS

Posted 9 October 1769

photos

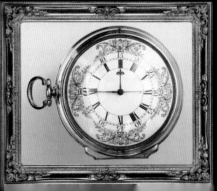

[NA]VIGATION AID

[di]fficult to know how far round the world [we] have gone without an accurate clock. [I] say that the new marine chronometer [Joh]n Harrison is developing for the navy will [...]. Maybe I'll carry one on my next voyage.

[Post]ed 2 February 1769   **22 COMMENTS**

MY MAP OF NEW ZEALAND

It took me six months to survey the entire coastline and produce this detailed map.

RIP CAPTAIN COOK

Tragic news! Captain Cook has been stabbed to death in a violent dispute with islanders on Hawaii during his third voyage of exploration. Just four years ago, on his second voyage, Cook became the first person to sail round Antarctica.

Posted 14 February 1779   281 COMMENTS

LAND AHOY!

It's two weeks since we left New Zealand, which turns out to be two islands separated by a narrow channel. At 6am this morning, Lieutenant Hicks shouted that he had sighted land. As we got closer we could see a coastline of low hills covered in trees extending northwest. I'm going to sail along it to see where we end up.

Posted 19 April 1770   203 COMMENTS

BOTANY BAY

Since we landed a week ago, the botanists Joseph Banks and Daniel Solander have found so many plant specimens that I have named the place Botany Bay. Their collections clutter up the ship dreadfully! We've seen a creature as big as a stag that bounds along on its hind legs like a rabbit. We've also spotted some natives. They were stark naked and seem very shy of us.

Posted 6 May 1770   152 COMMENTS

SHIP IN TROUBLE

Disaster has struck! *Endeavour* ran aground on part of the great coral reef that runs parallel with the coast here, and the sharp coral gouged a hole in her keel. I have put ashore to make repairs, but we may be stuck here for weeks.

Posted 11 June 1770   75 COMMENTS

HOMEWARD BOUND

Today we sailed into the Indian Ocean. As I thought, the 4,828-km- (3,000-mile-) long coastline I have been charting is the eastern shore of a huge island. I claimed the entire length for the British crown, naming it New South Wales, before heading for home. It'll be months before we see good old England, but I know I'll soon be itching to go exploring again.

Posted 22 August 1770   88 COMMENTS

SAIL AWAY FROM SCURVY!

"Not a single sailor died of scurvy on my voyage."

CAPTAIN JAMES COOK

Click here for FREE pickled cabbage recipes

COME TO TAHITI

we are arriving in this tropical paradise.
slanders seem very friendly.

d 13 April 1769   30 COMMENTS

ANY BAY

n Banks thinks this would be a suitable
to start a British colony one day.

d 6 May 1770   28 COMMENTS

JUMPER

s one of those strange animals I was telling
bout. Must think of a name for it.

d 6 May 1770   49 COMMENTS

The convict's tale

WILLIAM WADE

This is me after my arrest

My name is William Wade and my story starts in the Old Bailey law court in London, England. I couldn't believe my ears when I heard the judge say "It is therefore ordered by this court that you be transported upon the seas to such place as His Majesty shall think to direct, for seven years." That meant they were sending me to a penal colony at Botany Bay on the other side of the world, in Australia. And all I'd done was nab a bundle of clothes from off a washing line.

The boat I travelled on — the Neptune

We were months at sea. Conditions were terrible — there were 500 of us convicts crammed beneath deck and I had to share my wooden berth with three others. It was suffocating, especially when we reached the warm tropics. The only air and light came in from the covered hatchways above, which were kept padlocked at all times. As if we could have escaped! There were armed soldiers watching our every move. The food was pretty vile, but not much worse than what the sailors had. A lot of people got sick and died.

Nothing had prepared me for the sights and sounds of Australia. It's like the world turned upside down — different birds, different animals, different trees and shrubs. At first we were housed in the convict prison in Port Jackson and sent out to work every day in a chain gang. I must say, you meet all sorts that way. A lot of the blokes had been done for petty crimes like forgery. One kid, hardly in his teens, had stolen a loaf of bread to feed his starving brothers and sisters. There was a large group of Irish rebels and others who had been making trouble for the government. But there were some pretty violent types, too — murderers, even.

We were put to work on a farm, which was tough on me because I'm a city lad and know nothing of the outdoor life. It was

My pal Frank was convicted for killing a man

This is me

The Aboriginal girl's tale

My name is Alkira. My childhood was a happy time. We lived in a large family group and moved around the country, following the

This is me on a fishing trip

paths our people have always done. My mother told me about our ancestral spirits, who gave us the land. They had brought it into being during the Dreamtime – the time when animals and plants were created. We do not own the land, we are its keepers.

Our people knew where to find food. The women carried digging sticks to search for grubs and roots, and the men had spears to hunt for bush animals. My people lived beside the ocean and I remember fishing in the sea.

One day we were making our way to a watering hole when we found a long fence barring our way. We didn't understand. Who could have done this?

Soon after, we went to a corroborree, a ritual meeting with a neighbouring tribe when the elders discussed important matters. They told us about the white settlers who were taking

Here's everyone gathered at the corroboree

long hard work from dawn to dusk, and we'd get a thrashing if one of the guards thought we were idling. One day I made up my mind to escape with some other convicts — we'd noticed the windows were never barred at night, so it wasn't difficult. No wonder — the officers knew we'd soon come crawling back! The heat

A cat-o-nine-tails whip has nine lengths of rope, each with knots tied in. Ouch!

out there in the bush was unbearable, and we had no means of getting water. We couldn't find anything to eat — oh, how I longed for a nice juicy rabbit to poach. I don't know how the native Aboriginals manage to survive.

time if you break the rules, but life was much cushier after that.

At last my seven years was up, but blow me if I didn't decide to stay in Australia. I'd met a nice girl — Mary her name is. Funnily enough, she was on the same transport ship as me. We decided to settle down together and start a family. After all, the weather's a lot nicer here than back home in Britain!

This guard was very nasty. He had it in for me from the start

So back we went, and I was given a severe flogging with a cat-o-nine-tails, a mean kind of whip, and put into solitary confinement for a bit. I decided then and there that the best way to survive was to go with the flow. So I did all that was asked of me, and after a while I earned myself a ticket-of-leave from the governor — that's a piece of paper that allows you to work for a private individual for a wage. It can be torn up at any

Here I am with Mary and our kids. They are little angels... well most of the time

land to keep strange animals – cattle and sheep I later learned they're called.

Some young men and boys from my tribe decided to raid one of the white settlements. Soon afterwards white men with guns came to attack our people. They seized the young men and led them off to prison in chains. They took our land away from us, so we had to move onto land belonging to another tribe. This was a terrible thing to do, and it caused a war between us. Most of our men were killed.

My mother and I managed to escape. We went to live on the edge of a farm belonging to white people, where we were set to work fetching water and doing

The young men decided to raid a white settlement

So many people died

other hard tasks. My mother fell sick with an illness. She'd caught it from the Europeans – they said it was measles. She died of it, and now I'm all alone.

PETER the GREAT

1672 – 1725

THE ZANY ADVENTURES OF THE RUSSIAN TSAR...

THIS NEW CANNON OF MINE IS GREAT. OO-ER, THAT'S DONE IT!

BOOM

PETER WAS A LONELY BOY. HE LOVED PLAYING AT SOLDIERS – WITH REAL GUNS AND MEN!

TAKE THAT, SIS!

PUSH OFF, IVAN! I'M RUNNING RUSSIA NOW.

HE SHARED THE THRONE WITH HIS SICKLY BROTHER IVAN, BUT HALF-SISTER SOPHIA WAS IN CHARGE. HE DREAMED OF THE DAY HE'D BE RID OF THEM BOTH.

THERE GOES PETER! WHAT A GIANT!

WHAT'S THE WEATHER LIKE UP THERE, TSAR PETER!

WHAT A WHEEZE – I'LL PRETEND TO BE A SHIPBUILDER SO I CAN BUILD MY OWN RUSSIAN NAVY WHEN I GET HOME.

WHEN PETER WAS GROWN UP HE WENT ON A TOUR OF EUROPE. FOR SOME REASON, HE WAS RECOGNIZED WHEREVER HE WENT.

I'M BORED. C'MON, GANG – LET'S GO OUTSIDE FOR SOME WHEELBARROW RACES!

BAH! THESE RUSSIANS HAVE WRECKED ALL MY BEST FURNITURE AND NOW THEY'RE STARTING ON THE GARDEN!

IN LONDON, PETER PROVED A TROUBLESOME GUEST...

BEARDS ARE SO OUT OF DATE!... NEXT PLEASE!

BUT I'VE SPENT YEARS GROWING IT!

BACK IN RUSSIA, PETER TOOK STEPS TO DRAG HIS NOBLES INTO THE 18TH CENTURY.

TAKE THAT!... AND THAT!

POW

BIFF

SWEDEN

TURKEY

HE WON GREAT VICTORIES OVER THE KING OF SWEDEN AND THE SULTAN OF TURKEY.

WHO'D EVER WANT TO LIVE IN A PESKY MARSH LIKE THIS?

DRAT THESE MIDGES.

HURRY UP, SERFS ... NOT FAR TO GO NOW.

ST PETERSBURG

PETER HATED MOSCOW. HE MOVED HIS CAPITAL TO ST PETERSBURG, A CITY HE ORDERED TO BE BUILT FROM SCRATCH BY THE BALTIC SEA.

LET ME BE YOUR CHIEF BOTTLEWASHER, SIRE.

NO, LET ME – I'M BETTER THAN HIM!

IT'S FUN SEEING MY COURTIERS SWEAT A LITTLE.

PETER INVENTED A NEW WAY OF CHOOSING PEOPLE FOR THE TOP JOBS, BASED ON TALENT AND MERIT INSTEAD OF BIRTH.

AARGH!!

HE HAD HIS ONLY SON ALEXIS THROWN INTO PRISON, WHERE HE DIED IN GHASTLY AGONY.

HANG ON! I'M COMING!

ONE DAY HE DIVED INTO THE ICY SEA TO SAVE SOME DROWNING SAILORS BUT CAUGHT A NASTY CHILL AND DIED. *THE END*

CATHERINE the GREAT
1729 — 1796

THE AWESOME STORY OF THE GERMAN PRINCESS WHO BECAME EMPRESS OF RUSSIA!

THESE RUSSIAN PRIESTS DON'T HALF DRONE ON...

SHE CAN LOOK DOWN HER NOSE ALL SHE LIKES BUT I AM THE GRANDSON OF *PETER THE GREAT.*

WHEN SHE WAS 16 CATHERINE LEFT HER NATIVE GERMANY TO MARRY THE HEIR TO THE RUSSIAN THRONE. THEY DID NOT GET ON.

WHOOPEE, I'M EMPRESS!! PETER WAS SUCH A DRAG...

18 YEARS LATER HER HUSBAND, PETER III, WAS MURDERED AFTER REIGNING FOR ONLY SIX MONTHS. CATHERINE WAS PROCLAIMED EMPRESS.

AH – THE LATEST VOLUME OF THE ENCYCLOPEDIA! I'VE BEEN WAITING FOR THIS –

MA'AM, THE PEASANTS ARE REVOLTING!

SEND MY SOLDIERS TO DEAL WITH THEM!

A BIT OF A SWOT, CATHERINE KEPT UP WITH THE LATEST FRENCH IDEAS. BUT ALL WAS NOT WELL IN RUSSIA...

THEY'VE RUMBLED MY WHEEZE OF PRETENDING TO BE PETER III.

OH, ALL RIGHT, THEN. *I SURRENDER.*

A MAN CALLED PUGACHEV CLAIMED TO BE THE DEAD KING AND STARTED A REBELLION. CATHERINE STAMPED IT OUT WITHOUT MERCY.

DAHHLINGS – I LOVE YOU ALL!

I'LL WIN HER HEART BY BASHING UP THE TURKS.

CATHERINE HAD MANY LOVERS BEFORE FALLING FOR THE CHARM AND GOOD LOOKS OF PRINCE POTEMKIN.

THANK YOU MY GOOD PEOPLE.

THREE CHEERS FOR THE GREAT EMPRESS CATHERINE!

PRINCE POTEMKIN TOOK CATHERINE ON A TOUR OF THE SOUTHERN LANDS HE CONQUERED FROM THE TURKS.

QUICK, LET'S LEG IT...

HE ARRANGED FOR A RENT-A-CROWD TO STAND AND WAVE BEFORE RUSHING ON TO THE NEXT PLACE.

THANK YOU MY GOOD PEOPLE.

PHEW, JUST MADE IT! ALL TOGETHER NOW... *THREE CHEERS FOR...*

AND HERE'S ANOTHER JOLLY CRIMEAN VILLAGE.

THE HOUSES BEHIND THEM WERE FAKE. IN FACT, THE WHOLE COUNTRYSIDE WAS ALMOST DESERTED.

CATHERINE BECAME KNOWN AS A BOSSY DICTATOR, OR AUTOCRAT. ALTHOUGH SHE HAD ONCE PLANNED TO IMPROVE CONDITIONS FOR PEASANTS, SHE FINISHED UP BY MAKING THINGS TOUGHER FOR THEM THAN EVER. SHE GAVE GENEROUSLY TO THE ARTS THOUGH, FILLING HER PALACE WITH PRECIOUS OBJECTS COLLECTED FROM ALL OVER EUROPE. AND SO SHE DIED.
THE END

IT'S A TOUGH LIFE BEING AN EMPRESS... MEMO TO SELF: ORDER A PORCELAIN DINNER SERVICE FROM MR WEDGWOOD TO GO WITH THE MEISSEN AND THE SEVRES – 1,200 PLATES SHOULD DO.

Frederick William I was a control freak who personally supervised the consumption of candles in the royal palace.

Frederick II had a rigorous military training and was woken each morning by the firing of a cannon.

Frederick II had a preference for the arts and studied philosophy, history, and poetry. He had aspirations to be a writer and composer.

FREDERICK II (THE GREAT)

My father never understood me. I'm a person of culture, a man of the Enlightenment. Even as a boy I loved art, literature, and music. He was a bully, always wanting to toughen me up. When I was six, I was even given my own regiment to drill! Aged 18 I tried to escape with my best friend, Katte. We were arrested and my father forced me to watch Katte's execution. But I'm a greater soldier than my father ever was. The territories I've conquered in wars against Austria have made Prussia a force to be reckoned with.

FREDERICK WILLIAM I

They called me the "soldier king". I loved military parades and smart uniforms. My Potsdam regiment, consisting of soldiers specially picked for their height, was my pride and joy. Frederick despised all that – he was always playing the flute, reading foreign books, and talking French with his arty friends. What's wrong with good honest German?

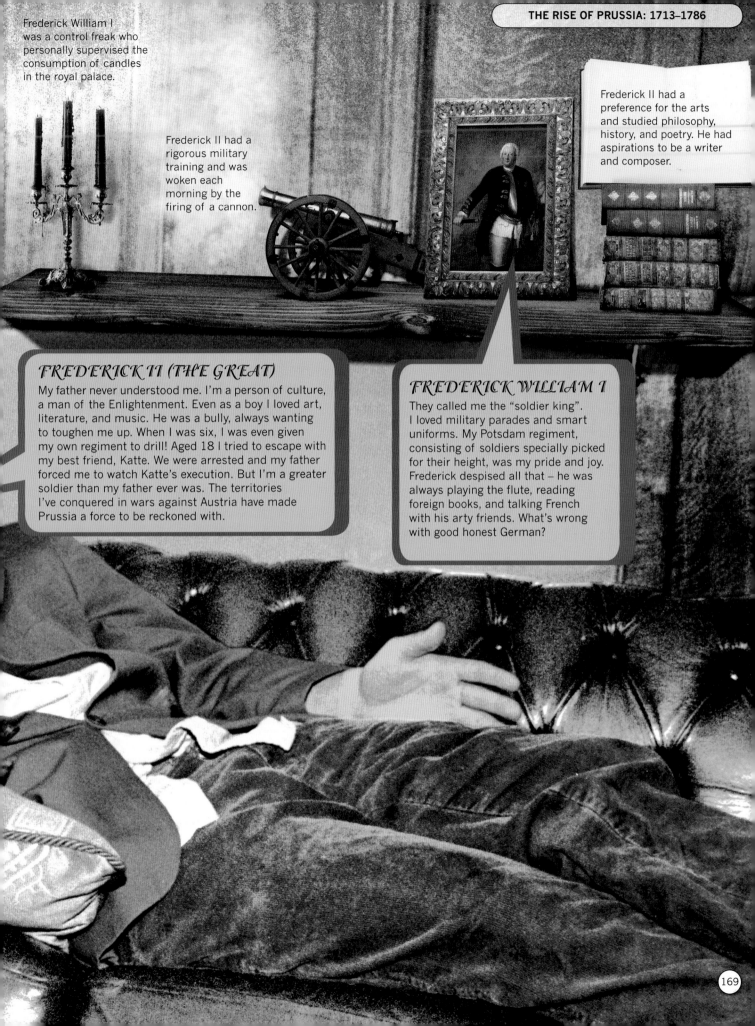

WORLD AT WAR!

Now listen up, all of you. We're here to tell you about a war that lasted from 1756 until 1763. The bright ones among you will have worked out that's why it's called the Seven Years' War. In Europe, the Prussians were fighting the Austrians and Russians. Britain agreed to support Prussia, and France backed Austria. Britain and France both had overseas colonies and they wanted to seize each other's territories, so the fighting spilled over to become a global war. Is that clear?

1 The British fleet arrive in July. Wolfe sets up camp below Québec.

2 On 12 September the British attack to the east of the city, but it is a trick to fool the French.

3 Wolfe moves upriver. At dead of night 4,500 men scale the cliff by a secret path.

ANOTHER NAME
In America, it's called the French and Indian War. That's the name of the war France and Britain had been fighting since 1754 for control of the continent. The Seven Years' War was simply the final stage.

EUROPEAN CAPERS
Frederick the Great, the king of Prussia, invaded Saxony (a region in northern Europe). Neighbours Austria, Russia, and France weren't having that. There were a lot of pitched battles. Prussia won some and lost some. Then Russia got a new tsar, Peter III. He thought Frederick was so great he stopped fighting him – lucky, or what?

BRITAIN VERSUS FRANCE
Britain and France were rivals for world power. The British drove the French out of India and from their colonies in the Caribbean, but they shot one of their own admirals, Byng, for losing the island of Minorca in the Mediterranean Sea. No job security there, then!

WHAT'S HAPPENING?

Let me put you in the picture. In North America, most of the fighting took place in New France – that's Canada to you. In 1759, British General James Wolfe sailed an army down the St Lawrence River to attack the key French fortress of Québec. It was a high-risk strategy that took the French by surprise.

4 Next morning they line up for battle on the Plains of Abraham, west of the city.

5 The French are astonished. They rush out to fight the British but are thrashed.

6 Québec surrenders but Wolfe, wounded in the fighting, dies on the battlefield.

CAPTURE OF QUÉBEC

Québec stands on a high cliff above the river and the French thought it could never be taken. Look here to see how Wolfe proved them wrong.

WHAT HAPPENED NEXT?

The Seven Years' War ended with the Treaty of Paris in 1763. France was forced to hand Canada over to the British. Spain, which had joined in at the last moment, had to give up Florida. Britain was now the world's leading colonial empire.

TRIANGLE OF TRADE

Between 1500 and the 1880s, up to 12 million Africans were forcibly transported across the Atlantic Ocean to work as slaves on plantations in the Americas. The well-organized trade triangle between Europe, Africa, and the Americas started in European ports. Merchants would load their ships with guns, cloth, liquor, and other goods and sail them to trading forts along the coast of West Africa.

Slave trade

SEIZED BY SLAVERS

At African ports, the European merchants exchange their goods for a new cargo — humans. Africans involved in the trade would raid distant villages to meet the unending demand for slaves. They seized men and women working in the fields and children herding animals and marched them in shackles to the coast to await the next ship.

JOURNEY FROM HELL

Crammed together, 600 at a time, many slaves did not survive the terrible conditions below deck in the ship's foul, unventilated holds. Often they died from suffocation, crushed beneath a weight of bodies when the ship rolled violently. Others starved themselves to death, overwhelmed by despair.

PLANTATION SLAVES

On arrival in the Americas or the Caribbean colonies, the slaves were put up for sale on the quay. Some were set to work growing sugar or coffee, others were shipped on to Virginia and New England to be sold into slavery on the cotton plantations. The ship's captain filled his holds with sugar, tobacco, cotton, or coffee and returned to England — another profitable trip completed.

ANTI-SLAVERY MOVEMENT

In 1787, English politician William Wilberforce and leaders of the Quaker religious group launched the anti-slavery movement. They faced fierce opposition. In 1807, after years of campaigning, Britain abolished the slave trade and gradually, over the next 70 years, other nations were forced to follow suit.

AMERICAN INDEPENDENCE

Join the 4 July party as Americans celebrate how they won their liberty. The struggle for independence began in the 1760s when Britain decided to raise money from its 13 American colonies by taxing goods like tea and paper. The Americans, who had no say in the matter and no voice in the British parliament, were furious. They declared there should be "no taxation without representation".

1. BOSTON TEA PARTY

In 1773, when a group of protestors dressed up as Mohawk Native Americans sneaked aboard a British ship in Boston's harbour, it was more than a storm in a teacup. They dumped the whole cargo of tea into the sea. The British government was furious and passed a series of punishing laws.

2. SIGN HERE

The laws (known as the "Intolerable Acts") pushed all 13 colonies into demanding a complete break with Britain. Lawyer Thomas Jefferson drafted the Declaration of Independence. It was agreed on 4 July 1776 and signed by the 56 delegates to the Continental Congress – a meeting of the provisional government held in Philadelphia.

3. WAR!

It was war, but while the British generals blundered, the Americans, led by their commander-in-chief George Washington, grew bolder and braver. Then the French joined in, supporting the Americans. It was too much for the British, who surrendered in 1781. In 1783 they recognized the independence of the United States of America.

4. FIRST PRESIDENT

Americans were free, but they still needed a constitution – written laws to say how the nation should be governed. To prevent any one person becoming too powerful they decided to have an elected president who would hold office for four years. In 1789, George Washington was the first chosen for the post.

FRENCH REVOLUTION

There are signs of growing unrest in France as we head into 1789. The luxurious lifestyle enjoyed by King Louis XVI and his Austrian-born wife Queen Marie Antoinette is coming in for mounting criticism. There are widespread food shortages and the King's government is bankrupt after a series of costly wars. Now the King has summoned the Estates General, the national assembly, to ask it to approve a rise in taxes...

TAXING ISSUE

17 June 1789 The commoners who make up the Third Estate today stormed out of the Estates General to set up a National Assembly of the people. "We intend to conduct the nation's affairs from now on," a spokesman said. Representatives from the clergy and the nobility, the First and Second Estates, declined to comment.

LOUIS LEGS IT

25 June 1791 The King and Queen's attempt to flee the country dressed as servants has failed. Their ruse was spotted and they are now under guard in Paris. Time will tell if Louis falls into line and accepts the new constitution, which gives power to parliament and leaves him as merely a figurehead.

EXCLUSIVE BREAKING NEWS

- July 1794 Robespierre arrested and sent to the guillotine...
- 8 June 1795 Ten-year-old heir to throne, Louis Charles, dies in prison...
- 5 October 1795 Corsican officer Napoleon Bonaparte crushes royalist uprising in Paris...

PRISON BREAK-IN

14 July 1789 Angered by rumours that the King has ordered the army to close down the National Assembly, rioters in Paris stormed the royal fortress of the Bastille, releasing all seven prisoners inside. Many were shouting "Liberty, Equality, Fraternity!" It's revolution.

DEMANDS FOR DOUGH

5 October 1789 Around 7,000 armed women marched on the royal palace of Versailles today to demand an end to the country's economic crisis, which has caused bread shortages. A palace official denies that when Queen Marie Antoinette was told the women had no bread, she said "Let them eat cake."

OFF WITH HIS HEAD

21 January 1793 Tensions were high in Paris this morning as Louis Capet, the former king, was executed. The crowd cheered when the guillotine severed his head from his body. Louis was found guilty several days ago of plotting against the French people. Long live the Republic!

REIGN OF TERROR

Spring 1794 France is awash with blood as the Committee of Public Safety, headed by Maximilien Robespierre, continues its war on the enemies of the Revolution. The accused are loaded onto wooden carts and driven through jeering crowds to the guillotine. Up to 40,000 people are reported dead in Paris alone.

- **27 October 1795** France has new government, the Directory…
- **9 November 1799** Bonaparte takes part in coup to overthrow the Directory…
- **7 February 1800** Bonaparte is confirmed as First Consul of France…

Napoleon Bonaparte

ONLINE NOW

My enemies accuse me of being a tyrant and a dictator but I was simply an army general who seized control of France, rescuing it from the chaos of the Revolution and restoring it to glory. I then fought a series of brilliant campaigns to bring liberty and enlightenment to the peoples of Europe. Unfortunately, my fabulous career went a little pear-shaped. I was forced to leave France in 1814, but regained control the following year Then things didn't go so well on the battlefield and I am now a prisoner of the British, exiled on a rocky island in the Atlantic Ocean.

Upload profile photo

Edit profile

Change skins I Change modules

Get a web badge

Age
51

Gender
Male

Last active
5 May 1821

Profile views
10657 times

Home town
Ajaccio, Corsica

Status update
Now stuck on island of
St Helena, South Atlantic

The other half of me

My wife Marie Louise Bonaparte with the apple of my eye, my son François-Charles-Joseph Bonaparte. I made him king of Rome.

Photos   View all I Upload I Choose top 10

Friends   3 of 3 friends I Choose top

Battle of Marengo (June 1800)

My first great victory in Europe, when I gave the Austrians a bloody nose. After that I could do no wrong in French eyes.

Battle of Austerlitz (December 1805)

My finest hour. I took on the combined forces of Austria and Russia and totally thrashed them. Europe was at my feet.

Battle of Waterloo (June 1815)

I'm sure I would have won this one too if the Prussians hadn't arrived in the nick of time to save the Duke of Wellington's bacon.

Joseph Bonaparte

My eldest brother – I made him king of Spain. Call me old-fashioned, but I'm a strong supporter of family values.

Auguste de Marmont

An old school chum, Auguste shared in all my early triumphs and it was a bitter blow when he deserted me in 1814.

Marshal Ney

My most loyal general, Ney came over to my side on my return to France in 1815 and fought like a tiger at the Battle of Waterloo.

Add a friend. Email: [   ] **Add**

Comments

View all | Post a comment

Napoleon was a virtual unknown when we married. It was thanks to me that he got his first big posting in Italy. Now he's divorced me for a 18-year-old who just happens to be the daughter of the Austrian emperor.

Josephine de Beauharnais

March 1810

It was a terrible mistake of his to invade Russia. He reached Moscow all right, but I'd ordered it to be burned, forcing him to retreat. Winter sets in early in Russia, and thousands of his men are reported to have perished in the snow. Not so powerful now, Napoleon!

Tsar Alexander I

December 1812

So old Boney's dead is he? Can't say I'm sorry. I know you should be gracious in victory, but he was a monster of ambition who threatened the safety of all the crowned heads of Europe. We're well rid of him.

Duke of Wellington

May 1821

Blog

View all | Write to my blog

Today I crowned myself emperor of the French in the presence of the Pope in Notre Dame Cathedral, Paris. Then I placed the empress's crown upon the head of my beloved wife, Josephine. It was a necessary act, to prevent the hated French kings from being restored to power. Frenchmen know how much I have done for them – reformed the legal system, invested in schools...

2 December 1804

My enemies thought they had said goodbye to me for ever when they exiled me to the island of Elba in the Mediterranean Sea. How wrong they were! After only nine months I managed to escape to France. As I marched north to Paris I was joined all along the route by cheering regiments while the European powers, meeting at Vienna, declared me an outlaw. I am preparing for war...

May 1815

My attempt to regain France is over. After leaving the battlefield of Waterloo I fled back to Paris but quickly realized the game was up. I made my way to the Atlantic port of Rochefort, hoping to find a ship to take me to the United States, but the British navy was there before me. I have surrendered to Captain Maitland of HMS *Bellerophon* and am to be exiled to a remote island where I will have little hope of escaping...

15 July 1815

INDUSTRIAL REVOLUTION

Between 1750 and 1850 life in Britain changed dramatically. Previously most people lived in the countryside, farming the land. Technological advances meant goods could be mass produced for the first time, and people flocked to towns and cities to work in the new factories. The landscape was transformed with factory chimneys billowing smoke over row upon row of cramped dwellings housing a new urban working class. Over time, this "Industrial Revolution" spread to other countries in Europe and to the United States. The world was suddenly a faster-paced, noisier place.

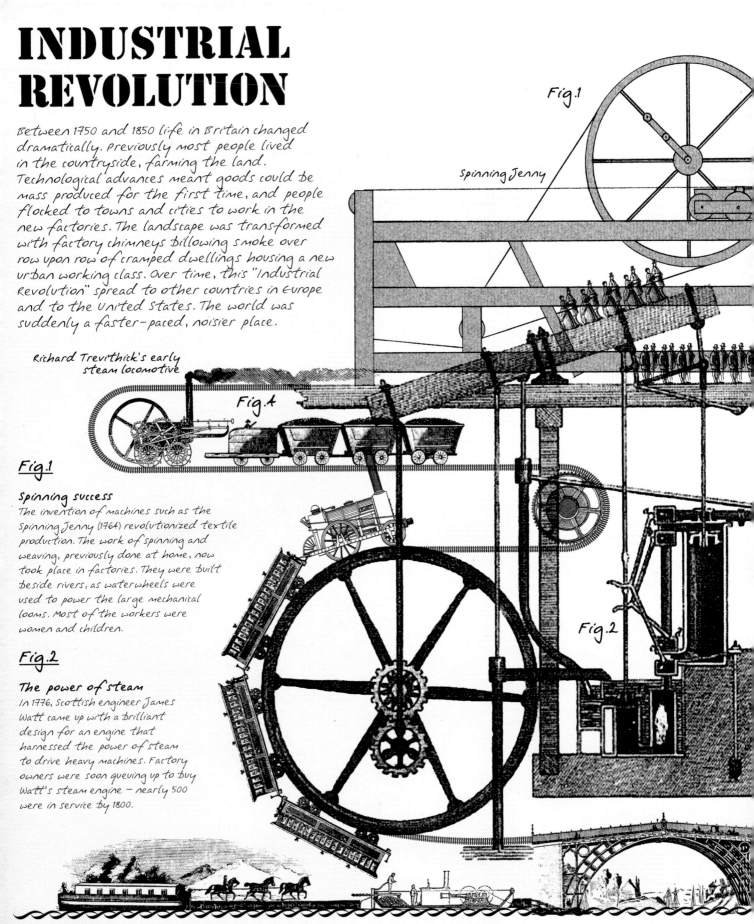

Fig.1

Spinning Jenny

Richard Trevithick's early steam locomotive

Fig.4

Fig.2

Fig.1

Spinning success

The invention of machines such as the Spinning Jenny (1764) revolutionized textile production. The work of spinning and weaving, previously done at home, now took place in factories. They were built beside rivers, as waterwheels were used to power the large mechanical looms. Most of the workers were women and children.

Fig.2

The power of steam

In 1776, Scottish engineer James Watt came up with a brilliant design for an engine that harnessed the power of steam to drive heavy machines. Factory owners were soon queuing up to buy Watt's steam engine – nearly 500 were in service by 1800.

Horses pulling a canal boat

An early steam boat

Abraham Darby's Iron Bridge (1779)

Fig. 3

Iron and coal

The boilers for the new steam engines had to be made of iron strong enough to withstand high pressure. They also burned enormous amounts of coal. Since the early 1700s, iron-makers had been experimenting with ways of making iron harder in coal-fired furnaces, and in 1779 Abraham Darby built the world's first cast-iron bridge. Canals were constructed to carry coal from mines to factories and finished goods on to ports and cities.

Fig. 4

Transport speeds up

Richard Trevithick exhibited the first steam locomotive to run on rails in 1804. The first public railway opened in 1825, and the railway network expanded rapidly to cover most of the country. Isambard Kingdom Brunel's railway bridges and tunnels were the engineering wonder of the age. Long-distance travel now took hours instead of days, while steamships cut the cost and time of sea journeys.

Fig. 5

Industrial growth

Rural poverty forced people to leave the countryside to work in mills and factories. Sprawling towns grew up around the new industrial centres – between 1800 and 1850, the population of Manchester, centre of the cotton industry, climbed from 75,000 to more than 300,000. Britain's factories made everything from textiles, china, and metal goods to machine tools, soap, and cement for the growing global market. Smoke and pollution made the towns filthy, unsanitary places.

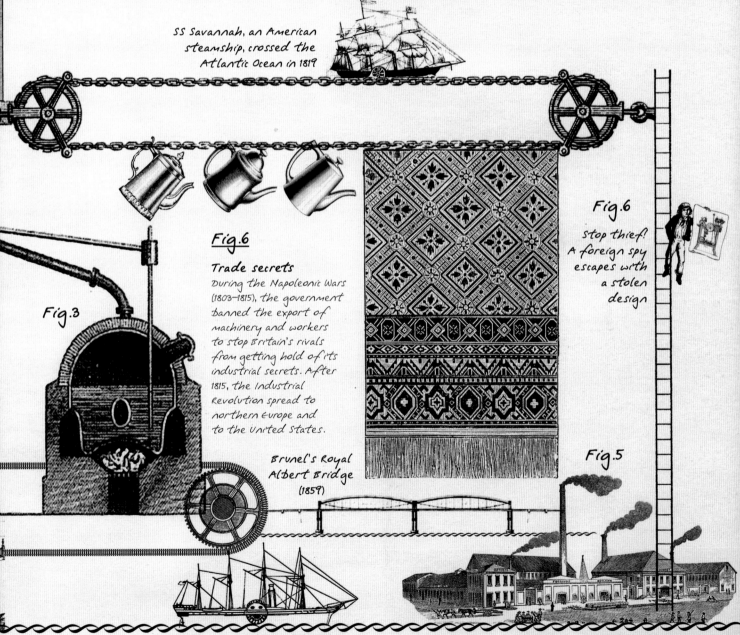

SS Savannah, an American steamship, crossed the Atlantic Ocean in 1819

Fig. 6

Trade secrets

During the Napoleonic Wars (1803–1815), the government banned the export of machinery and workers to stop Britain's rivals from getting hold of its industrial secrets. After 1815, the Industrial Revolution spread to northern Europe and to the United States.

Fig. 3

Fig. 6

stop thief! A foreign spy escapes with a stolen design

Brunel's Royal Albert Bridge (1859)

Fig. 5

Isambard Kingdom Brunel's Great Western, a paddle steamer, took a record-breaking 15 days to reach New York in 1837

Black smoke from factory chimneys

Lewis and Clark's daring journey into the unknown

This is the true story of the first overland expedition across America, of the great discoveries made and the dangers and setbacks faced.

In May 1804, a boat and two canoes left Camp Dubois on the east bank of the Mississippi, upstream from St Louis, to journey northwest up the great Missouri River. Loaded with supplies including a tonne of dried pork, medicines, and writing materials, the expedition's progress was slow.

Leading the expedition was Meriwether Lewis, secretary to US President Thomas Jefferson, and William Clark, an army officer. The President had chosen them to head a "Corps of Discovery" to explore the unknown heart of America and find a river route to the Pacific Ocean.

As they sailed up river they were relieved to find the Native American tribes living there were friendly, and they exchanged gifts. While Clark charted their route, making maps, Lewis made notes about the rocks, animals, and plants they found.

By November the weather was growing cold, and they decided to over-winter at a place they called Fort Mandan. Here they hired a French fur trapper, Toussaint Charbonneau, and his wife Sacagawea, a Native American from the Shoshone tribe, to act as guides.

NEW SPECIES

Lewis and Clark had instructions from President Jefferson to make a scientific survey of the lands they visited.

Very little was known about the lands the USA had gained from France in the Louisiana Purchase (see right), so Jefferson planned the expedition to be a voyage of scientific discovery. Lewis and Clark sent maps, drawings, plant and animal specimens – and even a live prairie dog – back to Jefferson. In all, they identified more than 300 previously unknown species.

Osage orange

Bobcat

Not all the Native Americans Lewis and Clark met were friendly. They only just avoided a fight with the Teton Sioux.

…AND BIGGER

They set off again in April, but danger lay in wait for them at the Missouri Falls. At the waterfall's base and blocking their way were perilous rapids. Risking life and limb, they struggled on. Snow was already falling as they started to cross the treacherous Rocky Mountains on horses procured from a Shoshone village. The journey took them 11 days and they nearly starved – but their luck held out. A group of Nez Percé Native Americans on the other side of the mountains lent them canoes to descend the swift Snake and Columbia Rivers.

On 7 November 1805, Clark wrote in his journal they could see the ocean – "O! the joy". But he was mistaken, and the Corps had to struggle on for another three weeks to reach the coast. They spent the winter there and set out for home in March 1806, reaching St Louis in September. They had been away for two and a half years, covered an incredible 12,375 km (7,690 miles), and succeeded in opening up a route to the west.

HOW DID IT GET SO BIG?

The USA expanded steadily throughout the 19th century. Much of the new land was purchased from old colonial powers and some territory was gained through war.

1803 The Louisiana Purchase saw France sell all the land it owned between the Mississippi River and the Rockies to the USA for $15 million. The deal was struck because Napoleon was desperate for cash to fight his wars in Europe. The USA more than doubled in size.

1819 East Florida was purchased for $5 million from Spain.

1836 Texas, then a province of Mexico, declared its independence. At the Battle of the Alamo, a force of 160 Texans and US citizens held out for 11 days against overwhelming odds. Mexico eventually lost the war but refused to recognize Texan independence.

1845 Texas joined the USA as the 28th state. This led to another war with Mexico, easily won by the USA, and in the peace that followed it gained almost the whole of the southwest (New Mexico, Arizona, Utah, and California).

1846 The fixing of the border with Canada at the 49th Parallel (an imaginary line of latitude running horizontally around the globe used to aid navigation) added the states of Washington, Oregon, Idaho, and parts of Montana and Wyoming in the northwest.

1853 In the Gadsden Purchase, an area of land (now part of Arizona and New Mexico) was bought from Mexico for the construction of the Southern Pacific Railroad, at a cost of $10 million.

1867 Alaska, a Russian colony since 1744, was purchased for $7.2 million. At the time this seemed a high price, but within a few years gold had been discovered there.

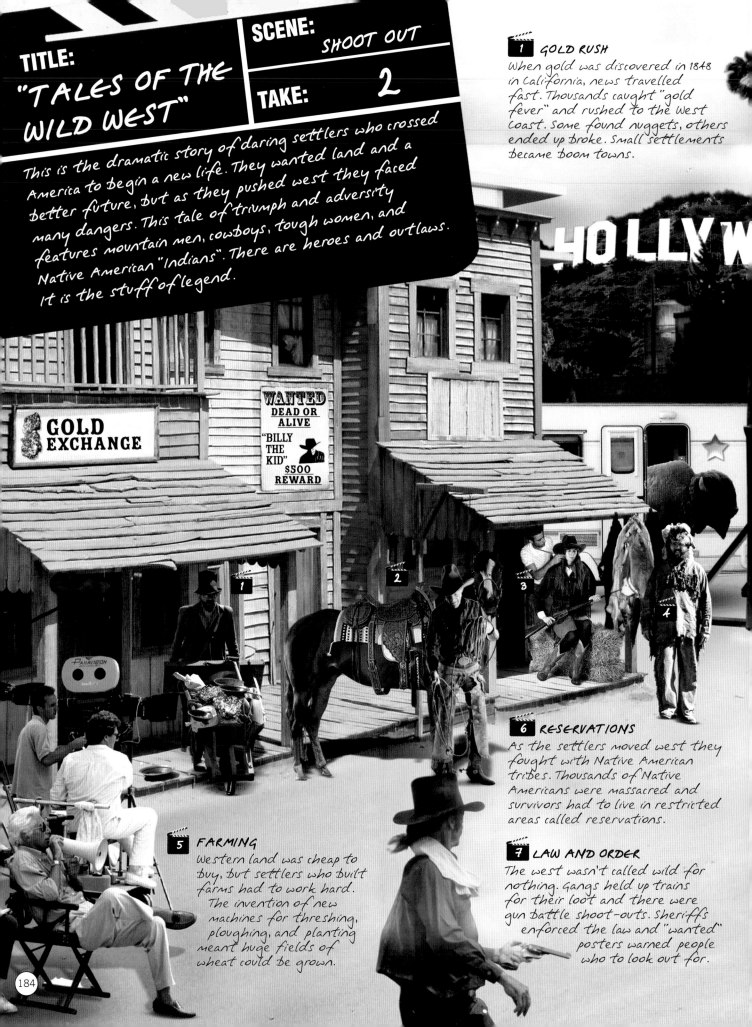

TITLE: "TALES OF THE WILD WEST"

SCENE: SHOOT OUT

TAKE: 2

This is the dramatic story of daring settlers who crossed America to begin a new life. They wanted land and a better future, but as they pushed west they faced many dangers. This tale of triumph and adversity features mountain men, cowboys, tough women, and Native American "Indians". There are heroes and outlaws. It is the stuff of legend.

1 GOLD RUSH

When gold was discovered in 1848 in California, news travelled fast. Thousands caught "gold fever" and rushed to the West Coast. Some found nuggets, others ended up broke. Small settlements became boom towns.

GOLD EXCHANGE

WANTED
DEAD OR ALIVE
"BILLY THE KID"
$500 REWARD

6 RESERVATIONS

As the settlers moved west they fought with Native American tribes. Thousands of Native Americans were massacred and survivors had to live in restricted areas called reservations.

5 FARMING

Western land was cheap to buy, but settlers who built farms had to work hard. The invention of new machines for threshing, ploughing, and planting meant huge fields of wheat could be grown.

7 LAW AND ORDER

The west wasn't called wild for nothing. Gangs held up trains for their loot and there were gun battle shoot-outs. Sheriffs enforced the law and "wanted" posters warned people who to look out for.

184

2 COWBOYS

Cowboys looked after cattle and spent hours in the saddle. They worked on ranches and took the herds on long trail drives to the railroads, where the cattle were traded.

3 WOMEN IN THE WEST

Life for women out west was tough. Many were farmers and others ran hotels and saloons. Calamity Jane and Annie Oakley became famous as expert shooters and riders.

4 FUR TRADERS

Fur traders roamed the mountains collecting beaver pelts to exchange for supplies such as whisky and gunpowder. These buckskin-clad trappers worked closely with Native Americans.

INDIAN RESERVATION

MOVE WEST FOR FREE LAND!

8 WAGON TRAIL

The Homestead Act of 1862 offered up patches of free land to pioneers. In search of a better life, families set off in wagon trains. They covered thousands of kilometres, and faced hunger, harsh weather, and raids by Native Americans.

Brainse Sráid C
Kevin Street
Tel: 4753

185

PEOPLE OF SOUTH AMERICA, WE ARE FREE!

From Mexico to Argentina, our armies have taken on the forces of the Spanish Empire and won! After 200 years we have thrown off our colonial chains to take our place among the independent nations of the world. The kingdom of Brazil, too, has severed its links with Portugal.

✦ ✦ ✦ ✦ ✦ ✦ ✦

Our national heroes

We salute the brave men who took up arms against the Spanish and, in a series of daring campaigns from 1810 to 1823, won our freedom. Long live the liberators of South America!

Simon Bolivar (1783–1830)

As a young man Bolivar studied in Europe and returned home to Venezuela full of democratic ideals, and determined to end Spanish rule. Though he failed time and again, he would not give up. Finally, in 1819, he led an army of 2,500 men on a daring march across the mountains to capture Bogota, capital of Colombia. He then liberated Venezuela and Ecuador before driving the Spanish from Peru. To South Americans, he will always be "the liberator".

ANTONIO JOSÉ DE SUCRE (1795–1830)

A brilliant soldier and Bolivar's closest companion, Sucre was only 15 when he joined the liberation struggle. A general at 25, he captured Quito (Ecuador), high in the Andes, in 1822 and routed the Spanish army at Ayacucho in 1824 to take control of northern Peru (Bolivia). He was elected its first president.

Miaaa**OW**
¡Hola Guapo!

MIGUEL HIDALGO (1753–1811)

On 16 September 1810, this Mexican parish priest rang the bells of his church as a signal for revolt, shouting "Death to bad laws! Death to the Spaniards!" More than 80,000 people joined him on the march to Mexico City. He won two victories on the way, but stopped short of capturing the capital. The Spanish had time to recover and Hidalgo was executed. He is remembered as the Father of the Mexican Revolution, which was eventually won in 1821.

JOSÉ DE SAN MARTIN (1778–1850)

The national hero of Argentina, San Martin had served in the Spanish army against Napoleon, returning to his native country to fight for its independence in 1812. He then raised an army with Bernardo O'Higgins and marched across the Andes to defeat the Spanish in Chile in 1818. He invaded Peru in 1821 and liberated its capital, Lima, but later handed over the country to Bolivar.

BERNARDO O'HIGGINS (1778–1842)

The son of an Irish-born Spanish administrator of Chile, Bernardo was educated in England. It was here he joined the struggle for South American independence. With San Martin, he led the war against the Spanish in Chile and became its first independent leader.

Scientific advances

Get set for the future with our exciting range of gizmos and discoveries. Sourced from the best science brains of the 19th century, wow your friends and family with amazing innovations including electrical power, a cutting-edge theory on the origins of humans, and an incredible talking machine. Terms and conditions apply.

PERFECT PRESENT FOR BRIGHT SPARKS

- Can't be beaten for current value
- Shock your friends with Faraday's electric generator

It's electrifying!
A spinning copper disc held between the opposing poles (ends) of a horseshoe magnet produces a continuous electric current. Simple when you know how!

- The most talked-about book of the 19th century – has he made a monkey of us?
- This month's "natural selection"!

NOW MILK IS GOOD FOR YOU

- Prof Pasteur's ingenious heating process destroys harmful germs
- Pasteurise, then pour it past your lips!

FREE TOY MONKEY WITH EVERY BOOK

A **GENERATOR** Invented by English chemist and physicist Michael Faraday, famous for his experimental work in the field of electricity and magnetism, we predict that this simple device will prove to have thousands of practical uses. A real technological breakthrough.

MF 1831 Electric generator
£10 20 weeks at 10 shillings

B **ON THE ORIGINS OF SPECIES** As a young man Charles Darwin visited the Galápagos Islands and got to thinking about why animals and plants evolve (change). Twenty years later he published his controversial theory of evolution by natural selection. Life on Earth will never seem the same after this must-read blockbuster!

CD 1859 Book
5 shillings 20 weeks at 3 pence

C **GERM-FREE MILK** Until French chemist Louis Pasteur came along, no one really understood how germs (bacteria) cause disease. Now he's discovered you can kill them by heating milk and other liquids to just below boiling point. Pasteurisation saves lives!

LP 1862 Pasteurisation kit
£8 20 weeks at 8 shillings

D PISTON POWER

- Knocks sparks off other designs
- Compresses the fuel mixture in the cylinder before ignition

G LOOK RADIANT

- Own your own piece of radium – it glows in the dark!
- Gives out high-energy particles

E

- Give us a Bell, they said – and he did!
- Transmits the human voice down an electric wire
- Every home should have one!

EXCITING SOUND EFFECTS

ADDS UP TO A GREAT BUY!

F

- The world's first mechanical computer
- Will take the headache out of calculation – if it's ever built!

NEW FOR 1898

H

- Are you receiving me loud and clear?
- Tune in with your own Marconi radio set

F **COMPUTER** Charles Babbage has devoted years of his life to designing an "analytical engine" that can carry out any mathematical task and is programmed by punched cards. Be ahead of your time and order one today.

CB 1835	Analytical engine
	£50 25 weeks at £2

G **RADIUM** Marie Curie's studies into radioactivity (the emission of high-energy particles), which she carried out with her husband Pierre, has led to the discovery of two new elements – radium and polonium, found in uranium ores. We think she deserves a Nobel Prize (or two)!

MC 1898	Radium
	£12 10 weeks at 24 shillings

H **RADIO RECEIVER** We're proud to present Italian scientist Signore Guglielmo Marconi's new invention for sending and receiving radio signals through the air. A microphone converts sound waves into electromagnetic waves, which are picked up by a receiver and fed to a loudspeaker that converts them back into sound waves. Just like that – no wires are needed at all. The wonders of modern science!

GM 1898	Radio receiver
	£18 30 weeks at 12 shillings

D **FOUR-STROKE ENGINE** German engineer Nikolaus Otto's design for a four-stroke internal combustion engine is the first that really works. Fellow German Karl Benz hopes to use this model to power the world's first petrol-driven car.

NO 1876	Internal combustion engine
	£24 30 weeks at 16 shillings

E **TELEPHONE** We're told Alexander Graham Bell became interested in the transmission of sound through his work as a teacher of the deaf. Looks like he's got a good head for business – he's already patented his invention and founded the Bell Telephone Company to promote it. Who knows, people may soon be able to speak to each other in different cities, even different countries – all by the power of electricity!

AGB 1876	Telephone
	£4 10 weeks at 8 shillings

YEAR OF REVOLUTIONS

It's 1848 and in one European capital after another angry protestors take to the barricades. Their demands vary – ONE MAN, ONE VOTE! FREEDOM OF THE PRESS! AN ELECTED PARLIAMENT! FAIRER LAWS! In countries under Austrian rule, nationalists seek the right to govern themselves. Shaken by the violence, a few rulers promise reforms, but within months the revolutions are over. Little has changed.

FEBRUARY: FURORE IN FRANCE

Angry crowds in Paris overthrow the country's ruler Louis-Philippe and declare a second republic, which quickly guarantees all males the right to vote and all citizens the right to work. By December it is all change again as Louis Napoleon (nephew of Napoleon Bonaparte) is elected president.

JANUARY: SICILY SIMMERS

A popular uprising in Sicily is the first flashpoint. Angered by King Ferdinand II's refusal to allow an elected parliament, a group of nobles set up their own government in the island's capital, Palermo. King Ferdinand II launches a military invasion from Naples, and the rebels surrender after nine months.

MARCH: UNREST IN AUSTRIA

Inspired by events in France, protestors in Vienna force the downfall of hardline minister Prince Metternich. Lajos Kossuth, a Hungarian nationalist, starts a revolutionary war against Austrian rule that spreads to other parts of the Empire. Emperor Ferdinand stands down and the army restores order by late 1849.

MARCH: GERMAN GRIEVANCES

Revolutions calling for greater freedoms break out in many German states, including Prussia. A national parliament meets in Frankfurt from May 1848 to draw up a political constitution for a unified Germany, but its chances of success are wrecked by Prussia's refusal to cooperate. The revolutions fizzle out.

APRIL: BLUSTER IN BRITAIN

Encouraged by what is happening in France, the Chartists organize mass meetings in London and Manchester. The aims of this mostly working-class political movement include giving the vote to all males and a secret ballot. Fearing revolution, the government calls in the army in force, but things pass off peacefully.

MARCH: IRATE ITALIANS

Protests against Austrian rule in northern Italy spread through the Italian states, and republics are set up in Milan and Venice. After the Pope flees Rome in November, Italian nationalists proclaim a people's republic there, but it is overthrown with French help. Austrian rule returns to the north.

WORKERS UNITE!

In February, German political writer and activist Karl Marx publishes the *Communist Manifesto* calling for a working-class revolution. Few are then aware of its existence but with its rallying cry of "Workers of all lands, unite!", the manifesto will become the most famous political pamphlet of modern times.

191

Adayinthelife

Monday 5 August 1850

The mill owner

JAMES WILSON
Age: 47
Career experience: Began work in his father's cotton mill aged 10. Travelled in Germany and France before being made partner in family textile business. Now sole owner. Married to Sarah, daughter of a textile merchant. They have two daughters, 21 and 16, living at home and a son, 19, at university.
Address: Fellside Hall, Lancashire. Seven servants including cook and butler.

James Wilson owns four cotton mills in England. Here's how he spends a typical day...

I am woken at seven by a servant and, after a breakfast of grilled kidneys and scrambled eggs, I head to my office at Deepdale, the largest of my four mills. I employ nearly 2,000 people in my factories, spinning and weaving cotton cloth.

The factory overseer, or manager, gives me his daily report. He tells me that the power looms (machines for weaving cloth) in one room had to be stopped to rescue a girl working as a "scavenger" who had slipped and fallen while she was crawling beneath the looms to pick up fluff and cotton waste from the floor. This is irritating – lost time is lost money – but luckily the girl was only badly bruised. Sometimes fingers and limbs can be crushed in the machinery.

In my father's day very young children worked in mills and were often badly treated. A series of Factory Acts has changed things. Now children must be nine years old and can work no more than a 10-hour day. I'm not keen on all this government interference. I look after my workers. I provide the children with a daily meal of soup and bread and have even built a school for them at Deepdale.

At the end of the morning's business, I visit the engine house. I love to watch the great steam engine at work driving all the factory's machines.

I have dinner at home, and in the afternoon I take the train into town where I make a number of business calls and attend a committee meeting for the installation of public drains – I'm very active in local affairs.

Later I drop in to my gentlemen's club. The members are all businessmen and mill owners like me and, over a drink or two, we discuss the latest news. I return home for a late supper and am in bed by 11.

NELLIE DAWSON
Age: 19
Career experience: Started at Wilson's mill as a scavenger aged 9; upgraded to piecer, repairing broken threads. Became a spinner last year. Further promotion unlikely.
Address: Lives in a two-roomed cottage with her mother, sister Louie, 17 (who was badly injured in a mill accident), and brothers, Tom, 11, a piecer, and Jack, 4. Their father and sister Kate died of cholera two years ago.

The mill worker

Employment number
1345

Nellie Dawson works as a spinner at Wilson's Deepdale Cotton Mill. Here's how she spends a typical working day...

At 6.15am, the sound of wooden clogs on the cobbled streets tells me it's time to get up. I hurry to join the stream of mill workers in the street. It's a long walk and my pay will be docked if I get to Wilson's mill a minute after the factory hooter goes at seven.

I climb the three flights of stairs to the spinning room where I guide the mule — a large machine that moves backwards and forwards twisting cotton into yarn or thread, filling 1,200 spindles at a time.

My job is to check that the yarn is running smoothly and to lift off the full spindles. It is very hot and the air is thick with dust and oil. I get an hour's break for dinner, but by 7pm I'm aching all over. I still have to walk home, and tomorrow will be the same. I work a half-day on Saturdays, with only Sundays off. But if I didn't work there would be nothing to eat at home.

SHOW'S OVER FOR SHOGUN

1868 MEIJI EMPEROR HANDED POWER

THE RISING SUN

Japan's daily news

US soldiers steam into Edo

JAPAN ON TRACK FOR SUCCESS

1872   NATION'S FIRST RAILWAY OPENS

The Emperor honoured with his presence today the opening of Japan's first railway line, which runs between Tokyo and Yokohama. It is a great step forward in the modernization of Japan and will lead to many more advances. Industry is growing rapidly, and the army and navy are to be reformed. It won't be long before Japan can be counted among the world's great powers.

It's full steam ahead as first train departs

Meiji Emperor

The shogun, Japan's military ruler, has been overthrown. Imperial rule is restored and all Japan should now unite around the figure of the Meiji Emperor, a spokesman said today. The days of the samurai warriors are numbered. We will break with the customs of the past that have been holding Japan back. There's much to learn from the outside world – but learn we will, and quickly.

DRAGON BOATS!

8 July 1853

Four strange ships, carrying guns, entered Edo Bay (Tokyo) this morning. Smoke poured from their funnels, and bystanders thought they were dragons. Commodore Matthew Perry of the United States navy later came ashore with a letter from the US president demanding that Japan's ports be opened to foreign trading ships. Does this mark an end to Japan's 200 years of isolation from the rest of the world?

1905 JAPAN'S MODERN NAVY DESTROYS RUSSIAN FLEET – SEE INSIDE FOR MORE DETAILS

After the Battle of Gettysburg, President Abraham Lincoln made a famous speech declaring the war as "a new birth of freedom" for all citizens.

UNION

Number of states 23
Population 21 million
Total number in army 2.5 million
Colour of uniform blue
Flag the Stars and Stripes
President and commander-in-chief Abraham Lincoln
Generals George B McLellan, Ulysses S Grant, William Sherman
Casualties 634,703 (359,528 dead, 275,175 wounded)

AMERICAN CIVIL WAR

By the mid 1800s the issue of slavery had become a big problem for the United States. It had long been outlawed in northern states, but plantation owners in the south insisted on their right to keep slaves. In 1860 Abraham Lincoln, a candidate for the anti-slavery Republican Party, was elected president. Southerners were horrified. Fearing that Lincoln would pass laws to end slavery, 11 southern states broke away from the Union to form a government of their own – the Confederacy. Lincoln was determined to save the Union from breaking up. The result was a terrible and bloody civil war.

WAR BREAKS OUT

In April 1861 Confederate troops attacked Fort Sumter – a Union military base in South Carolina – signalling the start of hostilities. The Confederate army, commanded by Robert E Lee, won several early successes. The cost was appallingly high as rapid-fire guns inflicted terrible slaughter and injuries on both sides. Lee's defeat at the Battle of Gettysburg was a major turning point in the war.

196

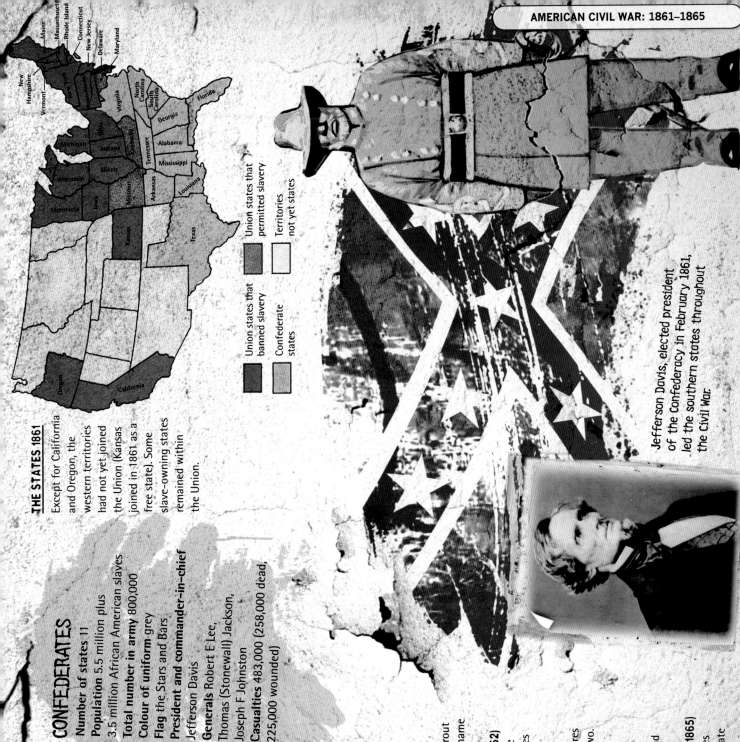

THE STATES 1861

Except for California and Oregon, the western territories had not yet joined the Union (Kansas joined in 1861 as a free state). Some slave-owning states remained within the Union.

Union states that banned slavery

Confederate states

Union states that permitted slavery

Territories not yet states

New Hampshire
Vermont
Maine
Massachusetts
Rhode Island
Connecticut
New Jersey
Delaware
Maryland
New York
Virginia
North Carolina
South Carolina
Florida
Georgia
Alabama
Tennessee
Kentucky
Ohio
Indiana
Michigan
Illinois
Wisconsin
Minnesota
Iowa
Missouri
Arkansas
Louisiana
Texas
Kansas
Oregon
California

Jefferson Davis, elected president of the Confederacy in February 1861, led the southern states throughout the Civil War.

CONFEDERATES

Number of states 11

Population 5.5 million plus 3.5 million African American slaves

Total number in army 800,000

Colour of uniform grey

Flag the Stars and Bars

President and commander-in-chief Jefferson Davis

Generals Robert E Lee, Thomas (Stonewall) Jackson, Joseph F Johnston

Casualties 483,000 (258,000 dead, 225,000 wounded)

SURRENDER

Union general Ulysses S Grant's campaign in the west, ending with the capture of Vicksburg, cut off Arkansas, Louisiana, and Texas from the rest of the Confederacy. William Sherman led a Union army through Georgia to Atlanta and then on to the sea, destroying everything in its path and leaving the economy of the south in ruins. Richmond, the Confederate capital, fell to Grant on 3 April 1865. Within days Lee had surrendered and the war was over.

KEY BATTLES

Bull Run, Virginia (21 July 1861)
First major battle of the war. Confederates rout Union army. "Stonewall" Jackson wins nickname for standing firm against Union assault.

Antietam, Maryland (16–18 September 1862)
Heavy casualties on both sides. Inconclusive result but Union claims victory. Confederates checked from advancing north.

Vicksburg, Mississippi (May–July 1863)
After six weeks' siege Ulysses S Grant captures Vicksburg, splitting Confederate forces in two. Union controls Mississippi River.

Gettysburg, Pennsylvania (1–3 July 1863)
Union victory ends Lee's second attempted invasion of north. Costliest battle of war and a major turning point for Union.

Appomattox Court House, Virginia (9 April 1865)
Last military engagement of war. Lee's forces are surrounded and he surrenders Confederate army to Grant.

Made in the USA!

The late 1800s were boom years for American industry. Its success was built on business dynamism, inventiveness, and mass production methods – making goods on a large scale by using standardized parts. From sewing machines to reapers, cars to skyscrapers, American tycoons made them, and made them big. Detach and assemble these parts for your own model of American enterprise.

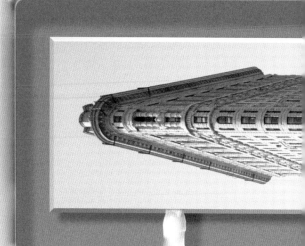

BLACK GOLD

An oil strike in Pennsylvania in 1859 saw the birth of the US oil industry, with petroleum quickly replacing smelly whale oil as a fuel for heating and lighting. John D Rockefeller, founder of Standard Oil, became the first dollar millionaire.

LIGHTING UP

In 1876, inventor Thomas Alva Edison founded an industrial research laboratory at Menlo Park, New Jersey, taking business enterprise to a new level. Among the products he developed was the electric light bulb. He went on to invent a system for generating and distributing electricity to light up America's cities.

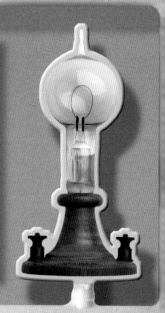

BUILDING HIGH

Cities grew outwards – and upwards. The first skyscraper, built for the Home Insurance Company of Chicago in 1885, used a steel-girder construction and was 10 storeys high. New York's famous Flatiron Building, 22 storeys high, was built in 1902.

A CAR FOR EVERYONE

When German engineers Gottlieb Daimler and Karl Benz developed petrol-driven cars in the 1880s, Americans soon picked up on the idea. Henry Ford pioneered the use of modern assembly line techniques to build the world's first popular car, the Model T Ford, telling the public they could have it any colour – "so long as it's black".

UNITING THE NATION

Railroad kings like Cornelius Vanderbilt and Jay Gould became fabulously rich through investing in the expanding railroad network. The first coast-to-coast railroad, completed in 1869, brought the vast nation together as never before and facilitated the transportation of foodstuffs, iron, and coal. Retailers could distribute their goods to a new mass market of customers right across the USA.

GIANT MACHINES

As the urban population grew, swollen by immigration from Europe, so did the need for America's farmers to produce more food. The McCormick Harvesting Machine Company developed huge agricultural machines, capable of doing the work of several men. Grain was stored in giant hoppers by the railroad, then transported in bulk to the cities.

1. BEGIN WITH PRUSSIA

Germany isn't a single country but a "confederation" of states. King Wilhelm of Prussia and his prime minister Otto von Bismarck have plans to make Prussia top dog nation. They start by building a strong army.

2. USE BLOOD AND IRON

In 1864, Prussia and Austria seize two small states from Denmark. Prussia takes charge of Schleswig and later snatches Holstein from Austria. In 1866, it invades Austria in a lightning seven-week campaign. Bismarck calls this his "blood and iron" strategy.

5. SEW IT ALL UP

The southern German states now join the rest. Just to make the French feel even worse about losing Alsace and Lorraine, Wilhelm is declared German emperor in the palace of Versailles.

Schleswig-Holstein

North German Federation

Southern German states

Alsace-Lorraine

3. FOOL THE FRENCH

Europe is stunned. Prussia now controls all the northern German states. Bismarck has his eyes on the rich industrial regions of Lorraine and Alsace in eastern France. He tricks the French emperor into declaring war.

4. INVADE!

Prussia invades France (1870) and inflicts a crushing defeat. Napoleon III abdicates. The German army lays siege to Paris. Before it falls in January 1871, starving Parisians resort to eating the zoo animals.

1871
8 MARKS

UNIFIED GERMANY

Easy to follow instructions show how Prussia sewed up the rest of Europe and stitched together the German states to create an empire.

Otto von Bismarck

Wilhelm I

Paper pattern included. In addition you will need:
• 1 army
• invasion plans
• an iron will
• 1 ruler

A COMPLETE GUIDE TO UNITING GERMANY

1870
12 LIRA

UNITED ITALY

Follow this guide to the *risorgimento* – the nationalist uprising that turned a patchwork of Italian states into a single country, united by language and culture.

Victor Emmanuel II

Camillo di Cavour

Giuseppe Garibaldi

Paper pattern included. In addition you will need:
- a dash of Italian spirit
- invasion plans
- material for 1,000 red shirts
- 1 ruler

SUCCESSFULLY UNITE ITALY USING THIS SIMPLE STEP-BY-STEP PATTERN

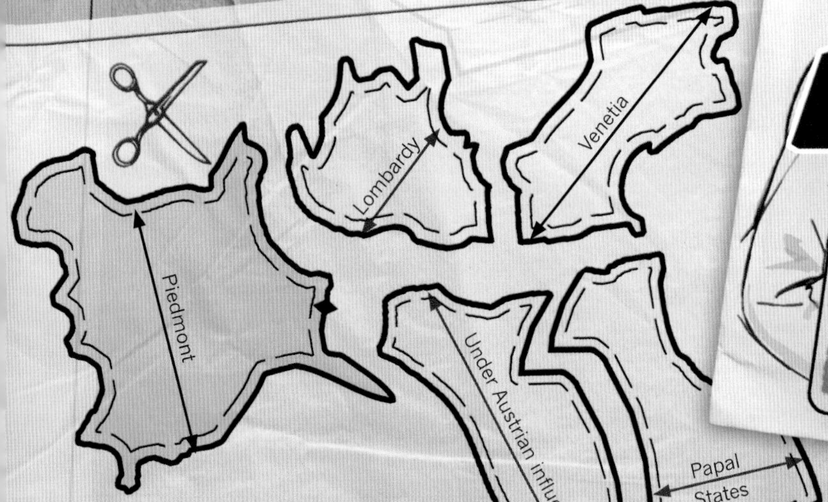

Lombardy

Venetia

Piedmont

Under Austrian influence

Papal States

Rome

Naples

Sardinia

Kingdom of two Sicilies

Sicily

1. BEGIN WITH PIEDMONT
Camillo di Cavour, prime minister of Sardinia-Piedmont, persuades King Victor Emmanuel II to put his energies into a campaign to unite Italy. First step is to free Lombardy from the Austrians, which they achieve in 1859 with French help.

2. JOIN MORE PARTS
In 1860, the other states of northern Italy, with the exception of Austrian-controlled Venetia, vote to join Sardinia-Piedmont.

3. ENTER A HERO
Adventurer Giuseppe Garibaldi invades Sicily and Naples with an army of 1,000 red-shirted volunteers. Cavour sends troops to secure the Papal states. Garibaldi hands his conquests over to Victor Emmanuel who is crowned king of a united Italy in 1861.

4. DO A DEAL
Victor Emmanuel agrees to support Prussia during its invasion of Austria in 1866. After Austria's defeat, the Prussians give him Venetia.

5. SEW IT ALL UP
Napoleon III of France prevents Garibaldi from marching on Rome. But after Napoleon's downfall, the Pope has to give the city up. In 1870 it becomes Italy's new capita[l]

201

CANADA

UNITED
KINGDOM

WEST
INDIES

SIERRA
LEONE

GOLD
COAST

NIGERIA

EGYPT

ANGLO-
EGYPTIAN
SUDAN

BRITISH
EAST
AFRICA

RHODESIA

SOUTH
AFRICA

INDIA

BURMA

CEYLON

SINGAPORE

MALAY
STATES

HONG
KONG

PAPUA

AUSTRALIA

NEW
ZEALAND

ALL MINE!

It is said that the "Sun never sets" on the British Empire. It spans right around the world, so it is always daytime in one part of it. By flexing our military muscle we have bcome the global superpower of the 19th century, ensuring that our culture, laws, business practices, and education system dominate. Even if we lose our colonies (not that one can imagine such a terrible event), our glorious English language will no doubt continue to reign supreme.

AUSTRALIA
Our Australian colonies contribute to the Empire's wealth with exports of wool and gold. In 1901, they will come together to form the self-governing Commonwealth of Australia under the British crown.

NEW ZEALAND
British settlers have introduced sheep farming to these islands. The native Māori claim they are sharing power, but they granted Britain sovereignty in a treaty. Perhaps they didn't know what they were signing?

SOUTH AFRICA
Britain must take control of the gold- and diamond-rich area of Transvaal if South Africa is to prosper and grow. We fear tensions with the Boers (Afrikaner farmers of Dutch descent) may shortly lead to war.

WEST AND EAST AFRICA
The Asante people of the Gold Coast proved hard to subdue, but West Africa is now exporting rubber and cocoa to Britain. East Africa is attracting white settlers – anyone for coffee?

SINGAPORE AND MALAYSIA
The British port of Singapore is a busy trading hub. Behind it lie the Malay States where rubber trees from South America are being planted to meet world demand for automobile tyres – whatever they are.

FIJI
Fiji is one of several British colonies in the sunny Pacific. It may not be so sunny, though, for the thousands of Indian migrant workers we have shipped there to work in the sugar plantations.

Rule Britannia

This year, 1897, we are celebrating our Diamond Jubilee, marking the 60 years that have passed since we ascended the throne as Queen Victoria of Great Britain and Ireland (our title "Empress of India" came later, in 1877 – a charming gift from Prime Minister Benjamin Disraeli). We have been greatly touched by the many tokens of affection we have received from our loyal subjects all over the British Empire, which now covers nearly a quarter of the globe.

CANADA
The Canadian Pacific Railway, opened in 1886, has united the country, now a self-governing dominion of the British Empire. Gold has just been found in the far northwest, triggering a gold rush.

INDIA
The "jewel in the crown" of the Empire, more than two-thirds of India is under direct British rule, including Burma (Myanmar), conquered in 1885. Neighbour Ceylon (Sri Lanka) is also a British colony.

HONG KONG
Hong Kong island, a bustling centre of trade with China, has belonged to Britain since 1842. The capital, Victoria, is one of many places around the world to have the honour of bearing our name.

GIBRALTAR
The naval base on Gibraltar, a rocky peninsula at the bottom of Spain, is seen as vital for protecting the sea route to India. British since 1713, the Spaniards think it's time they got it back.

WEST INDIES
Jamaica and Trinidad are the largest of Britain's island possessions in the Caribbean. The sugarcane industry has long been in decline, and bananas have recently been introduced.

1886 **1886** 1886

28 June

GREAT EVENT

RAILROAD IN CANADA FROM COAST TO COAST

GRAND OPENING

OF THE

CANADIAN PACIFIC

RAILWAY

INDEPENDENT CANADA

A proud young nation will cheer tonight as the Canadian Pacific Railway makes her maiden voyage. The first train to cross the continent will depart from Dalhousie Station, Montreal, at 8pm. Passengers will enjoy six days aboard the world's longest rail route before arriving at Port Moody, British Columbia, on 4 July. This east–west transport link is a fitting tribute to the back-breaking labours of 12,000 men, 5,000 horses, and 300 dog-sled teams.

On 1 July 1867, the former colonies of New Brunswick, Nova Scotia, Ontario, and Quebec gained independence from Britain when they formed the self-governing nation of Canada. Manitoba joined the federation in 1870, with Prince Edward Island signing on in 1873. In 1871, the western province of British Columbia became part of Canada on the promise that a railway would link her to the east coast. Now, that promise has finally been met!

RAILWAY UNITES CANADIAN PROVINCES FROM COAST TO COAST

FROM SWEEPING PRAIRIES TO ROCKY RANGES, THE MODERN MARVEL OF RAIL FINALLY UNITES CANADA! THE EXOTIC FAR EAST IS ALSO IN REACH, AS JAPANESE SILKS AND TEAS ARE TRANSFERRED FROM SHIP TO TRAIN IN BRITISH COLUMBIA.

WITH PLUCKY PIONEERING SPIRIT, LADY SUSAN AGNES MACDONALD HAS SHUNNED THE FIRST-CLASS CARRIAGE, VOWING TO RIDE THE RAILS ON THE LOCOMOTIVE'S COWCATCHER! THE ADVENTUROUS WIFE OF PRIME MINISTER SIR JOHN A MACDONALD PROMISES THAT SHE WILL BRAVE SITTING ON A BOX STRAPPED TO THE V-SHAPED GRILL "FROM SUMMIT TO SEA". A RAILWAY REPRESENTATIVE STATES THAT THE CREW IS "VERY WORRIED" ABOUT THE UNUSUAL SEATING ARRANGEMENT, BUT WILL SUPPLY THE FIRST LADY WITH "PLENTY OF WARM BLANKETS".

THE SCRAMBLE FOR AFRICA

Before 1870, European colonization of Africa was limited to a handful of small coastal settlements.

Then diamonds were found in South Africa. Suddenly every colonial power wanted a share of Africa's mineral wealth — and the unclaimed Congo basin was a prime target. The race for colonies grew so frantic that in 1884 a conference was held in Berlin to settle rival claims. African resistance was powerless against European guns, and by 1914 almost the entire continent was under European rule.

PORTUGAL
We used to ship slaves to Brazil from our forts along the coasts of Mozambique and Angola, which we've owned since the 1500s. But now that business is over, we've moved inland to claim land there.

BRITAIN
We took over the Cape colony of South Africa from the Dutch in 1814. That gave us a base to move into southern Africa, with its wealth of gold and diamonds. Leading the way was imperialist Cecil Rhodes, who dreamed of building a railway from Cairo in Egypt to the Cape.

GERMANY
Our leaders, Kaiser Wilhelm I and Chancellor Bismarck, were determined that the great German Empire should not be left out of the African land grab, so we carved out four widely scattered colonies for ourselves from what remained. We may have been last on the scene but, hey, we deserve our place in the sun, too, don't we?

BELGIUM
I am King Leopold II of Belgium. I ran this enormous chunk of central Africa as my personal estate and made a huge fortune from its rubber plantations and copper. People said I mistreated my African workers, and maybe it is true that within 15 years half the population had been worked or starved to death. But was it really necessary to make me hand the Congo over to the state of Belgium? So unfair!

Madagascar · Tanzania · Malawi · Mozambique · Swaziland · Burundi · Zimbabwe · South Africa · Lesotho · Zambia · Botswana · Namibia · Angola

LAND OCCUPATION
(Borders and country names are modern)

Belgium · France · Germany · Great Britian · Italy · Portugal · Spain · Independent

QING CHINA

The Qing Dynasty may have been founded by foreigners (the Manchu clan from northeast Asia), but once in charge of China, the Qing emperors wanted nothing to do with the rest of the world. Despite the policy of trade isolation, for 150 years the country enjoyed a period of prosperity and territorial expansion. By the 19th century, however, political rebellions were rife and economic pressures mounting. China was in crisis.

Kangxi (1661–1722) was the first great Qing emperor

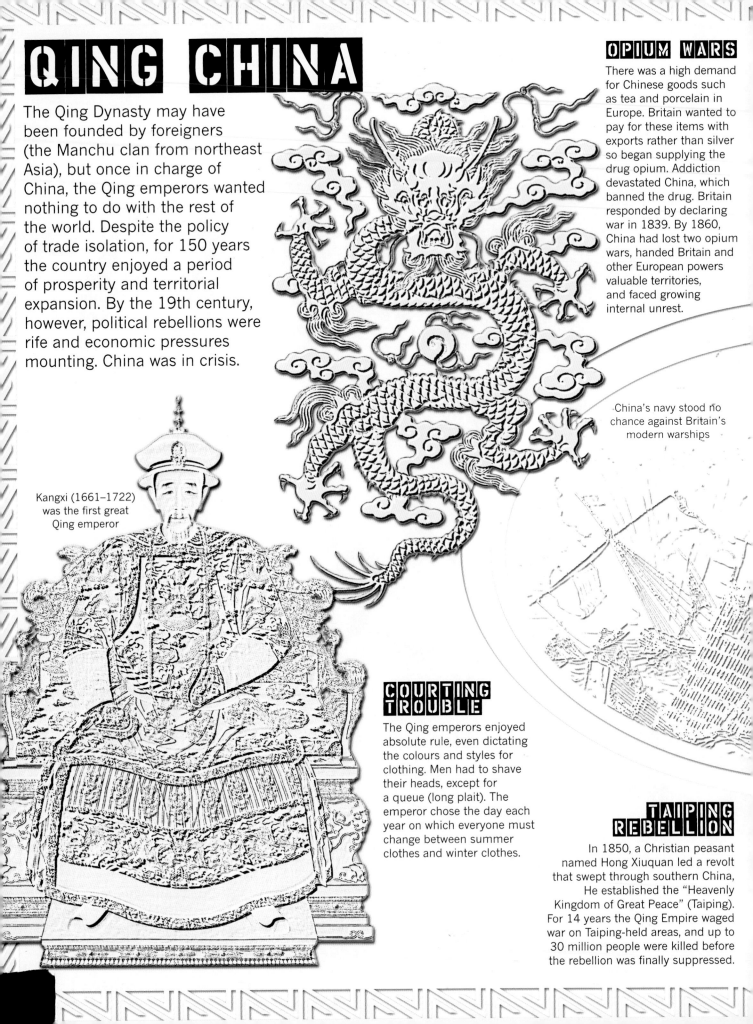

OPIUM WARS

There was a high demand for Chinese goods such as tea and porcelain in Europe. Britain wanted to pay for these items with exports rather than silver so began supplying the drug opium. Addiction devastated China, which banned the drug. Britain responded by declaring war in 1839. By 1860, China had lost two opium wars, handed Britain and other European powers valuable territories, and faced growing internal unrest.

China's navy stood no chance against Britain's modern warships

COURTING TROUBLE

The Qing emperors enjoyed absolute rule, even dictating the colours and styles for clothing. Men had to shave their heads, except for a queue (long plait). The emperor chose the day each year on which everyone must change between summer clothes and winter clothes.

TAIPING REBELLION

In 1850, a Christian peasant named Hong Xiuquan led a revolt that swept through southern China, He established the "Heavenly Kingdom of Great Peace" (Taiping). For 14 years the Qing Empire waged war on Taiping-held areas, and up to 30 million people were killed before the rebellion was finally suppressed.

MIDDLE GROUND

Following the humiliations of the Opium Wars and the Taiping Rebellion there were growing calls for change. In 1861, royal family members Prince Gong and Dowager Empress Cixi seized power. They opted for a middle path, hoping to appease both revolutionaries and conservative factions, but they pleased no one. Instead, army commanders turned into warlords, and rebellion brewed.

PULLING THE STRINGS

Dowager Empress Cixi ruled "from behind the curtain" for 47 years. Mother to Emperor Tongzhi, who ruled from the age of five until his death at 18 (1861–1875), and aunt of his successor Guangxu (1875–1908), she prevented either exercising their power.

Dowager Empress Cixi (1835–1908) was the widow of Emperor Xianfeng

Puyi (1908–1912) was China's last emperor

END OF EMPIRE

The death of Guangxu and Cixi in 1908 put the two-year-old Puyi on the throne. The Empire was vulnerable. An uprising in Wuchang in 1911 quickly led to full-scale revolt, and a Chinese republic was formed in 1912. Provisional president Sun Yatsen forced Puyi to abdicate, ending more than 2,000 years of empire.

Opium comes from the poppy plant

The Wright brothers achieve the first powered flight (p212) in The USA parties during the Roaring Twenties (p234), but pays the price in the Great Depression (p236). The USA and USSR compete to achieve new firsts in space (p262), while the civil rights movement (p266) and the Vietnam War (p268) keep America in the news.

Arctic explorers compete to see who will be first to reach the North Pole, while the race to the Antarctic South Pole challenges even the fittest (p214).

Archduke Franz Ferdinand's assassination (p218) triggers World War I (p220), with troops on the frontline firing from the trenches (p222). In 1919, a peace treaty is signed at Versailles (p224). A deadly flu virus (p226), probably spread by returning soldiers, kills more people than the war itself.

Communication: The way the world keeps in touch changes forever with the introduction of microchip technology and the Internet.

Feeling better: Healthcare in many countries improves dramatically after the discovery of penicillin and improved understanding of viruses and bacteria.

On the box: Television brings the world to an international audience and, for the first time, events can be followed as they happen.

Young people: The word "teenager" is invented and this age group enjoys a freedom previously unknown. Fashion, music, and art is created just for them.

Space invaders: After the Moon landing, the space programme opens up new frontiers with the construction of an International Space Station and exploratory craft sending back photos of Mars.

More mouths to feed: World population grows at a rate of 200,000 people every day.

Religion: Alternative ways of spending leisure time mean that fewer people attend church services. Marriage also goes out of favour.

Smallpox: After a successful vaccination programme, the World Health Organization certifies the eradication of this killer disease.

Horsepower: People no longer travel by horse. Fast-moving planes, trains, and cars put most horses out to pasture.

Environment: Countries suffer from the effects of a rising population and the pollution that it creates. Global warming becomes an international issue.

Going up ▲▲

Going down ▼▼

Take me back to the year 1900 and on to today

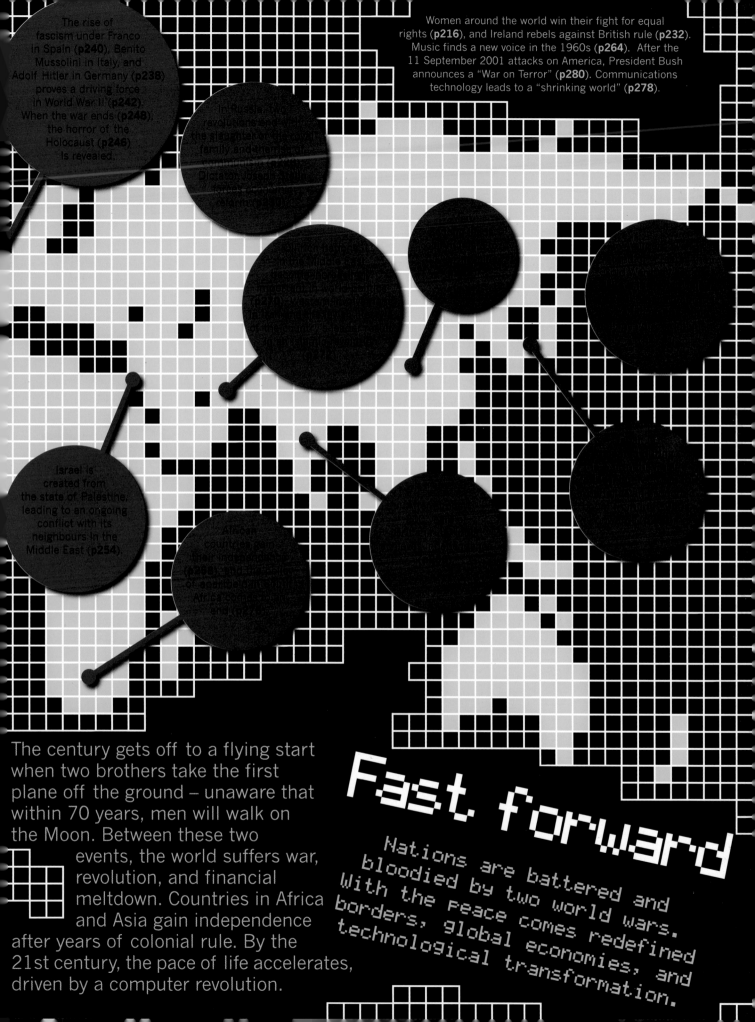

The rise of fascism under Franco in Spain (**p240**), Benito Mussolini in Italy, and Adolf Hitler in Germany (**p238**) proves a driving force in World War II (**p242**). When the war ends (**p248**), the horror of the Holocaust (**p246**) is revealed.

Women around the world win their fight for equal rights (**p216**), and Ireland rebels against British rule (**p232**). Music finds a new voice in the 1960s (**p264**). After the 11 September 2001 attacks on America, President Bush announces a "War on Terror" (**p280**). Communications technology leads to a "shrinking world" (**p278**).

In Russia, two revolutions end with the slaughter of the royal family and the rise of communism (**p226**). Dictator Joseph Stalin starts a reign of terror (**p234**).

Israel is created from the state of Palestine, leading to an ongoing conflict with its neighbours in the Middle East (**p254**).

African countries gain their independence (**p256**) and the regime of apartheid in South Africa comes to an end (**p274**).

The century gets off to a flying start when two brothers take the first plane off the ground – unaware that within 70 years, men will walk on the Moon. Between these two events, the world suffers war, revolution, and financial meltdown. Countries in Africa and Asia gain independence after years of colonial rule. By the 21st century, the pace of life accelerates, driven by a computer revolution.

Fast forward

Nations are battered and bloodied by two world wars. With the peace comes redefined borders, global economies, and technological transformation.

FIRST FLIGHT

Since the earliest times, people have dreamed of being able to fly. Hot-air balloons and gliders gave enthusiasts a taste of airborne adventure, but the real goal was to build a craft that could fly under its own power. Scientists said it was not possible, but the Wright brothers set out to prove them wrong. Now buckle up, ready for take-off!

Eleven-year-old Wilbur and seven-year-old Orville are fascinated when their father, the Reverend Milton Wright, gives them a toy helicopter. How does it work?

After building larger versions of his bamboo and paper toy helicopter, Orville starts to design and make kites. These fly well and are so popular that he makes extra pocket money by selling them to his friends at school. "Go fly a kite!" really brings in the bucks.

After they leave school, the brothers open a bicycle shop in Dayton, Ohio. The business takes off, so Orville suggests that they start making cars. Wilbur replies, "Why, it would be easier to build a flying machine." An idea is born.

In 1896, the death of German aviation pioneer Otto Lilienthal in a glider crash inspires the brother to return to their childhood interest – blue sky thinking!

The brothers become bird watchers (to study flight) and read up on aeronautics. They design a flexible wing so that the pilot can control the aircraft. But their glider doesn't perform as it should. It's back to the drawing board.

To recreate accurate conditions, the brothers build a wind tunnel. This will test their latest wing designs and prototype propeller. Wright Cycle Company employee Charlie Taylor helps them develop an engine that is light yet powerful enough to propel a plane. Hang on to your hats

DO NOT REMOVE THIS SAFETY CARD FROM THE AIRCRAFT

THE *WRIGHT FLYER*

2. Propellers face backwards and push the plane along

3. Vertical rudder keeps the plane stable and helps control sideways movement

4. Pilot lies on the lower wing to reduce wind resistance

1. Engine weighs just 36 kg (79 lb)

The result of their work is the *Wright Flyer* with its lightweight, 12-horsepower engine and flexible wing tips.

On 14 December 1903, Wilbur attempts to become the first person to make a powered, sustained flight, but he crashes soon after take-off. It takes three days to repair the damage.

On 17 December 1903, at 10.35 am on a clear day at Kill Devil Hill, Kitty Hawk, North Carolina...

...Orville makes the first flight. It lasts just 12 seconds and covers less distance than the wingspan of a jumbo jet. It marks the start of the age of true powered flight.

✳ TALES OF TENACITY ✳

With summers of **bitter cold** and winters of **permanent dark**, the North Pole does not welcome visitors. Located in the shifting ice that covers the Arctic Ocean, the Pole was a no-man's-land for centuries, with adventurers falling foul of *sudden blizzards* and jagged ice floes.

By the 19th century many explorers were trying to conquer this remote region, with varying degrees of success. In 1871, the US newpaper publisher **Charles Hall** set off on the last of three Arctic expeditions. He was the first to reach northern Greenland, but failed to reach the Pole.

Norwegian scientist **Fridtjof Nansen** tried a novel tactic, setting sail in his wooden vessel, *Fram*, in 1893. His idea was to let the ship freeze into the ice, so it would drift north with the floes. *Fram* began moving across the Arctic, but progress was slow. Weeks turned into months. Nansen grew impatient and decided to continue north on foot. It was *a mad idea* to leave the safety of the ship and travel with just three sledges, two canoes, and a pack of dogs. However, on 8 April 1895, Nansen reached a point 260 km (160 miles) farther north than the previous record.

A very different attempt was made by Swedish engineer **Salomon Andrée**, who tried to reach the Pole by hot-air balloon in 1897. The mission, and Andrée's life, ended when a storm brought down the balloon two days later.

When American explorer **Robert Peary** and his African-American partner **Matthew Henson** claimed to have reached the Pole in April 1909, *many doubted* this, believing they could not have travelled so quickly. The first expedition to indisputably reach the North Pole is American **Ralph Plaisted** who arrived there by snowmobile on 19 April 1968.

"Alas! Alas! Life is full of disappointments; as one reaches one ridge there is always another and a higher one beyond, which blocks the view."

Fridtjof Nansen

NORTH POLE

RACE TO

SOUTH POLE

THE POLES

TRIUMPH AND TRAGEDY

Antarctica is the world's coldest and least explored continent. Towards the end of the 19th century, the hostile terrain and severe cold took its toll on many adventurers, who tried to get there but turned back in defeat or persisted and lost their lives.

The real race to the South Pole began in 1911. Dreaming of personal glory and national pride, two men prepared for the trip of a lifetime. Norwegian explorer **Roald Amundsen** set off from Antarctica's Bay of Whales on 20 October. With his team of four men, Amundsen set off across the treacherous ice using four sledges, each pulled by 13 dogs. The men later transferred to skis and headed for the snowy mountain range, shooting the dogs they no longer needed, or could feed.

At the same time, English scientist **Robert Scott** laid plans for his trip, full of confidence because he had already been further south than any other explorer. Twelve days after Amundsen departed, Scott left his base by the Ross Sea with 16 men, 10 ponies, and 23 dogs. While Amundsen's trip went to plan, Scott's quickly *ran into disaster*. The dogs got weaker and the ponies died in the bad weather, while the motorized sledges failed, leaving the men to haul the supplies. They also faced the strongest winds on record.

When Amundsen reached the South Pole on 14 December, he left a letter for Scott and a letter for the King of Norway in case his team did not make it back. By this time, hunger, fatigue, and *frostbite* had taken their toll on Scott's team. He chose five men to make the final push. The rest returned in groups to base camp. Scott reached the South Pole on 17 January 1912, only to learn that he had been beaten. Devastated and exhausted, none of his team survived the journey home. Amundsen's letters were found strapped to Scott's body, a testament to the **triumph and tragedy** of the race to the South Pole.

"We shall stick it out to the end, but we are getting weaker of course and the end cannot be far."

Sir Robert Scott

http://www.givewomenthevote.com/home/index.htm

Meetings | Jobs | Have your say | Legal advice

Suffragette online

| Home | Abroad | News | Protests | Hunger strikes |

Wear it with pride

This medal is awarded to the courageous women who have suffered force-feeding while in prison. The ribbon colours show green for hope, white for purity, and purple for dignity.

News and views on the votes for women campaign

Search: Suffragette

News

Battle continues on streets of New York City

6 May 1912

The campaign for women to get the vote – suffrage – stepped up a gear today as hundreds of female protesters marched through New York City. The rally passed off peacefully – much to the relief of police who had feared a repeat of the rioting that followed a demonstration in Washington, DC, two months ago. During that march, jeering bystanders spat on and attacked the 8,000-strong crowd of suffrage campaigners. Many women were hospitalized as a result of the clashes.

Tell your story   Take me back   Get in touch

Mystic Mary

Here are my predictions for when the vote will be won by our sisters worldwide.

Denmark, Iceland: 1915
Great Britain: 1918 (but only women over 30 until 1928)
Austria, Canada, Germany, Poland, Sweden: 1918
Luxembourg, Netherlands: 1919
Czechoslovakia, USA: 1920
Ecuador: 1929
Spain: 1931
Greece: 1934
India: 1935
France: 1944
Italy, Japan: 1945
Argentina, Romania, Yugoslavia: 1946
Belgium: 1948
China: 1949
India: 1950
Switzerland: 1971
Liechtenstein: 1984

Not listed!
Remember that women of some countries already have the vote: **Pitcairn Islands** (1838), **New Zealand** (1893), **Australia** (1902), and **Finland** (1906). Time for the rest of the world to catch up!

WOMEN OF THE WORLD UNITE

HEADLINES

Poster pararde

We've collected some of the best suffrage posters from around the world. Now it's up to you to vote for your favourite in our online poll. We will be offering T-shirts of the winning poster.

Some leading characters

France

Madeleine Pelletier
Nicknamed "the French suffragette" in the 1890s, Pelletier was the first person to use the word feminism.

UK

Emmeline Pankhurst
Founded the British Women's Franchise League in 1889. She and her daughters have been arrested several times.

USA

Susan B Anthony
Worked tirelessly for the rights of African-Americans. In 1872, she was arrested for voting in the presidential election.

Have your say

- **Voting**
- **Marriage**
- **Divorce**
- **Children**
- **Women in the workplace**

Quotes of the week

"It is our duty to make this world a better place for women."
Christabel Pankhurst

"Failure is impossible!"
Susan B Anthony

"In the courts women have no rights, no voice; nobody speaks for them. I wish woman to have her voice..."
Sojourner Truth

Say no to force-feeding!

These women are demonstrating against the assault on suffragettes, and the rally is a reminder of the solidarity with our European sisters. The protest is aimed at the British government's cruel practice of force-feeding suffragettes. These women, often imprisoned for minor offences, are refusing to eat as a protest. Prison authorities are forcing milk and egg into them through a tube inserted in the nostril. This barbaric procedure must stop!

Death at the track
4 June 1913

Emily Wilding Davison, who ran out in front of the King's horse at a British racetrack, has died in hospital. Ms Davison sustained serious internal injuries and did not regain consciousness after the incident. Although her purpose was unclear, she is being heralded as a martyr to the cause of women's suffrage.

War looms in Europe
1 August 1914

Politcial pundits are saying war looks ever more likely in Europe. Experts on suffrage believe that a war can only strengthen the position of women, as they will take over the work of men while they are at war. Let's hope our true value will be recognized so that we can swiftly win the vote.

THE BEST BLOGS

Suffragette online

Arrests Up-to-date news of our sisters around the world who have been arrested for their activities (left). Some are blogging from prison cells.
Cat and Mouse Act A new law in the UK has led to hunger-striking prisoners being released until they recover their strength, then re-arrested.
Is it torture? Join the debate on whether force-feeding suffragettes in prison should be classified as torture.
Meek or militant? Is it OK to break the law to gain publicity for the cause?

SUFFRAGETTES

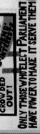

THE DAILY SCOOP

23 JULY 1914

Serbia given ultimatum

Austria has taken a hard line with the Serbian leadership, essentially calling for the province to obey the rule of the Austrian government. The shooting of the Austrian Archduke and his wife is being used as a way of settling old scores in European politics. Depending on Serbia's response, the current crisis could spiral into a large, Europe-wide conflict.

Russia, who supports Serbian independence and fears Germany, is allied with Britain and France. If Serbia is attacked, Russia may well jump in to defend its ally, and Britain and France may be pulled in too. Likewise, Austria is strongly allied with Germany, and Italy can perhaps be relied upon to support them.

WAR IS DECLARED

4 August 1914

Britain today joined the list of nations caught up in the conflict waging across Europe. This latest declaration of war followed the German invasion of Belgium, an old ally of Britain's. Germany is allied with Austria in its war against Serbia. That conflict was sparked by Serbia's refusal to agree to one of Austria's key demands – to hand over Archduke Ferdinand's assassin to Austrian courts. This small point has spelled war for Europe, but many believe the conflict will be brief and could even be over before Christmas.

SUNDAY NEWS

28 JUNE 1914

ARCHDUKE ASSASSINATED

Austrian heir shot dead on streets of Sarajevo

The heir to the Austrian throne, Franz Ferdinand, has been assassinated by the Archduke Franz Ferdinand. The Sarajevo Archduke assassination group: the Black Hand group to Gavrilo Black Hand an official Serbian crowd and was 19-year-old Serbian wife. The when Princip ran and his pregnant range. The shot him and his point-blank Serbian Sophie, at point-blank demand Black Hand, who

Archduke Franz Ferdinand

independence from Austria, the incident when the took a wrong. With pounced when vehicle to reverse. high Archduke's vehicle running Austria turn and began already states, strongest feeling European take the ill response. is expected to action possible in

---

THREAT OF WAR

6 JULY 1914

Germany is rumoured to have offered Austria complete support in any action they take against Serbia. This "blank cheque" will most likely be cashed by declaring war on Serbia. Germany is itching for a short successful war to test out its new technologies and to prove its power to its old foe Britain. Britain's military – especially its navy – is believed to be the best in the world, and this could soon be put to the test.

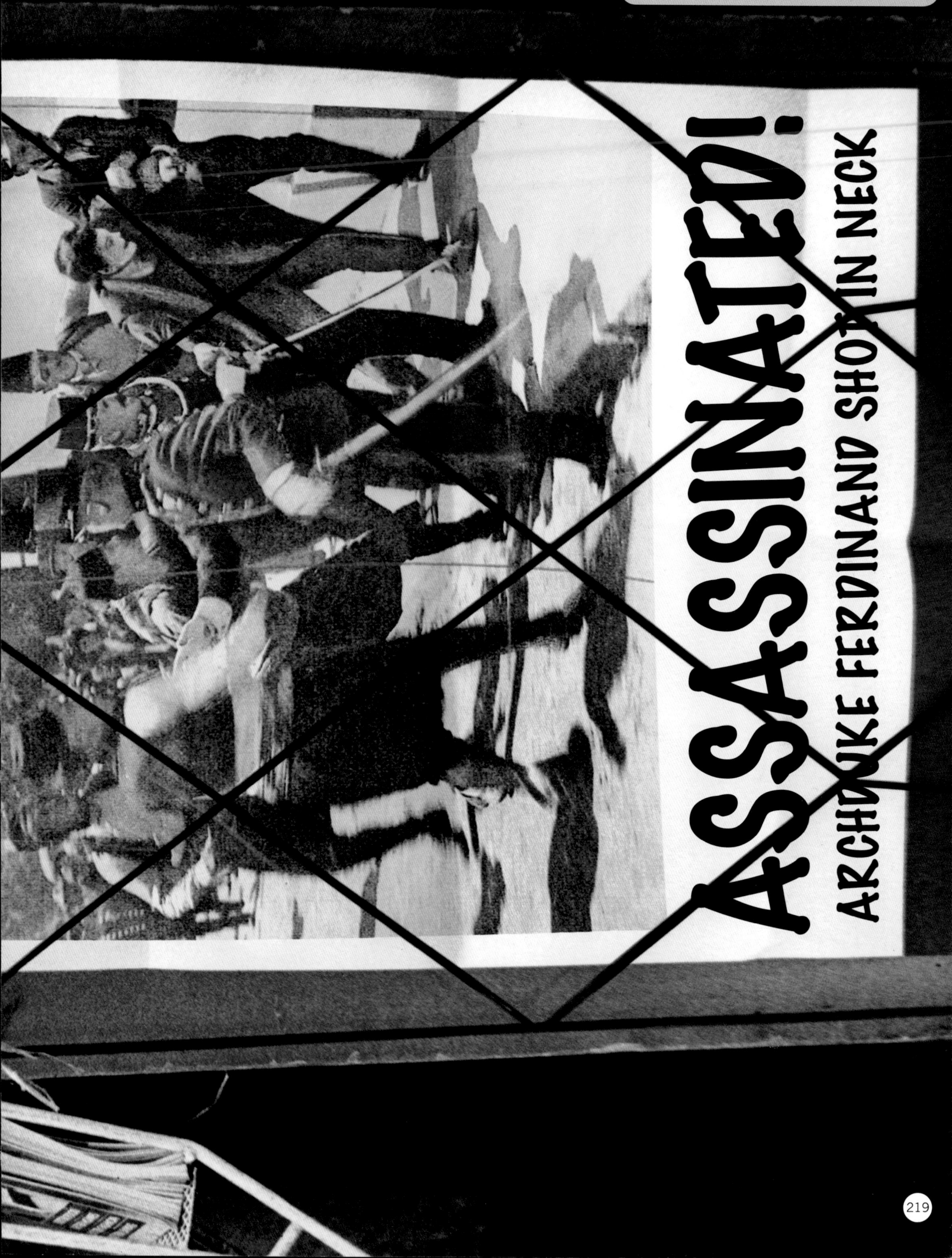

ASSASSINATED!

ARCHDUKE FERDINAND SHOT IN NECK

The Great War

In the summer of 1914, Europe was plunged into war. Most nations joined one of the opposing sides – the Central Powers (led by Germany, Austria-Hungary, and the Ottoman Empire) and the Allies (led by Britain, France, Belgium, and Russia). Both sides were initially

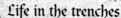

The war begins

In July 1914, Austria went to war with Serbia and the other nations of Europe were quickly drawn into the conflict. After Germany invaded Belgium, Britain declared war on 4 August 1914.

Life in the trenches

Much of the war was fought from long fortified ditches called trenches. Conditions in the trenches were horrific. As well as attacks by the enemy, soldiers often had to contend with thick mud and hungry rats.

Joining up to fight

To begin with, men on both sides volunteered to fight for their countries. Recruitment posters appealed to people's sense of duty. Later, conscription was introduced – men were required to enlist or face jail.

Christmas truce

On Christmas day 1914, after months of intensive trench warfare, German and British troops called a temporary truce. They sang carols together and even played football matches.

Fighting with fire

Trench warfare demanded weapons that could be used over short distances. Flamethrowers – mechanical hoses that propelled a stream of burning liquid – were first used at the Battle of Verdun in 1916. They were used to cause injury, or force soldiers out into the open.

The Somme

The Battle of the Somme, fought in northern France between 1 July and 18 November 1916, was one of the most terrible battles of the war. On the Allied side, more than 100,000 men were killed and 630,000 left wounded. Germany lost more than 500,000 men.

Sea battles

While fighting continued in the trenches, battles also raged at sea. German and British fleets fought for control of vital shipping routes. The Battle of Jutland, 31 May–1 June 1916, was one of the biggest contests. It involved 250 vessels, but there was no clear winner.

Tank warfare

The tank was a British invention, designed to withstand heavy fire and to cross trenches and the barbed wire in no-man's-land (the space between the trenches). However, when they were first introduced at the Battle of the Somme in 1916, these armoured vehicles got stuck in the mud and as many as one-third of them broke down.

convinced that the war would be over in months, but it raged for four long years, involving more and more countries, and causing unprecedented bloodshed. By the time it ended in 1918, it was a global conflict and had cost the lives of more than 20 million people.

Poison gas

In the trenches both sides used poison gas as a weapon, with deadly effect. The chemicals caused burns and blindness, and attacked the respiratory system leading to suffocation and a slow, painful death.

Sinking of the *Lusitania*

The *Lusitania*, a British liner, was sunk by a German submarine in May 1915, killing 1,201 passengers. Of that number, 128 were American. This event turned public opinion in the USA against Germany.

The Battle of Gallipoli

When the Ottoman Empire entered the war, they blocked crucial sea routes. On 25 April 1915, Australian and New Zealand Allied troops landed on the Gallipoli peninsula in Turkey to try to take control of one of these routes, the Dardanelles Strait. More than 200,000 soldiers died in the fighting that followed, and the Allies were forced to withdraw.

U-Boats

German submarines, or U-Boats, played a key role in the war at sea. They targeted the Allies' merchant ships to cut off vital supplies of food and ammunition.

Aerial bombing

While fighting raged abroad, those at home also found themselves in danger. Civilian targets were bombed from the air by bomber planes and airships. Buildings were destroyed and people lost their lives. World War I was called "total war" because it involved the whole population.

Artillery

US troops entered the war on the Allied side on 6 April 1917. They fired their first shots in trench warfare using the quick-firing artillery gun "Bridget", boosting the morale of the Allies.

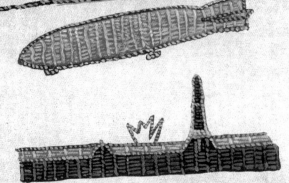

The Red Baron

At the beginning of the war, aeroplanes were used mostly for observation. But when a machine gun was invented that was capable of firing between a plane's propeller, the Germans developed tactics for fighting in the sky. Their most famous fighter pilot was Baron Von Richthofen, nicknamed the "Red Baron".

Zeppelins

The German Zeppelin was a rigid airship – a metal balloon filled with helium. Zeppelins were used to bomb Britain, killing 500 British civilians over the course of the war.

Armistice at last

On 11 November 1918, after four years of fighting, Germany was overwhelmed by the Allies and signed an armistice (an agreement to stop fighting). The war was finally over.

TRENCH WARFARE

Much of World War I was fought in flat, open countryside, so both sides dug deep trenches from where they could attack as well as defend themselves. By mid-October 1914, two lines of trenches faced each other from the Belgian coast to Switzerland. It became known as the Western Front, and the land between the trenches was called no-man's-land. Life in the trenches was appalling – dominated by mud, the sound of explosives, and constant bursts of enemy fire. But death could come from disease as well as from a sniper's bullet.

LETTERS FROM HOME
For the ordinary soldier, trench life was exhausting and uncomfortable, and letters from loved ones were often the highlight of the day. More than 12 million letters were sent to the Western Front every week. Although soldiers were encouraged to reply, many chose to hide the true horror of war.

"...the sound of the big guns somewhere not so many miles away has begun again. It is hard to tell which way one could go and not find someone shooting someone else."

RAIN AND MUD
When it rained, which it often did, the trenches filled with water. There was mud everywhere, and men had to eat, sleep, and fight in wet uniforms. After heavy rainfall, trenches could collapse, so soldiers cut drains to run off the water. Even so, trenches were a nightmare of dirt, slime, and rotting bodies.

"This is the wettest muddiest country I ever saw, it has been raining steadily for seven weeks. I stepped in a mud hole the other night and went up to my waist in mud..."

SHELL SHOCK

Early in the war, soldiers began suffering a new condition. Symptoms included headaches and giddiness. Doctors thought it was caused by the noise of shells, and called it "shell shock". But the real cause was the horror of war. Some disoriented soldiers were accused of deserting and shot by firing squad.

" THE RATS HERE ARE PARTICULARLY REPULSIVE, THEY ARE SO FAT — THE KIND WE CALL CORPSE-RATS. THEY HAVE SHOCKING, EVIL, NAKED FACES, AND IT IS NAUSEATING TO „ SEE THEIR LONG, NUDE TAILS.

TRENCH FEVER

Soldiers had to fight disease as well as the enemy. With hundreds of corpses littering the trenches, infection was inevitable. Trench fever was a problem for all soldiers, with fever, headaches, leg pains, and skin rashes. Some men also suffered trench foot, caused by the cold and wet conditions.

RATS AND LICE

The trenches were infested with millions of huge rats, which spread infection and stole food. Men would tempt them out of hiding with hunks of stale bread, then bash them with spades. Lice were also a problem, causing a constant itching. Lice fed on living bodies; rats thrived on the dead.

UNITED STATES
I'm going to push some of my pet schemes at Versailles. My "Fourteen Point Plan" will hopefully lead to economic prosperity, end land disputes around the world, and will stop future wars by founding a League of Nations. We'll keep Germany from building up their army – we'd rather stay on our side of the Atlantic than fight another war in Europe. And we must break up these old empires: the people living under them want their own nations.

THE COST OF WAR
Germany was ordered to accept full responsibility for the war and to pay reparations (compensation) to the tune of $33 billion over 42 years, mostly to France.

US President
WOODROW WILSON

A LEAGUE OF THEIR OWN
The League of Nations was set up to provide a forum where countries could discuss conflicts before they escalated into open warfare. In the end, the US didn't join, and with no armed force the League had little influence and no power.

TREATY OF VERSAILLES

Described as the "war to end all wars", World War I ended in 1918 and the world's leaders gathered in Versailles palace, near Paris, to pick up the pieces of a shattered Europe. Britain, the USA, and France won the war and dictated the terms to the losers – Germany, Austria, the Ottoman Empire, and Bulgaria. The decisions they made would have a major impact on Europe for decades to come.

KEY

New countries created after World War I

Alsace and Lorraine

Rhineland

Borders

Old Russian Empire

Old German Empire

Old Austrian Empire

NORTHERN IRELAND

IRISH FREE STATE

BRITAIN

NETHERLANDS

BELGIUM

FRANCE

SWITZERLAND

PORTUGAL

SPAIN

The German military was not allowed to enter the Rhineland

Alsace and Lorraine were taken over by France

MINISCULE MILITARY
According to the treaty, Germany's army was reduced from around 4 million soldiers to just 100,000. They were also not allowed to have any aircraft, ships, or submarines.

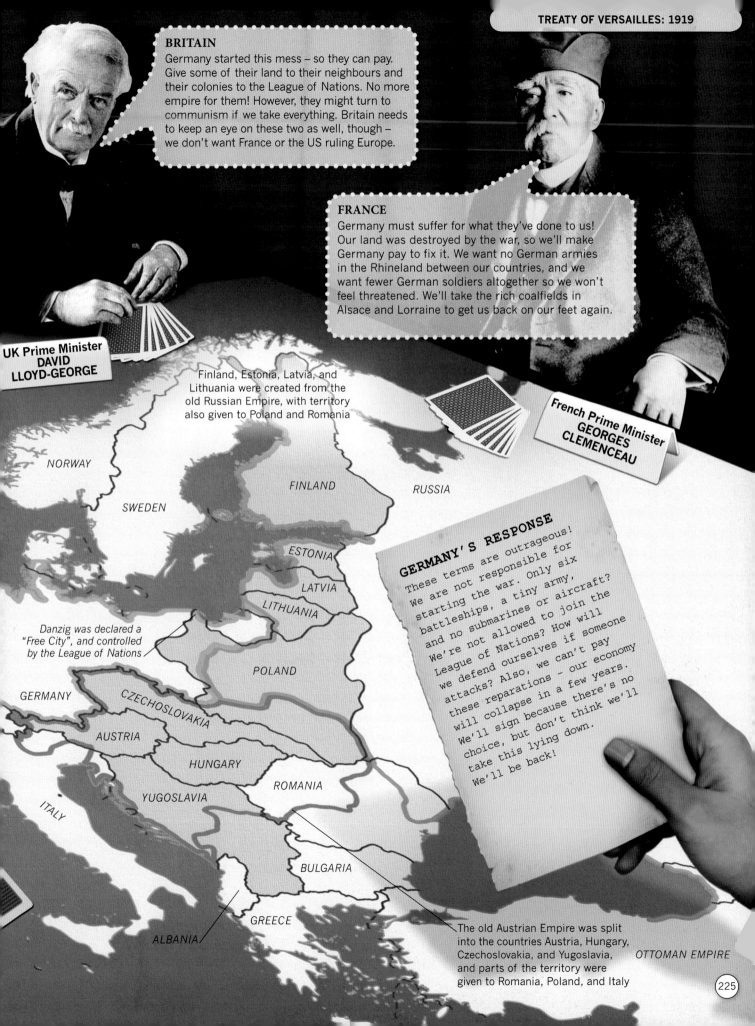

BRITAIN
Germany started this mess – so they can pay. Give some of their land to their neighbours and their colonies to the League of Nations. No more empire for them! However, they might turn to communism if we take everything. Britain needs to keep an eye on these two as well, though – we don't want France or the US ruling Europe.

UK Prime Minister
DAVID LLOYD-GEORGE

FRANCE
Germany must suffer for what they've done to us! Our land was destroyed by the war, so we'll make Germany pay to fix it. We want no German armies in the Rhineland between our countries, and we want fewer German soldiers altogether so we won't feel threatened. We'll take the rich coalfields in Alsace and Lorraine to get us back on our feet again.

French Prime Minister
GEORGES CLEMENCEAU

Finland, Estonia, Latvia, and Lithuania were created from the old Russian Empire, with territory also given to Poland and Romania

NORWAY

SWEDEN

FINLAND

RUSSIA

ESTONIA

LATVIA

LITHUANIA

Danzig was declared a "Free City", and controlled by the League of Nations

POLAND

GERMANY

CZECHOSLOVAKIA

AUSTRIA

HUNGARY

YUGOSLAVIA

ROMANIA

ITALY

BULGARIA

GREECE

ALBANIA

OTTOMAN EMPIRE

GERMANY'S RESPONSE
These terms are outrageous! We are not responsible for starting the war. Only six battleships, a tiny army, and no submarines or aircraft? We're not allowed to join the League of Nations? How will we defend ourselves if someone attacks? Also, we can't pay these reparations – our economy will collapse in a few years. We'll sign because there's no choice, but don't think we'll take this lying down. We'll be back!

The old Austrian Empire was split into the countries Austria, Hungary, Czechoslovakia, and Yugoslavia, and parts of the territory were given to Romania, Poland, and Italy

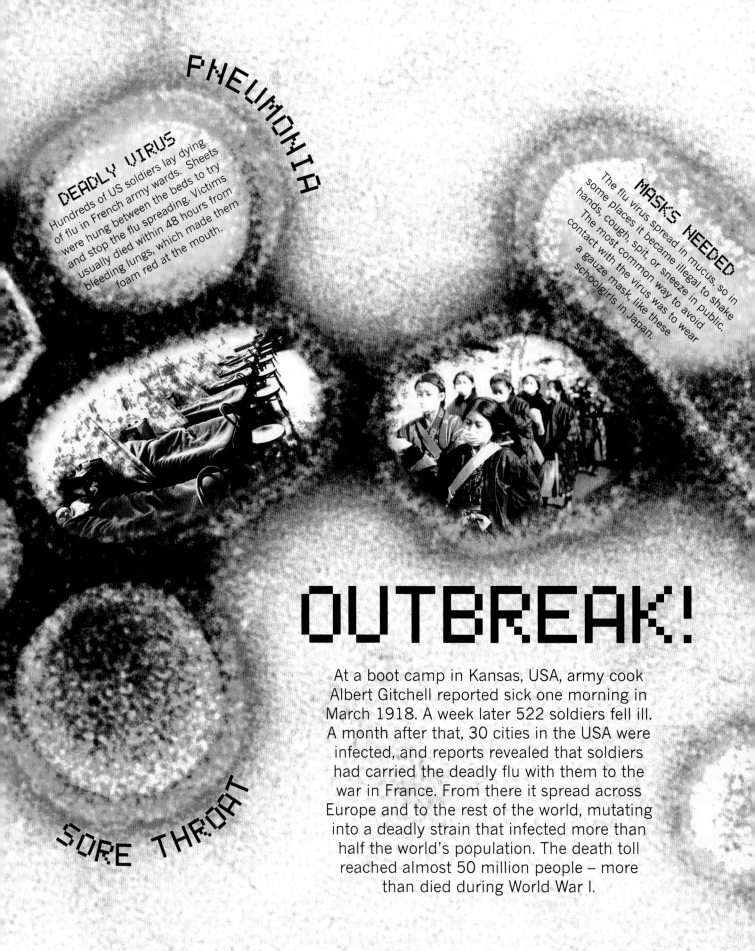

PNEUMONIA

DEADLY VIRUS
Hundreds of US soldiers lay dying of flu in French army wards. Sheets were hung between the beds to try and stop the flu spreading. Victims usually died within 48 hours from bleeding lungs, which made them foam red at the mouth.

MASKS NEEDED
The flu virus spread in mucus, so in some places it became illegal to shake hands, cough, spit or sneeze in public. The most common way to avoid contact with the virus was to wear a gauze mask, like these schoolgirls in Japan.

SORE THROAT

OUTBREAK!

At a boot camp in Kansas, USA, army cook Albert Gitchell reported sick one morning in March 1918. A week later 522 soldiers fell ill. A month after that, 30 cities in the USA were infected, and reports revealed that soldiers had carried the deadly flu with them to the war in France. From there it spread across Europe and to the rest of the world, mutating into a deadly strain that infected more than half the world's population. The death toll reached almost 50 million people – more than died during World War I.

NOTHING HELPS

In the panic to avoid catching flu, people tried taking everything from aspirin, castor oil, and kerosene to cinnamon and onion soup. Nothing worked. These schoolboys wore bags of camphor round their necks, hoping that the strong-smelling vapour would kill the virus before it infected them.

BLOOD POISONING

STOP THE SPREAD

At the start of the outbreak, only a few infected people died. Injections using serum from patients were tested, but, as it spread, the disease became more dangerous, and the death rate rose to one person in every five. People were dropping dead in the streets and graveyards were full. By the end of 1918 the worst was over, and by the following summer the deadly virus had disappeared without a trace.

FRESH AIR

As the virus was airborne, many countries banned indoor gatherings and people were stopped from travelling. Indoor meeting places, including shops, theatres, and even churches, were closed. Here, a court in San Francisco is held in the open air to reduce the risk of infection.

HEADACHE

During one eventful year, two revolutions took place that turned Russia into the world's first communist state. The buildup to the unrest of 1917 began 30 years earlier, when poor workers began to demand rights from the ruling tsar. The workers were represented by the Mensheviks, who wanted change through negotiation, and the more radical Bolsheviks, who wanted change through violent action. In 1905, mass protests forced Tsar Nicholas II to grant the people an elected government, but he still kept an iron grip on the country.

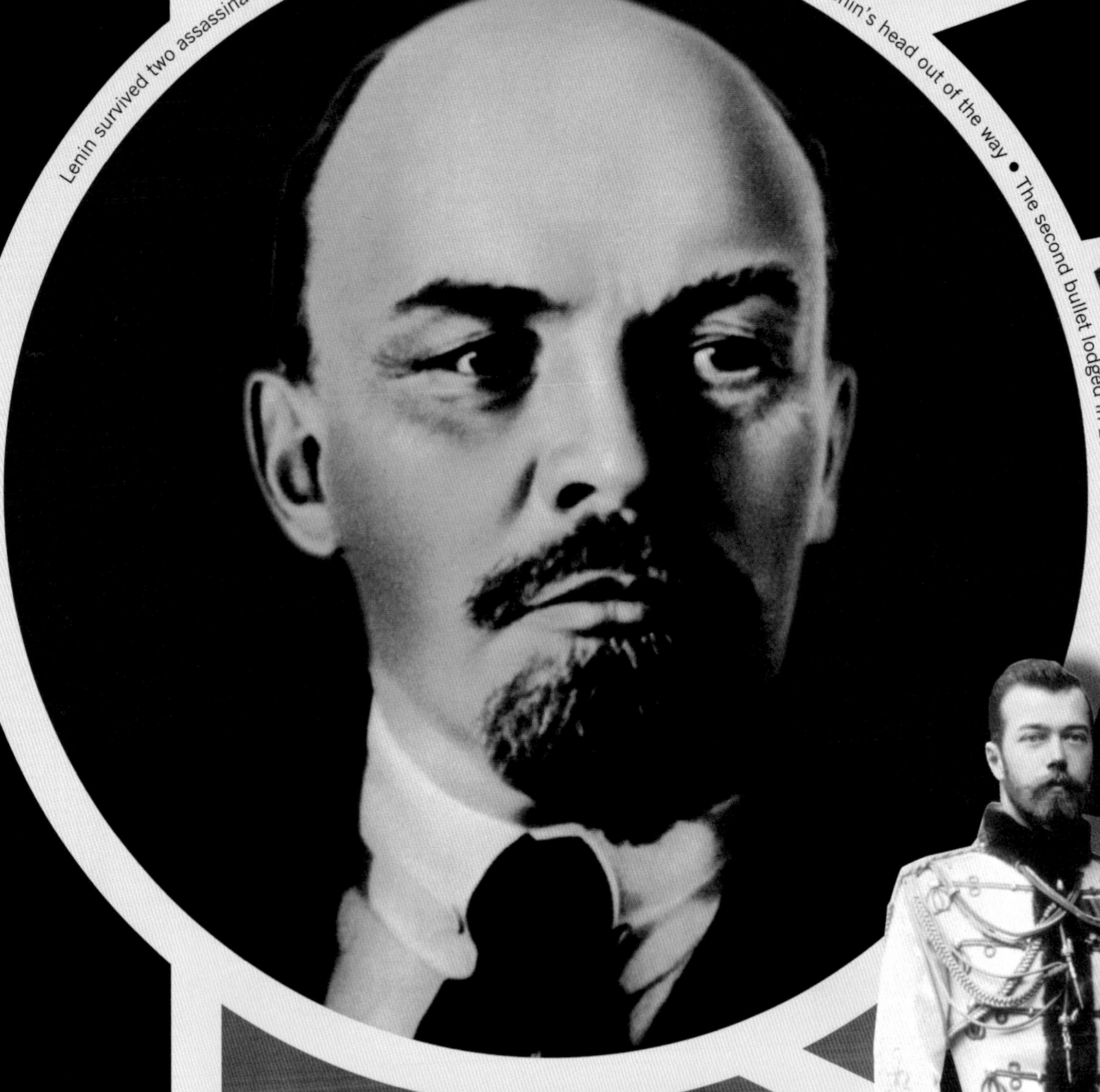

Lenin survived two assassination attempts • The first bullet hit a friend's hand when he pushed Lenin's head out of the way • The second bullet lodged in Lenin's neck

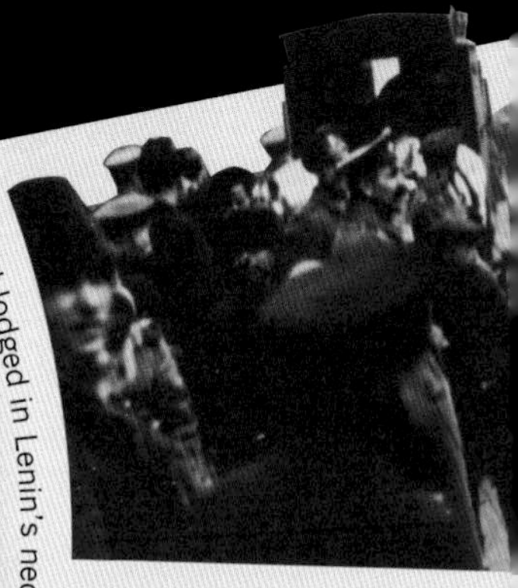

THE

COMMUNIST LEADER

In 1895, Vladimir Lenin was exiled to Siberia, a province in northern Russia, for his role in demanding political change. He led the Bolsheviks to power in the October Revolution and became Russia's first communist leader.

LAST OF THE TSARS

In July 1918, Tsar Nicholas II and his family were brutally murdered by the soldiers who were guarding them. First they said: "Your relatives have tried to save you. They have failed and now we must shoot you."

RUSSIAN REVOLUTION

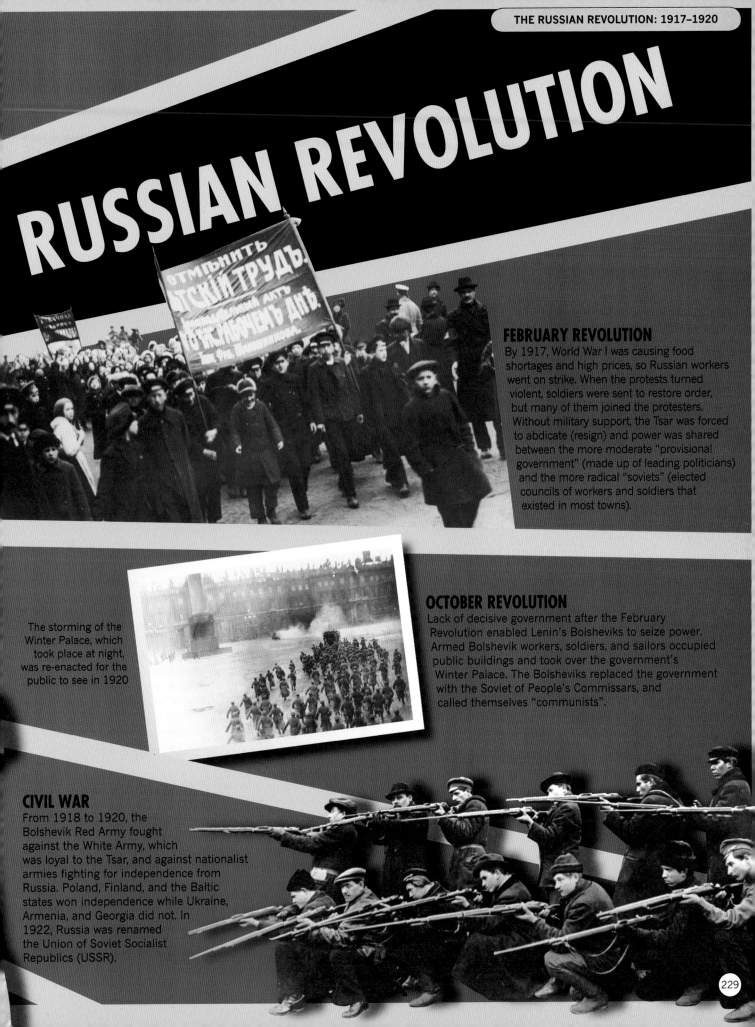

FEBRUARY REVOLUTION

By 1917, World War I was causing food shortages and high prices, so Russian workers went on strike. When the protests turned violent, soldiers were sent to restore order, but many of them joined the protesters. Without military support, the Tsar was forced to abdicate (resign) and power was shared between the more moderate "provisional government" (made up of leading politicians) and the more radical "soviets" (elected councils of workers and soldiers that existed in most towns).

The storming of the Winter Palace, which took place at night, was re-enacted for the public to see in 1920

OCTOBER REVOLUTION

Lack of decisive government after the February Revolution enabled Lenin's Bolsheviks to seize power. Armed Bolshevik workers, soldiers, and sailors occupied public buildings and took over the government's Winter Palace. The Bolsheviks replaced the government with the Soviet of People's Commissars, and called themselves "communists".

CIVIL WAR

From 1918 to 1920, the Bolshevik Red Army fought against the White Army, which was loyal to the Tsar, and against nationalist armies fighting for independence from Russia. Poland, Finland, and the Baltic states won independence while Ukraine, Armenia, and Georgia did not. In 1922, Russia was renamed the Union of Soviet Socialist Republics (USSR).

JOSEPH STALIN

This boy is a ruthless bully who will stop at nothing to get what he wants. However, he is the only pupil who shows the potential to turn the Soviet Union into a superpower to rival the USA.

SUBJECT	GRADE	COMMENT	TEACHER
History	A	Joseph is always trying to rewrite history. He doesn't like people to know that he became Soviet leader by putting his supporters in positions of power and exiling or murdering his rivals — even if they had done nothing wrong. When the old leader, Vladimir Lenin, died in 1924, Joseph was in a perfect position to take over.	Mr Gulag *Gulag*
Creative writing	A	Joseph writes amazing stories about himself and how he is a brilliant leader of the Soviet Union. He has taken control of Pravda, the state newspaper, which is calling him "the Man of Steel". Pravda means "truth" but many people think Joseph writes the articles himself and that they are not true.	Ivor Lotstosay
Languages	A	Joseph's performance has been very disappointing. He has not bothered to learn the languages of any of the eastern European countries he's taken control of since World War II. Instead, he expects them to do everything the way the USSR does it.	Mr Getoffski
Economics	A	Joseph is trying out some interesting economic ideas, which he calls Five Year Plans. He has taken land from farmers and forced them to grow their crops on state-run farms to make them more efficient. He calls this "collectivization" but it isn't working and thousands of people are starving to death. He has also forced mills and factories to modernize, which he calls "industrialization". This has been so successful that the USSR got richer while other countries suffered from the Great Depression.	Mr Lubianka
Sports	A	Joseph has excelled at war games. First he made a pact with Germany, which gave him time to build up his armed forces. When Adolf Hitler turned against him and tried to invade, Joseph was able to hold Germany back. Joseph then joined forces with the United States, Britain, and France and helped to win World War II.	Miss Korbutt

I will ~~not~~ bully my class mates, I will ~~not~~ bully my class mates,
I will ~~not~~ bully my class mates, I will ~~not~~ bully my class mates,
I will ~~not~~ bully my class mates, I will ~~not~~ bully my class mates,
~~not~~ bully my class mates, I will ~~not~~ bull my class mates, I will
bully my class mates, I will ~~not~~ bully my class mates, I will ~~not~~
my class mates, I will ~~not~~ bully my class mates, I will ~~not~~
class mates, I will ~~not~~ bull

Student assessment

Name: Joseph Stalin

Class: Working

No. of days absent: 0

No. of days late: 0

ASPECTS ASSESSED	COMMENT
Attitude	Joseph always thinks he is right, and will expel or murder anyone who dares to criticize him.
Behaviour	Joseph's bullying is out of control. From 1936–1938, thousands of people who didn't support him enthusiastically enough disappeared in what became known as the "Great Terror".
Friends	Joseph made friends with US President Franklin D Roosevelt and UK Prime Minister Winston Churchill during World War II, but since then he seems to have fallen out with them.
Team skills	Joseph has united much of central and eastern Europe in a military and economic unit made up of communist states.

Joseph is a disturbing child who has the

potential to become an adult tyrant!

Class teacher

This is Lenin. I call him baldy

That's me, the handsome one!

Trotsky never liked any of my ideas so I had him bumped off!

IRISH REBELLION

Britain had always found Ireland – closest neighbour and first conquest – its hardest colony to control. Intense pressure from Ireland and within Britain towards the end of the 1800s forced Britain to promise sovereignty (self-government) for Ireland in 1914. This was delayed when World War I broke out in Europe, leading to a series of momentous events, as told in these traditional-style ballads.

The Easter Rising
24–30 April 1916

On that Monday, did Dublin wake,
To a mighty big furore,
The Brotherhood, for Ireland's sake,
Rose on April 24. "Self-rule from
Britain's tight grasp!"
Cried the Republican army;
For independence they did gasp,
"Grant Éire Her Sovereignty!"

Patrick Pearse led the rebel stand,
A trained barrister was he.
The law he took into his hands,
Alongside James Connolly.
The team of Irish Volunteers,
With the Citizen Army,
Joined Cumann na mBan in sweat
and tears, in crying
"Grant Éire Her Sovereignty!"

For one whole week, the fighting raged,
The proud streets of Dublin warred.
Britain's troops would not be upstaged,
While that revolution roared.
On both sides gunshots were shared,
For each cause the blood ran free;
the Provisional Government declared,
"Grant Éire Her Sovereignty!"

The fight was lost, a white flag waved,
With rebels forced to disband,
Fifteen brave souls could not be saved,
From Britain's harshest reprimand.
Although they died, their spirit rose
in heroic dignity;
By legal vote, Ireland's people chose to
Grant Éire Her Sovereignty!

The Irish Republican Brotherhood (IRB) was a secret society that wanted Irish independence

"Éire" is the Gaelic Irish name for the island of Ireland

The Women's League, or Cumann na mBan (pronounced "come-on na mon"), was a women-only politcal group

Patrick Pearse announced the Irish Republic and Provisional Government from the steps of Dublin's General Post Office on the first day of the Rising

Fifteen leaders of the Rising – including Patrick Pearse and James Connolly – were executed, shocking many in both Ireland and Britain

Irish War of Independence
1919–1921

Irish rebels Sean Treacy and Dan Breen fired the first shots of the war

In 1919, war was sparked in
County Tipperary,
When Treacy and Breen fired at the
Royal Irish Constabulary.
Against the British Crown
the IRA keenly fought,
An Irish state was what the
Republicans sought.

The Royal Irish Constabulary was the police force in Ireland. It was controlled by the British

The Irish Republican Army (IRA) was the main rebel group during the War of Independence

For ten thousand pounds, the British
government wished one man dead,
This large bounty was placed on Irish
leader Michael Collins' head.
Two years of civil unrest ended in
a stalemate,
A wary truce was made,
11 July was the date.

Peace Treaty and Partition
1921–1922

After much bloodshed, a treaty was
signed between two fighting lands,
On 6 December of '21,
the Irish and Brits did shake hands.
Twenty-six southern counties became a
Free State on the following year,
Freedom was what the Republicans
sought; it was what they held dear.

In the Emerald Isle's north, six counties
remained under Britain's rule,
'Twas Northern Ireland (also called
"Ulster") – its naming was in dual.
But through partition, a simple solution
was not truly found,
Between Loyalists and Republicans,
the Troubles would resound.

The Irish Free State was the name given to the 26 counties of southern Ireland after independence

Partition meant the dividing of the mostly Protestant six counties in the north of Ireland from the rest of the island

Loyalists are people living on the island of Ireland who wish to be ruled by Britain

Irish Free State and Civil War
1922–1923

The Irish Free State was a dominion,
tethered by a string,
Narrowly passed in Ireland's Dáil,
citizens in great divide.
The treaty raised republican ire,
Éire answered to Britain's king,
The nation soon split in civil war,
terrible passion on each side.

National Army and IRA fought,
they warred across the land;
Cork, Limerick, Kilkenny, Ballina, Sligo,
and Galway.
Ceasefire was called in April '23.
Was this the final stand?
The war was done, amnesty declared.
Yet tensions they would stay.

Dominion status meant Ireland controlled most of its own affairs, but still had the British monarch as head of state

The Dáil (pronounced "dawl") is the name for the main house of Ireland's parliament. It passed the treaty confirming Ireland's dominion status with a slim majority of 64 votes to 57

The "Troubles" is the name given to the political and social problems created by the partition

The pre-independence IRA split to become the National Army of Ireland, which supported the treaty, and a branch of the IRA, which opposed it

Timeline to independence

1914: Home Rule, which promised self-rule for Ireland, is delayed on outbreak of World War I.

1916: Easter Rising breaks out in Dublin and is crushed after six days.

1918: Sinn Féin (which means "we ourselves") sets up an illegal parliament, Dáil Éireann.

1919–1921: Anglo-Irish War between the IRA and Britain.

1921: Anglo-Irish Treaty establishes Irish Free State (1922) as a dominion of Britain. The six counties of Ulster remain under British rule as Northern Ireland.

1922–1923: Irish Civil War breaks out between pro- and anti-treaty fighters. The anti-treaty side loses after a year.

1937: Ireland gains full sovereignty as Éire.

1949: Ireland becomes the Republic of Ireland, and leaves the British Commonwealth.

the ROARING TWENTIES

This was the decade that began with a boom and then went bust. After the hardships of World War I, the years that followed felt like one big party – when people spent their money on music, movies, dancing, and also on illegal booze. The party came to an abrupt end in 1929 with the economic ruin caused by the Wall Street Crash.

Hey there kiddo! What a swell party this is …

GOLDEN AGE

Stars like Charlie Chaplin and Buster Keaton made Hollywood the film capital. This was the golden age of silent movies, but *The Jazz Singer* became the first successful talking picture. It opened with the words "Wait a minute, you ain't heard nothin' yet."

FASHION FLAPPERS

During the 1920s, young women dared to be different. Flappers wore short skirts, bobbed hair, high heels, and make-up. They just wanted to have fun, dancing the night away to the *Charleston*, the *Black Bottom*, and the *Shimmy*.

HIGHER AND HIGHER

As American cities attracted more people, and space became scarce, buildings began to reach upwards in ever more daring designs. The Chrysler Building in New York City, begun in 1928, was the first structure in the world with more than 75 storeys. The top was designed to look like a car ornament.

BAN THE BOOZE

In 1920, the United States went dry. Breweries and bars were forced to close as prohibition outlawed the making and selling of alcohol. Soon "bootleggers" began producing illegal liquor. People began to drink in secret bars, known as speakeasies, because they had to speak through a hole in the back door to be let in.

Barrels of illegal beer were emptied into the sewers during prohibition

Top speed of this Model T car was a hair-curling 72 km/h (45 mph)!

Hand over the money, you dirty rat! Or I'll fill you with holes!

ON THE ROAD

The booming economy meant that people had money to spend, and cars proved a main attraction. Touring holidays became popular, but motorists had to plan carefully as there were long distances between petrol stations and breakdowns were common.

GANGSTERS RULE, OK?

Prohibition meant that bootlegging was big business, and gangsters made a lot of money from running speakeasies and protection rackets. Chicago was the gangster capital, and Al Capone was the big cheese of gangsters. Anyone who got in his way was bumped off.

THE JAZZ AGE

Theatres and speakeasies were always packed with fellas and flappers keen to catch the latest jazz bands. These joints would really jump when stars such as Louis Armstrong or Bessie Smith were playing. People could also listen to jazz at home on the new commercial radio stations.

GREAT DEPRESSION

When Americans woke up on Monday 28 October 1929, they had no idea how quickly the good times would turn to bad. Trouble had been brewing for a while. To get rich quickly, people had invested money in the New York Stock Exchange. On this fateful Monday, stock prices fell rapidly, but when investors tried to sell their shares, they were worthless. The crash caused widespread panic, with banks refusing to lend money and companies going broke. Within a few days the extremely rich were very poor. The day became known as Black Monday.

HUMBLE HOMES

More and more families lost their homes because they couldn't make the mortgage payments. Across the USA, homeless people constructed shelters from whatever materials they could find. These shanty towns were known as "Hoovervilles" after President Herbert Hoover, who refused to give government aid to the poor.

STOCK SHOCK

Businessmen wept in the streets following days of shocking news from the Stock Exchange on Wall Street, New York City. Stocks and shares suffered their steepest ever falls, which meant that thousands of people's fortunes were completely worthless. Newspapers called it the "Wall Street Crash".

DESPERATE FOR DOUGH

By 1930, the situation was getting worse. Thousands of banks and companies went out of business, which meant that millions of Americans no longer had jobs. The financial crisis spread to Europe, and the unemployed were forced to queue for handouts of bread and soup.

PRESIDENTIAL PROMISE

Fresh hope came in 1933 when newly elected President Franklin D Roosevelt spoke reassuringly to the nation on the radio. He called his friendly broadcast a "fireside chat", and told listeners that he understood people's hardships. He promised Americans a "New Deal" to end the Depression.

BACK ON TRACK

By the end of the decade, things were looking up, thanks to Roosevelt's package of ideas for getting the country back to work. As well as giving state aid to the unemployed, his government paid for big building projects, which employed millions of people and created new wealth.

DUST DISASTER

To make matters worse, severe droughts and over-farming caused dust storms to form in the central United States. This "Dust Bowl" led to farmland becoming useless and thousands had to leave their homes to search for work.

The election of a Republican government in Spain in 1936 spurred the Spanish army in Morocco to revolt. Army leader General Francisco Franco emerged as leader of a fascist party, the Falange Española Tradicionalista.

He became dictator of Spain in 1939, after victory in the Spanish Civil War. By keeping Spain neutral during World War II, he was neither defeated nor deposed at the war's end in 1945 like Mussolini and Hitler. He ruled until his death in 1975, when Spain began to move towards democracy.

Benito Mussolini founded the Italian Fascist Party in 1919. The fascists believed in the unity of the Italian people, and adopted the Roman symbol of the fasces — a bundle of sticks that are weak individually, but strong together. Black-shirted fascist squads used intimidation and violence to break the strikes that crippled the country after World War I. The party marched on Rome in 1922, and seized power when the weak government crumbled. Mussolini was declared dictator in 1925, and styled himself Il Duce ("the Duke"). He dragged Italy into World War II in support of Germany, but was executed by Italian communists in 1945.

MUSSOLINI

FRANCO

THE RISE

World War I left Europe poor, disheartened, and anxious about the rise of communism in the USSR. Germany felt humiliated by the Versailles peace treaty, and Italy was angry that it had not gained any territory. Extreme nationalist groups obsessed with traditional values sprung up, determined to champion national identity and combat the threat of communism

Inspired by Mussolini's march on Rome, Adolf Hitler launched an ill-fated attempt to take over Germany in 1923. After failing, he spent a year in prison, writing his manifesto *Mein Kampf* ("My Struggle"). Economic depression brought supporters flocking to his National Socialist German Workers'— or Nazi— Party. Hitler became chancellor of Germany in 1932 and declared himself Führer (meaning "leader") in 1934. He promoted his vision of a racially pure Germany that could only be achieved by purging Germany of Jews, communists, and other groups deemed undesirable. He broke the terms of the Versailles Treaty by joining with Austria and parts of Czechoslovakia in 1938. His invasion of Poland the following year sparked World War II.

Even states that did not fall to fascist dictators harboured fascist groups. One would-be dictator was Oswald Mosley, who set up the British Union of Fascists in 1932. He was impressed with Mussolini's Italy, and set up his own black-shirted group who guarded his rallies and attacked communist and Jewish groups. He was imprisoned during World War II, ending his political career. Elsewhere, leaders who were in power could be sympathetic to fascism without becoming fascist themselves. One was Miklos Horthy in Hungary, who became an ally of Hitler's before World War II, but was ultimately overthrown in 1944 on Hitler's command.

HITLER

MOSLEY

OF FASCISM

Led by charismatic leaders who promised prosperity and national pride, these fascist groups wore smart uniforms, embraced strict discipline, and looked to a society bonded by race. The strong leadership and powerful message were attractive to a disenchanted public and by the time the

SPANISH CIVIL WAR

When the Spanish people lost faith in their king, they voted in a Republican government for a more free and equal society. Instead of making things better, this led to a bitter power struggle between left-wing Republicans and right-wing Nationalists – groups with different ideas of how to run the country. In 1936, military leader General Franco tried to bring down the government by force, triggering a bloody civil war. In 1939, the Republican armies collapsed and Franco became dictator of Spain.

GENERAL FRANCO

In 1934, Francisco Franco became Spain's youngest ever general. When the Republican government suspected that Franco might start a rebellion, they tried to keep him out of the way by sending him to the Canary Islands. But Franco took over the islands and flew to Morocco, where he seized control of the Spanish Army of Africa (Spanish troops garrisoned in Morocco) and invaded Spain.

EL FRENTE POPULAR DE

AL FRENTE POPULAR DE

REPUBLICANS

Socialists and communists from across the western world supported the Republican cause. They formed volunteer groups called International Brigades to join the fight against Franco. One of their main aims was to keep Franco out of Spain's capital, Madrid.

SOVIET TANKS

The Soviet Union assisted the Republican army by providing more than 250 light tanks, as well as tank crews and specialists to train the Republicans in tank warfare. The tanks helped the Republicans win the Battle of Guadalajara in 1937, a victory that stopped the Nationalists from surrounding Madrid.

GERMAN AIR BARRAGE

The Nationalists were helped by the German Luftwaffe (air force). One of the worst atrocities was when the Luftwaffe destroyed the town of Guernica, with the first ever, large-scale air raid aimed at civilians. The Nationalists captured Madrid in 1939, securing victory.

NATIONALISTS

Franco's supporters were known as Nationalists. When Franco's Army of Africa joined forces with Nationalist troops in Spain, they expected to easily overthrow the Republican government. In the end it took three years, even with military support from Germany and Italy.

SPANISH REFUGEES

By October 1937, Nationalist troops had overrun most of northern and western Spain. From the start of the war, women, children, and the elderly from both sides were evacuated from war zones to refugee camps in Europe, Mexico, and the Soviet Union.

WAR IN EUROPE

From the safety of a bomb-proof cellar under central London, staff monitor progress of the war as German planes drone overhead. For more than five years, in these cramped, airless quarters, men and women work round the clock to plot enemy activity on large-scale maps as Hitler's troops invade Poland and begin their ruthless march across Europe. Chiefs of staff from the army, air force, and navy are making decisions that will help the Allies (countries fighting against Axis countries led by Germany) to victory in 1945.

GREAT BRITAIN

FRANCE

During the Battle of the Atlantic, German submarines operating from Norway and France try to sink ships carrying supplies from America.

Germans send secret messages using special machines. Thanks to Polish intelligence, and a captured Enigma machine, codebreakers can read many of the messages.

ABGR DLSL. PNCRQT. WJDKSIR.

AIR RAID. LONDON. TONIGHT.

1. OUTBREAK OF WAR
At precisely 04.26 hours on Friday 1 September 1939, the German air force begins bombing Polish cities, the German navy shells the port of Danzig, and more than a million German troops force their way into Poland. Two days later, Britain and France announce that a state of war exists with Germany.

2. SURPRISE ATTACK
Caught unawares by the speed and surprise of the air and land attack (a tactic known as blitzkrieg), Europe is unable to repel the enemy. Germany invades Denmark, Norway, Holland, Belgium, Luxembourg, and France. In May 1940, more than 340,000 Allied soldiers are rescued from the French beaches of Dunkirk. On 22 June, France surrenders.

3. LIVING WITH THE ENEMY
German soldiers occupy the countries they have invaded. Across Europe, resistance groups are willing to risk their lives to bring down the enemy. The French Resistance supplies the Allies with vital intelligence reports as well as undertaking dangerous missions to disrupt German supply and communication lines within France.

In 1941, the USA joins the war. From a converted broom cupboard, British Prime Minister Winston Churchill has secret talks with US President Franklin D Roosevelt.

1

3

5

6

4 ATLANTIC LOSSES
To gain total control of Europe, Hitler needs Britain. To conquer Britain he launches a bombing campaign on towns and cities, but British defences hold firm and Hitler abandons his plans. Instead, he tries to starve Britain into submission by attacking supply ships that are bringing food and weapons from America.

5 STALINGRAD
At the start of the war, Germany and USSR are allies, but in 1941 Hitler invades the USSR. At first, his blitzkrieg method works, but then the Soviet Red Army and the freezing Russian winter prevents the advance. After Soviet victories at Stalingrad and Kursk in 1943, the Germans are driven out.

6 D–DAY LANDINGS
Just after midnight on 6 June 1944, with a full moon and the right tides, 150,000 Allied troops cross the English Channel, and land on the beaches of northern France, and begin liberating the occupied countries of western Europe. Soviet troops attack from the east and, by May 1945, Germany is forced to surrender.

WAR IN THE PACIFIC

When Japan launched an attack on the USA in 1941, the war already raging in Europe turned overnight into a global conflict. Japan and the USA are separated by the Pacific Ocean, which turned into a vast theatre of war including many countries and countless islands of strategic importance. During the war for control of the Pacific, thousands of planes were shot down and more warships were sunk than in all the other sea battles of the 20th century combined.

❶ JAPAN EXPANDS

In the past, Japan had fought both China and the USSR for control of disputed territories. To continue expanding its Pacific empire, Japan first had to battle with the US navy. Although US President Roosevelt appealed to Japan to avoid war, he was ignored.

❷ PEARL HARBOR

Without any warning, Japanese torpedo planes attacked the US fleet in Pearl Harbor, Hawaii, on 7 December 1941. The two-hour raid killed 2,403 people and damaged or destroyed 18 ships and 292 planes. The US entered the war the following day.

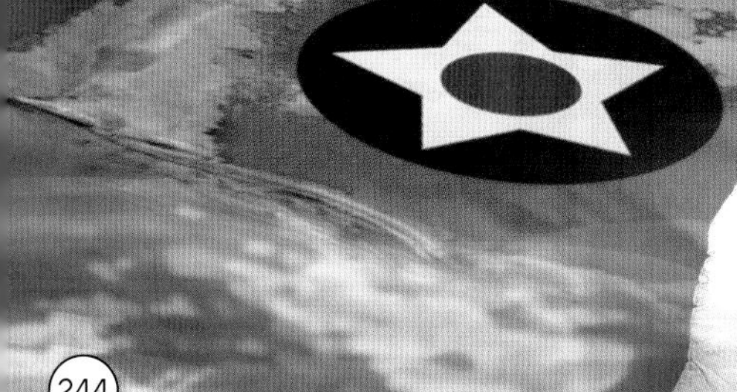

❸ BATTLE OF CORAL SEA

It seemed impossible to halt Japan until the US discovered their secret plans in 1942. This allowed them to lay in wait for Japan's attack in the Coral Sea. Although two US aircraft carriers were sunk, Japan's invasion of New Guinea was scuppered.

❹ BATTLE OF MIDWAY

A month later, Japan tried to destroy the US fleet by attacking in two places at once, hoping to trick the US into dividing, and weakening, its strength. But the US was prepared for the attack and destroyed four Japanese aircraft carriers. At last, the US was winning the battle for control of the Pacific.

❺ LEYTE GULF

After Midway, the US slowly regained control of the Pacific and started taking back Japanese-occupied territory. In 1944, US forces landed at Leyte in the Philippines. They wiped out Japanese forces in the biggest ever naval battle.

❻ IWO JIMA

The US desperately needed an island they could use as an airfield to launch an air offensive on Japan. It took 36 days and cost 5,931 lives to capture and secure Iwo Jima, a volcanic island south of Tokyo. The island was then used to support air raids on 66 Japanese cities.

❼ ATOM BOMBS

When Japan refused to surrender, the US unleashed the awesome power of a new weapon – the atom bomb. The cities of Hiroshima and Nagasaki were vaporized, killing 198,222 people outright. Japan's Emperor Hirohito surrendered on 2 September 1945.

JAPAN SURRENDERS

THE HOLOCAUST

IN 1933, JUST THREE MONTHS AFTER COMING TO POWER IN GERMANY, ADOLF HITLER'S NAZI PARTY PASSED THE FIRST OF 400 ANTI-JEWISH LAWS. A CLIMATE OF FEAR DEVELOPED AS JEWS WERE SACKED FROM THEIR JOBS AND SIDELINED FROM SOCIETY. EVEN CHILDREN STOPPED PLAYING WITH THEIR JEWISH FRIENDS.

AS YOU KNOW, THIS PASSOVER MEAL IS A CELEBRATION OF OUR JEWISH HERITAGE. BUT I'M SAD TO SAY THAT MANY GERMANS DON'T LIKE JEWS SO LIFE MAY GET HARDER FOR US.

TWO YEARS LATER...

THE NAZIS PASS THE NUREMBERG LAWS. THESE STATE THAT JEWS ARE NOT GERMAN CITIZENS AND CANNOT MARRY GERMANS OR VOTE.

JEWS ARE HUMILIATED AND EVEN FORCED TO SCRUB THE STREETS.

WE'VE DECIDED TO GO AND LIVE WITH YOUR UNCLE AND AUNT IN THE NETHERLANDS.

YOU CAN TAKE THREE FAVOURITE TOYS. WE'LL HAVE TO LEAVE EVERYTHING ELSE BEHIND.

IN AMSTERDAM, JEWS ARE TREATED LIKE EVERYONE ELSE AND THE CHILDREN PLAY HAPPILY WITH THEIR COUSINS.

BACK IN GERMANY, LIFE IS GETTING WORSE. ON 9 NOVEMBER 1938, GERMANS ATTACK JEWISH HOMES, SHOPS, AND SYNAGOGUES. IT IS CALLED *KRISTALLNACHT* – THE NIGHT OF BROKEN GLASS.

... 7,500 SHOPS DESTROYED, 400 SYNAGOGUES IN FLAMES, MORE THAN 90 JEWS KILLED.

MOTHER AND FATHER THANK GOD THEY TOOK THEIR CHILDREN TO AMSTERDAM, WHERE THEY ARE SAFE FROM THE NAZIS.

BUT THEY ARE NOT SAFE FOR LONG. IN MAY 1940, GERMANY INVADES THE NETHERLANDS.

JEWS ARE NO LONGER ALLOWED ON TRAMS...

AND ARE REFUSED ENTRY TO THE CINEMA.

DON'T CRY. ONE DAY THE NAZIS WILL LEAVE.

RUMOURS ABOUND THAT JEWS ARE NOT SAFE. THE FAMILY DECIDE TO HIDE, BUT IT'S TOO LATE...

JEWS? YOU'RE COMING WITH US. PACK YOUR THINGS – JUST ONE SUITCASE EACH.

HUNDREDS OF JEWISH FAMILIES ARE PACKED IN AN AIRLESS TRAIN.

WHEN THE TRAIN ARRIVES AT THE CONCENTRATION CAMP, PEOPLE ARE CONFUSED.

DADDY, I'M REALLY SCARED.

STAY BY ME AND YOU'LL BE SAFE.

SAY GOODBYE TO YOUR DADDY. WOMEN AND GIRLS OVER THERE. NOW!

WHY DO WE ASK THEM TO BRING SUITCASES?

IT MAKES THEM THINK THEY MIGHT BE GOING HOME ONE DAY. HA HA. LITTLE DO THEY KNOW!

GUARDS TAKE THEIR VALUABLES AND CLOTHES AND GIVE THEM CAMP UNIFORMS.

ALL PRISONERS HAVE THEIR HEADS SHAVED...

...AND AN IDENTIFYING NUMBER TATTOOED ON THE OUTSIDE OF THEIR LEFT FOREARM WITH NEEDLE AND INK.

KEEP STILL OR IT WILL HURT MORE. FROM NOW ON YOU HAVE NO NAME AND WILL ANSWER ONLY TO YOUR NUMBER.

PLEASE DRINK A LITTLE OF THIS SOUP. EVEN IF IT IS WATERY AND THERE'S NO BREAD, IT WILL HELP TO KEEP YOUR STRENGTH UP.

MANY THOUSANDS OF PRISONERS STARVE TO DEATH BECAUSE THEY ARE FORCED TO WORK HARD AND ARE NEVER GIVEN ENOUGH FOOD. RATS FEED ON THOSE WHO BECOME TOO WEAK TO MOVE.

PRISONERS WHO ARE UNFIT FOR WORK ARE KILLED IN GAS CHAMBERS AND THE BODIES BURNED OR BURIED IN MASS GRAVES.

IT SAYS "SHOWERS" ON THE DOOR BUT I DON'T BELIEVE IT. ANYONE WHO GOES IN THERE IS NEVER SEEN AGAIN.

THAT NIGHT, THE DAUGHTER HAS A NIGHTMARE ABOUT HER PARENTS GOING TO THE SHOWER BLOCK AND NEVER COMING BACK.

HAVE FAITH AND WE'LL SEE OUR FAMILIES AGAIN ONE DAY.

SHE GOES BACK TO SLEEP AND DREAMS OF HAPPIER DAYS BEFORE HITLER CAME TO POWER.

MY GOD! THEY LOOK LIKE LIVING SKELETONS...

...SOME ARE TOO WEAK EVEN TO WALK.

ARE WE REALLY FREE TO LEAVE? OR IS THIS ANOTHER DREAM?

ON 27 JANUARY 1945, THE SOVIET RED ARMY LIBERATES AUSCHWITZ CONCENTRATION CAMP. THE SOLDIERS CANNOT BELIEVE THE HORROR THEY FIND INSIDE – DEAD BODIES LYING WHERE THEY HAVE FALLEN OR PILED INTO HOLES IN THE GROUND, AND THOUSANDS OF STARVING SURVIVORS DYING AT A RATE OF HUNDREDS EVERY DAY.

AN ESTIMATED 10 MILLION PEOPLE DIED IN CONCENTRATION CAMPS, INCLUDING SIX MILLION JEWS – MORE THAN A THIRD OF EUROPE'S ENTIRE JEWISH POPULATION. ONLY 300,000 JEWS SURVIVED LIFE IN THE CAMPS.

THE COLD WAR

For more than 40 years the world lived with the threat of nuclear war between the capitalist (market-driven) West and communist East. It was called the Cold War, and the threat came from tensions between two superpower nations – the USSR and the USA – and their allies. The stakes were high at each of the Cold War's many flash-points. Both superpowers had enough nuclear weapons to destroy the planet.

NEW ALLIANCES

After World War II the USSR took control of Estonia, Latvia, Lithuania, and the countries referred to as the "Eastern Bloc". Meanwhile, the USA was helping western European countries to rebuild themselves. This East–West divide became official in 1949, when the USA and Western European countries formed the North Atlantic Treaty Organisation (NATO), promising to defend each other in times of attack. In 1955 the USSR united the Eastern Bloc in a similar alliance called the Warsaw Pact.

■ NATO nations		■ Warsaw Pact nations
■ Other US allies		■ Other USSR allies

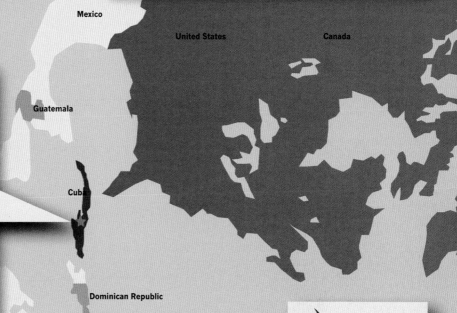

Alaska

Mexico

United States

Canada

Guatemala

Cuba

Dominican Republic

CUBAN MISSILE CRISIS

In 1961, Cuban leader Fidel Castro allowed the USSR to build missile bases on Cuba, within range of the USA. This led to a battle of wills between the USA's new president, John F Kennedy, and the experienced leader of the USSR, Nikita Khrushchev. Kennedy blockaded Cuba and demanded that the sites be dismantled, but Khruschev refused to back down. Nuclear war seemed inevitable. Frantic negotiations took place and finally, crisis was averted when the USSR agreed to dismantle the missiles in exchange for the USA agreeing not to invade Cuba.

John F Kennedy

Nikita Khrushchev

EASTERN BLOC

As World War II ended, the USSR drove the Germans out of Eastern Europe and stationed Soviet troops there. The USSR took control of these Eastern European countries, forming an "Eastern Bloc".

THE CHILL FACTOR

★★★★★
★★★★
★★★
★★
★

1948 Berlin blockade and airlift

1949 Chinese communists win a civil war and take over the country. The following year China forms an alliance with the USSR.

1962 Cuban missile crisis

1964 Vietnam War starts

1959 Cuba becomes a communist state.

1950 Korean War

1945 After WWII Germany is split. Britain, France, and the USA take control of West Germany. The USSR controls East Germany.

1947 The USA promises to help any free country fighting to defend itself against communism, a policy known as "containment".

1952 The US develops a hydrogen bomb, hundreds of times more powerful than the atom bomb. A year later, the USSR develops one, too.

1956 Hungarian Uprising

1961 Communist soldiers erect the Berlin Wall, sealing off communist East Berlin from West Berlin.

KOREAN WAR

In 1950, the USA joined the war to help South Korea fight an invasion by communist North Korea. China sent troops to support North Korea, but US president Harry Truman resisted calls to bomb China, saying: "We are trying to prevent a world war, not start one."

WEAPONS AND TECHNOLOGY

During the Cold War, a range of weapons and technology was adopted by the superpowers.

U2 SPY PLANE

This plane could photograph Soviet territory from twice the height of an airliner. The Soviets shot one down in 1960 and released the pilot in exchange for a captured spy.

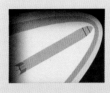

CRUISE MISSILES

These flying bombs can be loaded with nuclear weapons and programmed to find their own way to targets at supersonic speeds.

STAR WARS

The US plan to build a defence shield in space was called Star Wars. The idea was to put laser weapons in orbit to shoot down Soviet missiles fired at the US.

BERLIN BLOCKADE

The USSR tested its strength in 1948 by stopping Westerners reaching Berlin via road or rail. For 11 months British and US planes delivered food, fuel, and supplies to West Berlin until the Soviets lifted the blockade.

BRIEF UPRISINGS

In 1956, the Hungarian public revolted against their Soviet-controlled government. Thousands of people were killed as troops crushed the revolution. An uprising in Czechoslovakia in 1968 met a similar fate.

AFGHAN WAR

In 1979 the communist regime in Afghanistan was overthrown, and the USSR invaded to put the communists back in power. Muslim soldiers called Mujahidin ("holy warriors") fought against the invaders for a decade, until the USSR finally withdrew in 1989.

Japan
South Korea
Korea
China
India
Afghanistan
Pakistan
Iran
North Pole
Denmark
Netherlands
Belgium
West Germany
Austria
France
Switzerland
Yugoslavia
Italy
Albania
Greece
Turkey
Spain

1968 Uprising in Czechoslovakia, known as the "Prague Spring".

1975 Civil war breaks out in Angola. The USA gives arms to the anti-communist factions and Cuba sends troops to fight with the communists.

1983 US President Ronald Reagan calls the USSR "an evil empire", and announces plans to put weapons in space to defend the USA against nuclear attack.

1988–1991 Communist rule in Europe and the USSR collapses completely.

1970 After a 25-year "arms race" to build more nuclear weapons than each other, the USA and USSR start talks to reduce nuclear weapons.

1979 Soviet-Afghan war

1985 Mikhail Gobachev is appointed the Communist Party leader. His reforms lead to the end of the Cold War.

CHINESE REVOLUTION

The son of a wealthy peasant in Hunan province, Mao Zedong rose through the ranks to become one of China's most formidable leaders. Mao first tasted revolution in 1911 as a soldier against the Qing Dynasty. Moving to Beijing in 1919, he joined the May the Fourth Movement, a nationalist group that produced the Chinese Communist Party (CPC). As it grew in popularity, the CPC opposed the Chinese Nationalist Party government. Mao led a famous uprising in Hunan province in 1927, and organized the CPC's Red Army into a ruthless force.

The Long March

China's government set out to stop Mao and his Red Army by surrounding their strongholds. Scattered and threatened, Red Army groups around China set off on a "Long March" to Shaanxi, a communist haven in Hunan where the CPC's second army was based. Mao led his troops from Jiangxi in 1934, forming the main part of the march. The journey of 12,500 km (7,760 miles) took a year. They crossed mountains and deserts on foot, sometimes in sub-zero temperatures. Only a tenth of the number that set out survived. By the end, Mao emerged the undisputed leader.

Warring parties

During World War II, when China was at war with Japan, the communists helped the government. But when Japan surrendered in 1945, the struggle resumed, resulting in civil war. The Red Army took four years to crush the government. As chairman of the CPC, Mao declared the People's Republic of China in 1949.

Great Leap Forward

Immediately, Mao began a ruthless campaign against counter-revolutionaries and intellectuals, killing millions in mass public executions and harsh labour camps. Then, in the hope of revitalizing China, he produced two five-year plans. The first developed heavy industry, particularly steel production. The second, called the "Great Leap Forward", began in 1958. It was supposed to remodel Chinese society and the economy completely, but it was a disaster. People were forced to live in communes, all farmland was owned by the state, and many peasants were made to work in industry. Food production plummeted, causing the worst famine ever. Abroad, China claimed record harvests, but in reality, up to 40 million people starved.

Tough times

Mao was a charismatic and forceful leader who slaughtered anyone who spoke against his regime. This gave him a firm grip on power, despite the extremely difficult lives of the Chinese people. Living in poverty and needing permission to marry or move, the entire population suffered extraordinary hardships. However, speaking out meant exile to a labour camp or execution. Millions were desperate and suicide was rife.

Cultural Revolution

By 1966, Mao feared he was losing his grip on power, so he launched a "Cultural Revolution", intended to annihilate "bourgeois" opposition to communism. Keen to destroy the intellectual classes, Mao ordered all cultural objects to be destroyed and schools to be closed. Most party officials and educated people were sent away to be "re-educated". Forced to work in factories and fields, many of them died. Military gangs of young people loyal to Mao, known as Red Guards, beat and killed any suspected opponents of communism. These young guards had grown up with the cult of Mao and been exposed to political art that idolized him. In a panic, people accused each other of being counter-revolutionaries in the hope of escaping the terrifying Red Guards.

Death of a dictator

Mao declared an end to the Cultural Revolution in 1969. His health declined, and the CPC began to prepare for the power struggle that would follow his death. When he died in 1976, change was swift. Though Mao had wanted the Gang of Four (a group of supporters including his wife) to continue his policies, they were all arrested. The communist government introduced new measures to promote economic and social reform, and improve the lives of the Chinese people.

Israel's Changing Map

According to ancient scripture, God promised Palestine to the Jewish people, who were scattered throughout the world. From the 1890s on, the campaign for a Jewish homeland in Palestine – called the Zionist movement – began to gain momentum. However, Palestine is also a holy land to Muslim Arabs, who had lived there for centuries. After World War II, the United Nations (UN) – an international organization set up to promote peace – decided that Arabs and Jews should share the land, but the independent Jewish state of Israel was declared on the 14 May 1948. This infuriated the Arabs, and the tensions between Israel and its Arab neighbours have resulted in Israel's borders being redrawn many times.

FENCED IN

Palestinian Arabs refused to acknowledge Israel's right to exist. In 1964, several Arab groups united to form the Palestine Liberation Organization (PLO) to fight for the return of a Palestinian Arab state. The conflict has raged ever since, and part of Israel's response was to build the "West Bank Barrier" — a controversial security wall more than 645 km (400 miles) long, which has become a powerful symbol of the bloody dispute between the two peoples.

SYRIA

LEBANON

Golan Heights

West Bank

Dead Sea

Syria failed to recapture the Golan Heights in the Yom Kippur War of 1973

The West Bank Barrier encloses the most complicated area of dispute between Israel and Palestine

Israel invaded Lebanon in 1978 and 1982 to drive out the PLO, and again in 2006 while fighting the anti-Israeli militant group Hezbollah

Israel pulled its military forces from the Gaza Strip in 2005, ending nearly four decades of occupation

River Jordan

JORDAN

ISRAEL

EGYPT

Egypt attempted to reclaim the Sinai Peninsula in the Yom Kippur War of 1973, but failed. Israel handed it back to Egypt in 1982

PEACE PROCESS

Efforts have been made by the international community to negotiate peace in this troubled region. The 1978 Camp David Accords (agreements) resulted in a peace treaty between Israel and Egypt. The 1993 Oslo Accords led to Israel agreeing to withdraw from some of the occupied territories in return for the PLO rejecting violence against Israel. Despite this progress, tension in the region remains high.

1947: LAND CARVE UP

The UN decided to give more than half the land in Palestine to the Jews and much less to the Muslim Arabs. The Arabs argued that far more Arabs than Jews lived in Palestine, and therefore they should have a bigger share of the land. However, the decision was made, and the border stayed put.

1949: THE ARAB-ISRAELI WAR

Almost as soon as Israel was created it was invaded by the Arab countries of Egypt, Syria, Transjordan (later called Jordan), Lebanon, and Iraq. The Israeli army drove out the invaders and took control of more land than Israel had been given by the UN. Tens of thousands of Arabs were forced off their land.

1967: THE SIX DAY WAR

In June 1967, Arab forces began massing on Israel's borders. Rather than waiting to be invaded, Israel struck first and, in just six days, gained control of the Golan Heights, the Sinai Peninsula, and the remaining Palestinian territories of the West Bank and Gaza Strip. Israel later gave Sinai back, and withdrew from the Gaza Strip, but the other areas have been known ever since as the "occupied territories".

255

INDEPENDENT INDIA

At independence, north-west India became the Muslim state of Pakistan, which means "Pure Nation".

As night fell on 14 August 1947, people across the British colony of India waited with growing excitement for the most important moment in their history. At the stroke of midnight, the eerie sound of a man blowing into a conch shell signalled that India was free after more than 150 years of British rule. However, for millions of people the period was tainted by violence that broke out due to religious differences between Hindus, Muslims, and Sikhs.

Rising tensions

Many Indians resented British rule in their country, and in 1885 the Indian National Congress (INC) was formed to promote their rights and to campaign for independence. The INC was mainly Hindu, so in 1906 Muslim nationalists formed their own group called the Muslim League.

Gandhi rejected British-made clothes and urged INC members to make their own by spinning cotton.

Great soul

Mohandas Gandhi became a respected spiritual and political leader by advising nationalists to campaign for independence without using violence. To achieve this, his followers refused to cooperate with the British or to obey their laws, eventually causing the British to listen to the INC's demands. Gandhi's popularity in India gained him the name of "Mahatma", which means "Great Soul".

Pakistan after independence

Since independence, Pakistan has fought three territorial wars with India. The country has also suffered several military coups, in which generals deposed the elected government and seized control. An ongoing peace process with India has greatly reduced the risk of another war between the two.

Pakistan's Muslim faith is reflected in its flag. The crescent moon is a symbol of Islam, the star represents knowledge, and green is a colour sacred to Muslims.

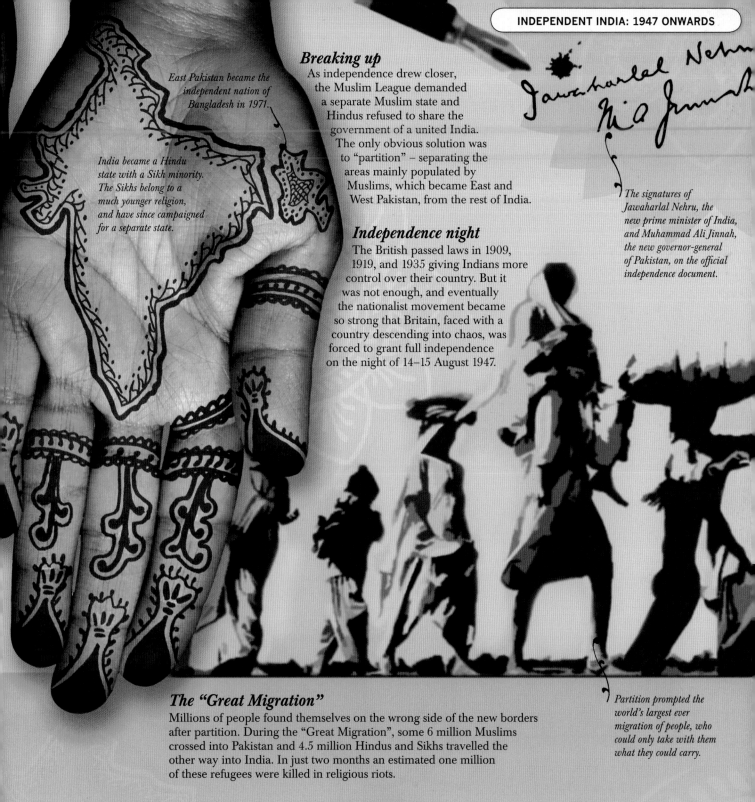

East Pakistan became the independent nation of Bangladesh in 1971.

India became a Hindu state with a Sikh minority. The Sikhs belong to a much younger religion, and have since campaigned for a separate state.

Breaking up

As independence drew closer, the Muslim League demanded a separate Muslim state and Hindus refused to share the government of a united India. The only obvious solution was to "partition" – separating the areas mainly populated by Muslims, which became East and West Pakistan, from the rest of India.

The signatures of Jawaharlal Nehru, the new prime minister of India, and Muhammad Ali Jinnah, the new governor-general of Pakistan, on the official independence document.

Independence night

The British passed laws in 1909, 1919, and 1935 giving Indians more control over their country. But it was not enough, and eventually the nationalist movement became so strong that Britain, faced with a country descending into chaos, was forced to grant full independence on the night of 14–15 August 1947.

The "Great Migration"

Millions of people found themselves on the wrong side of the new borders after partition. During the "Great Migration", some 6 million Muslims crossed into Pakistan and 4.5 million Hindus and Sikhs travelled the other way into India. In just two months an estimated one million of these refugees were killed in religious riots.

Partition prompted the world's largest ever migration of people, who could only take with them what they could carry.

India after independence

India has overcome religious violence and wars against Pakistan and China to become the world's largest democracy. Economic reforms since the 1990s have made it one of the world's fastest-growing economies.

The Indian flag features an ancient symbol of life and virtue called the Ashoka Chakra.

Rwanda's flag

A NEW AFRICA

From the 1950s onwards, the majority of African countries gained independence from their colonial masters. Independence brought new hopes and opportunities for some countries. Other nations had a harder time, with brutal civil wars and corrupt dictators seizing power. Natural disasters, such as drought and floods, also troubled Africa, leading to devastating famines and weakened economies. However, the future is looking up, as African nations begin to achieve economic growth and stability.

TRIBAL BLOODSHED

Rwanda gained independence from Belgium in 1962, but soon violence flared between the nation's two main ethnic groups – Hutu and Tutsi. The worst year of bloodshed came in 1994, when Hutu extremists went on a horrific killing spree that took more than 800,000 lives. Since 2000, the country has enjoyed a period of recovery and stability, reflected in the new Rwandan flag – the green stands for hope, blue for happiness, and yellow for light and prosperity.

Children were used as soldiers in Rwanda's civil wars

TEMPTING TOURISTS

Africa's only constitutional monarchy, Morocco, declared independence from France in 1956. Today, King Mohammed IV oversees the elected parliament. More than 7 million tourists visited in 2007, drawn to see the country's souks (markets), kasbahs (forts), and medieval Islamic architecture.

Money from tourism is a huge boost to Morocco's economy

King Mohammed IV has reigned since 1999

IRON RULE

In 1980, the British colony of Southern Rhodesia began self-rule as the nation of Zimbabwe. President Robert Mugabe established an independent government, but has turned from hero to tyrant over the course of his reign as he refused to let go of power. The country's food production collapsed in 2002, when white farmers were violently evicted from their land. Since 1999, the Movement for Democratic Change has campaigned for a fairer political system.

Robert Mugabe

Maize (corn) production has dropped due to recent bad harvests

FIGHTING FAMINE

Ethiopia managed to elude the European powers for all but a brief period in the 1930s. Famine has plagued the land-locked country since the 1940s, with 1 million Ethiopians starving in 1984. The following year, music lovers worldwide raised £150 million of famine relief through the Live Aid rock concerts, which helped to ease the situation. Ethiopia introduced coffee to the world about 800 CE, and coffee beans are still a successful export.

Coffee beans are the seeds of a cherry-like fruit

Gold mining is central to Ghana's economy

SUCCESS STORY

Since gaining independence from Britain in 1957, Ghana has gone on to be one of the most successful post-colonial African nations. Over the decades, Ghana has built a strong economy based mostly on its mineral wealth in the form of diamonds, gold, and oil.

Diamond mines are located close to Ghana's capital, Accra

Chinese president Hu Jintao shakes hands with Mozambique's president Armando Emílio Guebuza

BRIGHT FUTURE

Portuguese rule ended in Mozambique in 1975. Dangerous landmines spike the country after years of civil war, adding further misery to a country that has also endured natural disasters such as floods and droughts. In 2007, Chinese president Hu Jintao agreed to work with Mozambique to boost tourism, farming, and building projects.

PERIGO MINAS! EMINA!

Landmines are explosive devices buried in the ground

259

TIGER TYCOONS

With its defeat in World War II, and its economy in ruins, the chips were down for Japan. Prevented from building weapons, it turned its attentions to the growing market for consumer goods. Before long, the roar of its tiger economy reverberated around the world and "Made in Japan" was stamped across practically every household item. Singapore, Taiwan, Hong Kong, and South Korea wanted to get their paws on some profits too and followed Japan's economic model – training a skilled workforce to make mass-produced goods for export. Jackpot!

WIN

CRASH!

WIN

WIN

WIN

LOSE

WIN

LOSE

HEAVY METAL

With little to start from and nothing to lose, Japan began to develop its coal and steel industries. Soon, ships and cars rolled off production lines and out into the world. If they failed to sell it would all fall flat – the economic gamble had begun.

POWERING UP

With its eyes on the prize, Japan followed up with a glut of consumer goods – fridges, TVs, computers, cameras, and other electrical goods. Japan's neighbours joined the game from the 1960s – the tigers were beginning to claw their way to a fortune.

TIGER CUBS

As economies boomed, wages in the tiger nations rose, forcing up the price of goods. Nations with lower labour costs, such as Indonesia, Malaysia, Thailand, and Vietnam sold cheaper products, and a new generation of tiger cubs was born.

ENTER THE DRAGON

Communist China looked on from the sidelines with disdain – it believed the tigers were only fuelling expensive Western tastes. It wouldn't play the game until the 2000s, but now it has, its dragon economy is ready to set the world ablaze.

GAME OVER?

An economy built solely on exports is a high-risk strategy. When the world's lust for cars and hi-tech gadgetry wavered, the tiger tycoons crashed. In 1997, it looked as though the game was all over, but smart investment and new products lured the customers back, and the tigers roared again.

CRASH!

RACE TO THE MOON

PREVIOUSLY...

4 OCTOBER 1957: THE SPACE RACE BETWEEN THE USSR AND THE USA IS UNDERWAY. FIRST OFF THE LAUNCH PAD IS RUSSIA'S *SPUTNIK 1*, AN ARTIFICIAL SATELLITE...

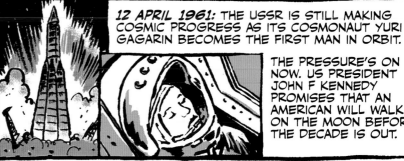

12 APRIL 1961: THE USSR IS STILL MAKING COSMIC PROGRESS AS ITS COSMONAUT YURI GAGARIN BECOMES THE FIRST MAN IN ORBIT.

THE PRESSURE'S ON NOW. US PRESIDENT JOHN F KENNEDY PROMISES THAT AN AMERICAN WILL WALK ON THE MOON BEFORE THE DECADE IS OUT.

16 JULY 1969: THE USA TAKES THE LEAD WITH THE LAUNCH OF THEIR APOLLO 11 MISSION. NO ONE HAS EVER SET FOOT ON THE MOON, BUT THE SATURN V ROCKET IS CARRYING THREE AMBITIOUS APOLLO ASTRONAUTS READY TO DO JUST THAT. *LET THE COUNTDOWN BEGIN...*

WE HAVE LIFT OFF – WHOOSH!

THE *APOLLO 11* CRAFT IS MADE OF THREE PARTS – THE LUNAR, COMMAND, AND SERVICE MODULES. NEIL ARMSTRONG, EDWIN "BUZZ" ALDRIN, AND MICHAEL COLLINS SIT INSIDE *COLUMBIA*, THE COMMAND MODULE, AT THE APEX OF THE HIGH-FLYING ROCKET.

PHOOMPH! WHIZZING INTO ORBIT AT TOP SPEED, THE ROCKET'S ENGINE BURNS HARD, PUSHING ITS PRECIOUS CARGO TO ITS FINAL DESTINATION.

ALREADY ATTACHED TO THE SERVICE MODULE OF SUPPORT SYSTEMS, *COLUMBIA* AND THE LUNAR MODULE, *EAGLE*, SEPARATE FROM THE ROCKET. *KA-BOOM!*

THE 384,400-KM (238,900-MILE) JOURNEY TO THE MOON TAKES A WHOPPING THREE DAYS. ON BOARD *COLUMBIA*, THE TRIO EAT AND SLEEP.

ON 20 JULY 1969, THINGS HEAT UP! *EAGLE* SEPARATES FROM *COLUMBIA* AND BEGINS ITS DESCENT TO THE LUNAR SUFACE. COLLINS STAYS BEHIND IN *COLUMBIA* AS THE COMMUNICATIONS LINK.

COLLINS IS A LUNAR LONE RANGER, OUT OF CONTACT WITH EARTH WHILE *COLUMBIA* ORBITS THE FAR SIDE OF THE MOON. HE IS ONLY THE SECOND ASTRONAUT TO BE THIS FAR FROM THE REST OF HUMANITY! THE FIRST WAS JOHN YOUNG ON THE APOLLO 10 MISSION IN MAY.

EEEEK! PANIC STATIONS IN THE FINAL DESCENT, AS ARMSTRONG AND ALDRIN REALIZE THAT *EAGLE* IS GOING TO MISS ITS TARGET. SYSTEMS ARE ON *HIGH ALERT!* THE NAVIGATION COMPUTER MUST SELECT A NEW LANDING POSITION...

... *BIG MISTAKE!* THE SITE TURNS OUT TO BE A CRAGGY CRATER.

ARMSTRONG MUST TAKE MANUAL CONTROL AND GUIDE *EAGLE* TO A SAFE LANDING SPOT...

BRAAM! BRAAM! THE LOW-FUEL ALARM SOUNDS! ARMSTRONG AND ALDRIN MUST HOPE THEY HAVE ENOUGH FUEL LEFT TO LAND SAFELY.

PHEW! FALSE ALARM. IT TURNS OUT THAT THE LOW LUNAR GRAVITY HAS AFFECTED SENSORS IN THE FUEL TANK – THIS CAN BE FIXED FOR LATER MISSIONS.

A *CLOSE ONE!* *EAGLE* LANDS SAFELY, WITH ONLY *30 SECONDS* OF SPARE FUEL.

ARMSTRONG CALLS HOME.

"HOUSTON, TRANQUILITY BASE HERE, *THE EAGLE HAS LANDED.*"

SIX HOURS AFTER LANDING, ARMSTRONG EXITS *EAGLE* AND BEGINS HIS *MOONWALK.*

"THAT'S ONE SMALL STEP FOR MAN, *ONE GIANT LEAP FOR MANKIND.*"

SOON AFTER, BUZZ ALDRIN IS OVER THE MOON TO JOIN ARMSTRONG...

"BEAUTIFUL! MAGNIFICENT DESOLATION."

TA-DAH! WATCHED BY THE WORLD, NEIL ARMSTRONG AND BUZZ ALDRIN MAKE HISTORY AS THE FIRST HUMAN BEINGS TO WALK ON THE MOON.

THE HEROES LEAVE BEHIND AN AMERICAN FLAG AND A PLAQUE THAT READS, "WE CAME IN PEACE FOR ALL MANKIND".

SWINGING SIXTIES

"All you need is love" sang the Beatles in 1967. The words spoke of a decade of change – a time of outrageous fashion, psychedelic art, and music with a message. Instead of doing what they were told, young people challenged all forms of authority and believed that love conquered all. But not everything in the hippy garden was rosy. The world was also rocked by demonstrations against the Vietnam War, the death of a president, and the continuing struggle for civil rights.

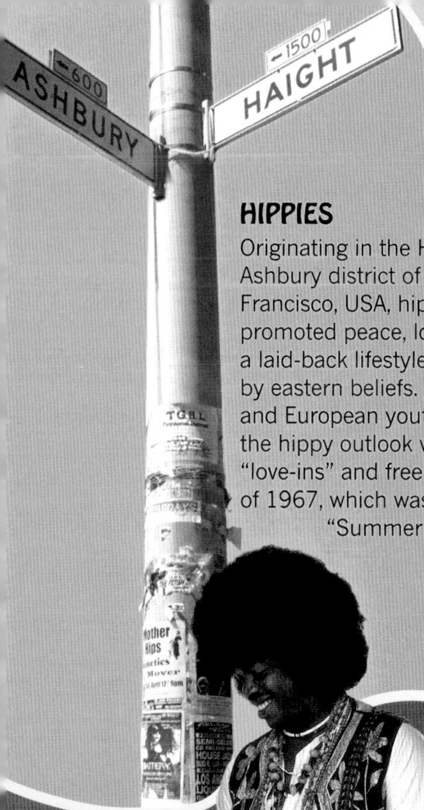

HIPPIES

Originating in the Haight-Ashbury district of San Francisco, USA, hippy culture promoted peace, love, and a laid-back lifestyle inspired by eastern beliefs. American and European youth copied the hippy outlook with the "love-ins" and free festivals of 1967, which was called the "Summer of Love".

....Or you'll sink like a stone...For the times...

Folk singer Bob Dylan was a musical icon

Hippy fashion included beads and embroidered clothes

GIVE PEACE A CHANCE

During the early '60s, the Campaign for Nuclear Disarmament (CND) protested against nuclear weapons. Later, the focus shifted to mass demonstrations against the Vietnam War.

TICKET TO RIDE

For the first time, young people had spare cash, and they were able to buy cars, motorbikes, and scooters, and take advantage of cheaper air tickets. In the UK, the scooter was the mode of transport favoured by gangs known as Mods. They travelled to coastal resorts to battle with motorbike-riding Rockers.

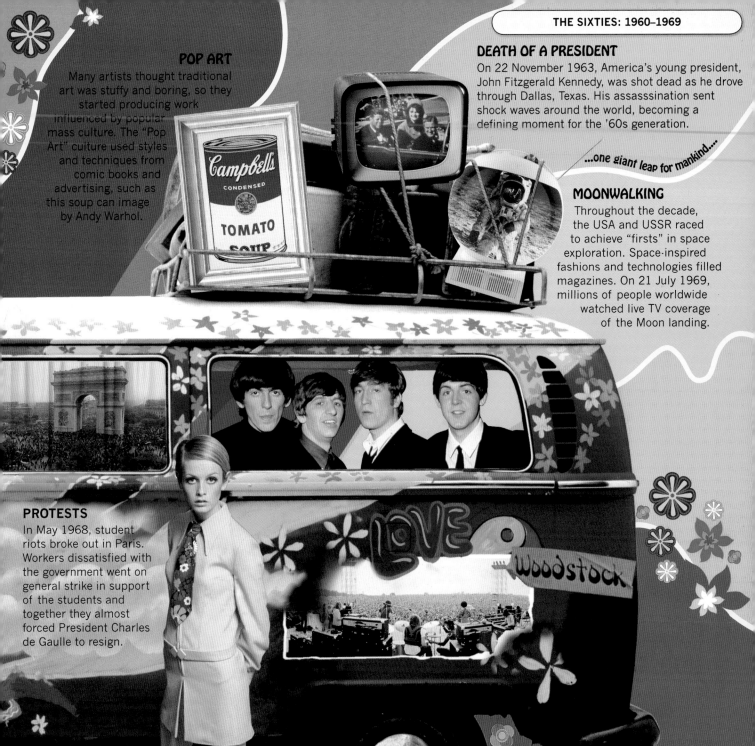

POP ART
Many artists thought traditional art was stuffy and boring, so they started producing work influenced by popular mass culture. The "Pop Art" culture used styles and techniques from comic books and advertising, such as this soup can image by Andy Warhol.

DEATH OF A PRESIDENT
On 22 November 1963, America's young president, John Fitzgerald Kennedy, was shot dead as he drove through Dallas, Texas. His assasssination sent shock waves around the world, becoming a defining moment for the '60s generation.

...one giant leap for mankind....

MOONWALKING
Throughout the decade, the USA and USSR raced to achieve "firsts" in space exploration. Space-inspired fashions and technologies filled magazines. On 21 July 1969, millions of people worldwide watched live TV coverage of the Moon landing.

PROTESTS
In May 1968, student riots broke out in Paris. Workers dissatisfied with the government went on general strike in support of the students and together they almost forced President Charles de Gaulle to resign.

FOLLOWER OF FASHION
The way people dressed in the '60s reflected their rebellious attitudes. Mini-skirts, tie-dyed shirts, Afghan coats, and flared trousers were all the rage, with long hair for both men and women. The hub of the fashion world was Carnaby Street in London, which *Time* magazine called the "Swinging City".

Twiggy was the world's first supermodel

FAB FOUR
The Beatles were so popular that they were mobbed by screaming girls wherever they went – a phenomenon called "Beatlemania". In 1969, about half a million young people attended the world's first pop festival, dancing in the mud in Woodstock, New York State.

Civil rights

Black citizens of the southern United States in the 1950s faced daily discrimination and oppression. Most were unable to vote, were forced into the lowest-paid jobs, and even had to use separate public transport and schools to white people. Civil rights groups challenged this inequality through lawsuits, marches, and non-violent protests, determined to achieve full citizenship rights.

KEEP OUT!
By state law, black Americans had to use separate areas of public facilities, including schools, restaurants, public transport, and even drinking fountains. This separation of races was known as segregation.

BUS BOYCOTT
In 1955, Rosa Parks was arrested for refusing to give up her bus seat to a white person. In protest, black people stopped using buses for more than a year. Loss of money forced the bus company to change its rules.

REAR WINDOW
ALFRED HITCHCOCK

DINER

B3 | Cleveland Avenue

NO BLACKS ON BUSES

WHITES ONLY

LITTLE ROCK RIOTS

A national court granted black children access to the same schools as white. In 1957, riots erupted when black children tried to enter Central High School in Little Rock, Arkansas, and paratroopers were deployed to protect the students.

SIT INS

In 1960, four black students ordered coffee at a whites-only food counter. When asked to leave, they refused. This non-violent protest was called a "sit-in" and inspired other "sit-ins" across the south.

FREEDOM RIDERS

Civil rights protestors organized "freedom rides" to test a court ruling ending segregation on interstate buses. Many freedom riders were attacked and beaten, but public support forced bus companies to relent.

MARCH ON WASHINGTON

In 1963, thousands of people marched through Washington, DC, calling on the government to pass civil rights laws. Martin Luther King, Jr addressed the crowd saying "I have a dream…". His dream was for black people to be treated fairly.

RIGHT TO VOTE

In 1965, demonstrators headed to the state capital of Alabama to protest that black people still could not vote. Police stopped the march, but the bad publicity forced the president to agree a new law enforcing equal voting rights.

CASSIUS CLAY

World-famous boxer Cassius Clay (later Muhammad Ali) won a gold medal at the 1960 Olympics, but threw it into a river when he was chased out of a whites-only café. At the 1996 Olympics, he lit the flame and was awarded a new gold medal.

VIETNAM WAR

Fearing that communism could spread across Asia, the USA began to support South Vietnam in its war against the Viet Cong communists, who were backed by North Vietnam. Pitting US military might against the underground tactics of the Viet Cong proved an almost impossible task. The war dragged on, devastating Vietnam and leading to international outrage at the massive loss of life on all sides.

1968: TET OFFENSIVE

US generals claimed they were winning the war, but in 1968 the communists launched the Tet Offensive – an all-out assault in which they captured many South Vietnamese towns and cities. The US eventually drove the communists out, but the success of the Tet Offensive strengthened US public opinion against the war.

1964: GULF OF TONKIN

Three North Vietnamese torpedo boats attacked USS *Maddox* in the Gulf of Tonkin. After a second attack, the US Congress gave President Johnson permission to use deadly force against the communists. The US was now officially at war.

MAYDAY...MAYDAY...THIS IS USS MADDOX REQUESTING AIR SUPPORT

This heat is killing me!

Air vents concealed by vegetation

Underwater entrance

Viet Cong soldiers and their families could stay underground for months at a time – some even got married there

The tunnels stretched for 250 km (155 miles)

Hospital
First-aid stations were located in the tunnels, and some areas even had operating theatres.

1965: ROLLING THUNDER

The US carried out an aerial bombing campaign called Operation Rolling Thunder. The bombs contained toxins to kill the vegetation concealing hiding places in the jungle. The US also sent out "search and destroy" missions to pick off small groups of the Viet Cong, but the communists were better at jungle warfare.

Hidden trapdoor leading to other parts of the tunnel system

Weapon store

ALPHA-BRAVO ARE YOU RECEIVING? THESE CHOPPERS ARE JUST PERFECT FOR JUNGLE WARFARE! OVER

DELTA-BRAVO RECEIVING LOUD AND CLEAR. ROGER THAT – WHEN IT'S OVER I BET THEY'LL CALL IT THE "HELICOPTER WAR"

1973: US PULL OUT

Following the Tet Offensive, the US government began peace talks with the Viet Cong. US troops pulled out five years later after the peace deal was signed. South Vietnam remained under threat from the North, and peace remained fragile.

platoon halt!

Defence post

As many as 10,000 people lived in the tunnels

Oh no! Not rice again...

Kitchen
Smoke from stoves was diverted by tunnel to areas far away from the main compound to fool US soldiers.

Can you hear choppers?

Air-raid shelter
Cone-shaped bomb shelters were sturdy and also amplified the sound of helicopters above.

With the US gone, we can take Saigon whenever we want

LIFE UNDERGROUND

The Viet Cong built an intricate network of tunnels. By using hidden entrances, they could quickly appear, attack, and then disappear back underground. Weapon factories, kitchens, dormitories, and makeshift hospitals enabled the soldiers and their families to survive.

Some of the tunnels were 18 m (60 ft) deep

1975: THE FALL OF SAIGON

Two years after US troops pulled out, the communists attacked South Vietnam again. This time, the US decided not to get involved, as the earlier war had proved dangerous, costly, and unpopular. On 30 April 1975, the North Vietnamese took over the South Vietnamese capital, Saigon. The war ended with a communist victory – the very thing the US had fought so long and hard to prevent.

Meeting room
All military decisions were made deep in the tunnel complex in meeting and conference rooms.

BLACK GOLD

A dark, sticky liquid formed deep underground has become the most sought-after, multi-tasking natural resource of modern times. Oil powers cars and planes, is used to heat homes, and can be manufactured into plastics. No wonder it is nicknamed "black gold". The global demand for oil means countries with large oil reserves benefit from booming economies and increased political power. Nowhere is this more evident than in the Middle East.

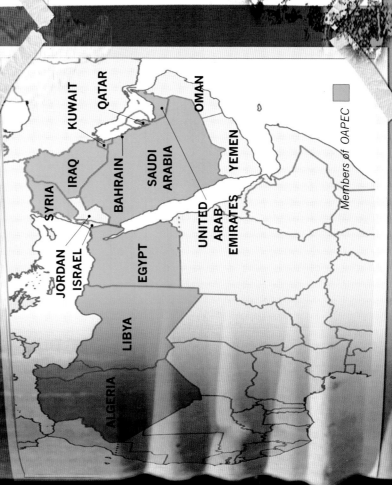

SLICKER CITIES

In the 1970s, the mining of oil and natural gas transformed the United Arab Emirates into a wealthy state. As the fastest-growing city on Earth, its capital, Dubai, is filled with luxury hotels and impressive skyscrapers. By comparison, Yemen is the poorest country in the Middle East. Although a small amount of oil was discovered in 1984, Yemen's oil reserves are expected to run out in the next decade.

NATIONS UNITE

Oil was first discovered in the Middle East in 1908 in Persia (now Iran). Oil companies rapidly moved into the region and soon oil wells dotted the landscape. In 1968, the Middle East's oil-producing nations set up an organization to discuss issues important to their industry and to ensure economic stability within the region. OAPEC (Organization of Arab Petroleum Exporting Countries) soon flexed its economic muscles on a global scale.

■ *Members of OAPEC*

SYRIA
JORDAN
ISRAEL
IRAQ
KUWAIT
QATAR
BAHRAIN
SAUDI ARABIA
UNITED ARAB EMIRATES
OMAN
YEMEN
EGYPT
LIBYA
ALGERIA

OIL CRISIS

In October 1973, OAPEC banned oil shipments to Western nations believing that they unfairly supported Israel during the Yom Kippur War (a conflict between Israel, Syria, and Egypt). By the next year, the global price of oil had soared by 400 per cent and petrol shortages led to many countries restricting car use. Some people resorted to more traditional horse power to get around.

BONANZA TO BUST

If the 1970s were an oil famine, then the 1980s were a feast. The overproduction of crude oil led to an excess on the market. With too much oil for sale, the price of barrels dropped by almost 60 per cent. From the 1990s, concern grew about oil supplies running out. The price of oil continues to rise steadily as scientists seek to discover alternative fuel supplies.

ALL FIRED UP

When Iraq invaded Kuwait to take control of the country's oil fields, a United States-led force of 34 nations sought to liberate Kuwait. On 17 January 1991, the allied countries launched the air offensive Operation Desert Storm. Iraq was bombed until President Saddam Hussein withdrew his troops from Kuwait on 26 February 1991. As the troops retreated, they set the country's oil wells alight.

Islamic Revolution

For years Britain and Russia tussled for control of the oil-rich country of Persia. Revolution at home forced Russia to withdraw, leaving the spoils to Britain. To keep a firm hold on Persia, Britain backed pro-West army general Reza Khan when he seized the throne to become shah (king). Reza Shah set about modernizing the country along Western lines. He renamed it Iran, replaced the Islamic curriculum in education, and discouraged Muslim practice. The seeds of discontent were sown...

1. Rising son

Reza Shah grew weary of British influence in Iran, so threw in his lot with Germany during World War II. But this decision cost him his job when British and Soviet troops invaded in 1941, forcing him into exile. His son, Mohammed Reza, rose to become the new shah. Under Mohammed Reza Shah, Islam was pushed further to the margins of Iranian society, but the population remained deeply religious.

2. Oil fight

Anti-Western feelings ran high in Iran and, in 1951, Mohammed Reza Shah was forced to share power with a radical nationalist prime minister, Mohammed Mossadeq. To the anger of the West, Mossadeq took charge of the country's oil reserves. Western nations responded by blocking Iranian oil sales, causing an economic crisis in Iran.

3. Rich and poor

In 1953, Britain and the US intervened again in Iran, overthrowing Mossadeq and returning Mohammed Reza Shah to full power. The Shah acted like a dictator and his lifestyle became increasingly extravagant, underlining the growing divide between rich and poor. The Shahyad Tower, built to celebrate the 2,500th anniversary of Iran's monarchy, became a symbol of decadence and injustice for many.

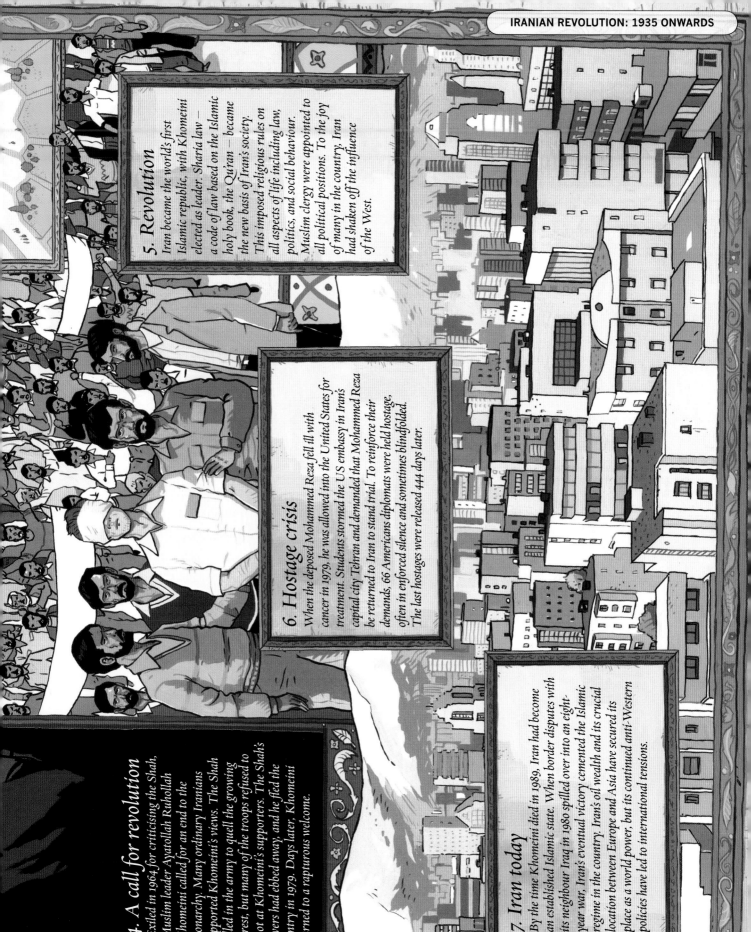

5. Revolution

Iran became the world's first Islamic republic, with Khomeini elected as leader. Sharia law — a code of law based on the Islamic holy book, the Quran — became the new basis of Iran's society. This imposed religious rules on all aspects of life including law, politics, and social behaviour. Muslim clergy were appointed to all political positions. To the joy of many in the country, Iran had shaken off the influence of the West.

6. Hostage crisis

When the deposed Mohammed Reza fell ill with cancer in 1979, he was allowed into the United States for treatment. Students stormed the US embassy in Iran's capital city Tehran and demanded that Mohammed Reza be returned to Iran to stand trial. To reinforce their demands, 66 Americans diplomats were held hostage, often in enforced silence and sometimes blindfolded. The last hostages were released 444 days later.

7. Iran today

By the time Khomeini died in 1989, Iran had become an established Islamic state. When border disputes with its neighbour Iraq in 1980 spilled over into an eight-year war, Iran's eventual victory cemented the Islamic regime in the country. Iran's oil wealth and its crucial location between Europe and Asia have secured its place as a world power, but its continued anti-Western policies have led to international tensions.

4. A call for revolution

Exiled in 1964 for criticising the Shah, Muslim leader Ayatollah Ruhollah Khomeini called for an end to the monarchy. Many ordinary Iranians supported Khomeini's views. The Shah called in the army to quell the growing unrest, but many of the troops refused to shoot at Khomeini's supporters. The Shah's powers had ebbed away, and he fled the country in 1979. Days later, Khomeini returned to a rapturous welcome.

273

EUROPE DIVIDED

After World War II, many of the countries of eastern Europe came under Soviet control. Germany was split into communist East and capitalist West. The city of Berlin, which was in East Germany, was also divided. In 1961 a wall was erected, splitting the city in two.

Following reforms made by Gorbachev (left), the Soviet Union collapsed in 1991. Yeltsin (right) became president of the new Confederation of Independent States.

School project, summer term 1991:
THE FALL OF COMMUNISM

THE GREAT ESCAPE

Another example of the East Germans' desire to escape the restrictions of a communist regime emerged last night with the news of another dramatic escape. The first underground tunnel to West Berlin was discovered accidentally by a mourner in a city graveyard. The theory is that the escapees pretended to mourn by a grave, before dropping into the tunnel and out of sight. This is the latest in a long line of escape attempts, as a result of the Berlin Wall's construction in 1961. Built to divide the part of the city controlled by communist East Germany from the part controlled by West Germany, the Wall is guarded by tanks. At first, people tried to climb the Wall to reach the West, but many were shot. Escape plans are becoming increasingly elaborate as the situation in East Germany worsens. More restrictions are in place, and those who complain are arrested.

This is a newspaper cutting from the West

GORBACHEV VISITS EAST GERMANY

The beginning of the end of communism came when Mikhail Gorbachev became head of the Soviet Union in 1985. A committed reformer, he visited East Germany in 1989 to urge the government to make changes. After his visit, millions attended pro-democracy rallies, the government fell, and the new regime granted East Germans freedom of movement across the borders.

RAISING THE IRON CURTAIN

Like a house of cards, communism began to collapse across eastern Europe in 1989. Hungary opened its borders, raising the symbolic 'Iron Curtain' that divided the continent. Hungary approved a new constitution, creating an independent, democratic state. The first multi-party elections took place in 1990. Changes also took place in Poland, the first Soviet bloc country since 1945 to elect a non-communist leader.

This banner shows support for the Polish Solidarity movement, a trade union that campaigned for democracy during the 1980s.

VELVET REVOLUTION

The communist regime in Czechoslovakia collapsed peacefully in November 1989. This followed the famous "Velvet Revolution", in which thousands of students staged peaceful, non-violent demonstrations. At the same time, Bulgaria's communist regime was also brought to a peaceful end.

A Czechoslovakian tram driver gives the peace sign during the Velvet Revolution of 1989. The poster shows the future president, Václav Havel.

A month later, the regime in Romania was violently toppled. Across Europe, people celebrated the end of communism. With the restrictions lifted, they could make choices and travel freely.

The name Trabant means "fellow traveller"

Nicknamed the Trabi, the Trabant car had been the only option for eastern Europeans. The plastic-body car could reach a top speed of only 100 km/h (62 mph). No longer manufactured, the Trabi is now a collector's item for car enthusiasts.

CHANGE IN EAST GERMANY

With the new freedom of movement, Western influences soon made an impact on the lives of East Germans in the range of consumer products available. Media restrictions were also lifted, giving people a wider view on world news.

BERLIN AFTER THE FALL

The demolition of the Berlin Wall led to the reunification of Germany on 3 October 1990. Once known for its Wall, Berlin is no longer a divided city. West Berliners do not need passports and visas to visit family members in the east of the city, and East Berliners can explore neighbouring streets for the first time.

Revellers at the Berlin Wall look forward to a unified Germany

THE END OF APARTHEID

Apartheid was the name given to the South African legal system that took away civil rights from anyone who was not white. For more than 40 years, black South Africans fought this discrimination, and many nations refused to trade or participate in sporting events with South Africa. The most famous protest leader was Nelson Mandela, who spent 27 years in prison before going on to become the first black president of a multi-racial, democratic South Africa in 1994.

A LIFELONG STRUGGLE

Nelson Mandela became a symbol of resistance to apartheid. As leader of the African National Congress (ANC) military wing, he battled to bring all Africans together as one people. After the ANC began sabotaging industrial and economic targets, Mandela was sentenced to life imprisonment. This is the speech he gave from the court in 1964...

THE DIVISIONAL COUNCIL OF THE CAPE
WHITE AREA
BY ORDER SECRETARY

DIE AFDELINGSRAAD VAN DIE KAAP

BLANKE GEBIED
OP LAS. SEKRETARIS.

WHITES ONLY

First introduced in 1948, apartheid segregated whites from non-whites in all areas of life. Most South Africans are black, but white people governed the country and made laws forcing non-whites to leave their land and live in separate "townships".

SHARPEVILLE MASSACRE

In 1960, police shot at anti-apartheid demonstrators in Sharpeville township, killing nearly 70 people. The government supported the police and banned all non-white political organizations. Worldwide rallies gave a clear indication of anti-apartheid support.

"DURING MY LIFETIME I HAVE DEDICATED MYSELF TO THIS STRUGGLE OF THE AFRICAN PEOPLE... I HAVE CHERISHED THE IDEAL OF A DEMOCRATIC AND FREE SOCIETY IN WHICH ALL PERSONS LIVE TOGETHER IN HARMONY WITH EQUAL OPPORTUNITIES. IT IS AN IDEAL WHICH I HOPE TO LIVE FOR AND TO ACHIEVE. IF NEEDS BE, IT IS AN IDEAL FOR WHICH I AM PREPARED TO DIE."

CONTINUED VIOLENCE

For decades waves of violence erupted across the country. When F W de Klerk became president of South Africa in 1989, he released Nelson Mandela from jail, repealed all apartheid laws, and announced that everyone over 18 would be allowed to vote.

THE RIGHT TO VOTE

On 27 April 1994, almost 20 million South Africans queued for days to vote in the country's first free elections. The ANC won easily and Mandela became president. As a sign that things had changed, South Africa adopted a new flag and national anthem, and 27 April became a national holiday known as Freedom Day.

ONE WORLD

The Earth seems to be getting smaller – but only because technology brings everything closer. Today, friends on opposite sides of the world can swap emails in seconds, jet across the globe in less than a day, and buy the same clothes from the same shops. This is known as globalization and, while it may be convenient, it also has a down side. The energy spent powering computers, the fuel burned for travel, and the increased production and packaging of consumer goods is affecting the environment.

A LOAD OF RUBBISH

Our wasteful consumer society creates a lot of rubbish. Most of what people throw away is transported to landfill sites where it is buried. But dumping rubbish in the ground releases toxins, and rotting rubbish gives off explosive gases and polluting liquids, which harm our environment.

A CALL FOR HELP

Many people believe that globalization exploits poor countries. Every year, leaders of the world's richest countries gather for the G8 summit meeting to discuss global issues. At the same time, demonstrators target the meetings to demand that rich countries do more to help developing nations.

BIG BRANDS

At one time, companies produced and sold goods on a local level. Today, the world's biggest companies make things wherever it is cheapest and sell them on every continent. Some of these multinational corporations make more money than entire nations, and their brand logos are recognized globally.

POP CULTURE

In the past, people from different countries had their own styles of music, films, and literature. With the advent of the Internet, many of those different ideas and styles have become part of a global culture. Japanese manga comics, for example, are now popular worldwide.

MASS TRAVEL

With 29.6 million flights in 2007, this really is a jet-setting age. Anywhere in the world is less than a day away, and people think nothing of flying to another continent for a business meeting or across the globe for a holiday. Aircraft are polluting gas-guzzlers though, and campaigners warn of the damage they cause.

A CLOSE CALL

New technology means that people and businesses can share information instantly, wherever they are. So, when you phone a helpline to sort out a computer problem, you might talk to someone in a call centre on the other side of the world. They can look at your screen from wherever they are and talk through problems.

THE WAR ON TERROR

NEW YORK CITY
When the first plane hit the North Tower of the World Trade Center, people thought it was an accident. When the second plane hit the South Tower, it was obviously a deliberate attack.

LONDON
On 7 July 2005, four British-born suicide bombers detonated bombs on three underground trains and a bus. The bombs killed 52 people and injured some 700 more. Al-Qaeda claimed responsibility.

MADRID
On 11 March 2004, ten bombs went off in crowded trains and railway stations, killing 191 people and injuring more than 1,700 others. The official verdict is that Al-Qaeda-inspired terrorists were responsible.

GUANTANAMO BAY
Since 2002, the United States has held any suspected terrorists in a detention camp at their naval base in Cuba. The camp detains terrorists flown there from all over the world.

IRAQ
Following claims that Iraq had links with Al-Qaeda and was producing weapons of mass destruction (WMDs), a US-led coalition invaded in March 2003 to overthrow Iraqi dictator Saddam Hussein.

On 11 September 2001, terrorists hijacked four US airliners. They flew two of them into the twin towers of the World Trade Center in New York City and a third into the Pentagon in Washington, DC, killing nearly 3,000 people. The fourth plane crashed into a field in Pennsylvania. Al-Qaeda, the organization responsible, claimed to be fighting a holy war (*jihad*) to end foreign influence in Muslim countries. US president George W Bush vowed to hunt down and eradicate those responsible, and declared a "War on Terror" against any of their supporters.

AFGHANISTAN

Al-Qaeda was known to have training camps in Afghanistan, so a US-led coalition invaded in October 2001. Osama bin Laden was hiding in the mountains, but the allies failed to catch him.

TIMELINE OF EVENTS

1990s: Al-Qaeda recruits Muslims in East Africa. In August 1998, they bomb US embassies in Nairobi, Kenya, and Dar es Salaam, Tanzania.

1993: Al-Qaeda plant a bomb in the car park of the World Trade Center. The bomb kills six and injures more than 1,000 people.

Sep–Oct 2001: In the wake of 9/11 the US announces the "War on Terror". US-led troops invade Afghanistan.

Jan 2002: US President Bush calls Iraq, Iran, and North Korea an "axis of evil". He says he will not permit "the world's most dangerous regimes to threaten us with the world's most dangerous weapons."

2002–2003: The United Nations (UN) requires Iraq to prove it has no weapons of mass destruction.

Feb–Mar 2003: Despite international protests against war in Iraq, US-led forces invade without UN authorization. The invasion code name is Operation Iraqi Freedom.

2003 onwards: Al-Qaeda uses the Western presence in Afghanistan and Iraq to encourage Muslims in Western countries to be more radical.

2003 onwards: The US establishes a counter-terrorist presence in Djibouti, northeast Africa, and attempts to prevent East African states being radicalized by Al-Qaeda.

2008: US president George Bush commits more troops to Iraq in a "surge" that the US hopes will bring the conflict to an end.

DELHI

On 29 October 2005, two days before the Hindu festival of Diwali, three bombs went off in crowded markets, killing 62 people. Investigators blame the Islamic terrorist group Lashkar-e-Toiba.

BALI

On 12 October 2002, terrorist group Jemaah Islamiyah (JI) killed more than 200 people in a Balinese bar and nightclub. Linked to Al-Qaeda, JI is probably responsible for other attacks in Indonesia.

KEY PLAYERS

GEORGE W BUSH

In his address to the nation after the 9/11 attacks, the President undertook to win the War on Terror and "to defend freedom and all that is good in our world."

OSAMA BIN LADEN

Mastermind of the 9/11 attacks, Bin Laden heads the FBI's most wanted list. He co-founded Al-Qaeda in 1988 to wage holy war against Western influence in Islamic affairs.

SADDAM HUSSEIN

Former dictator of Iraq, Saddam was found by US forces in 2003 hiding in a hole in the ground. He was hanged on 30 December 2006 for crimes against humanity.

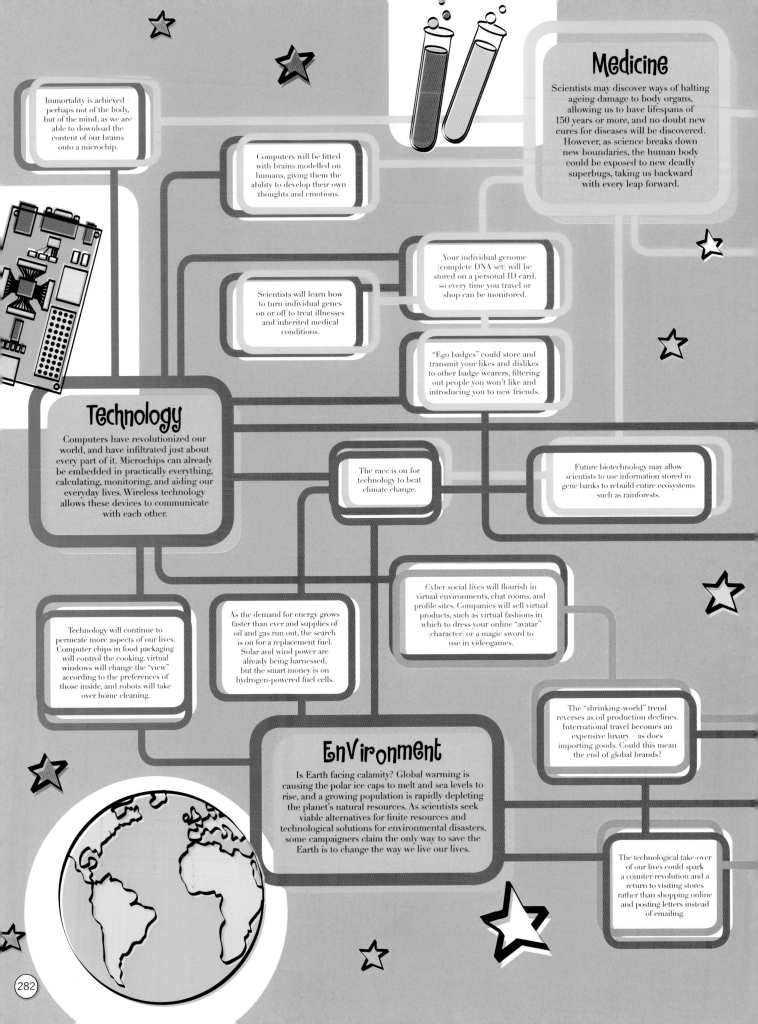

Medicine

Scientists may discover ways of halting ageing damage to body organs, allowing us to have lifespans of 150 years or more, and no doubt new cures for diseases will be discovered. However, as science breaks down new boundaries, the human body could be exposed to new deadly superbugs, taking us backward with every leap forward.

Immortality is achieved – perhaps not of the body, but of the mind, as we are able to download the content of our brains onto a microchip.

Computers will be fitted with brains modelled on humans, giving them the ability to develop their own thoughts and emotions.

Your individual genome (complete DNA set) will be stored on a personal ID card, so every time you travel or shop can be monitored.

Scientists will learn how to turn individual genes on or off to treat illnesses and inherited medical conditions.

"Ego badges" could store and transmit your likes and dislikes to other badge wearers, filtering out people you won't like and introducing you to new friends.

Technology

Computers have revolutionized our world, and have infiltrated just about every part of it. Microchips can already be embedded in practically everything, calculating, monitoring, and aiding our everyday lives. Wireless technology allows these devices to communicate with each other.

The race is on for technology to beat climate change.

Future biotechnology may allow scientists to use information stored in gene banks to rebuild entire ecosystems such as rainforests.

Cyber social lives will flourish in virtual environments, chat rooms, and profile sites. Companies will sell virtual products, such as virtual fashions in which to dress your online "avatar" (character) or a magic sword to use in videogames.

Technology will continue to permeate more aspects of our lives. Computer chips in food packaging will control the cooking, virtual windows will change the "view" according to the preferences of those inside, and robots will take over home cleaning.

As the demand for energy grows faster than ever and supplies of oil and gas run out, the search is on for a replacement fuel. Solar and wind power are already being harnessed, but the smart money is on hydrogen-powered fuel cells.

The "shrinking-world" trend reverses as oil production declines. International travel becomes an expensive luxury – as does importing goods. Could this mean the end of global brands?

Environment

Is Earth facing calamity? Global warming is causing the polar ice caps to melt and sea levels to rise, and a growing population is rapidly depleting the planet's natural resources. As scientists seek viable alternatives for finite resources and technological solutions for environmental disasters, some campaigners claim the only way to save the Earth is to change the way we live our lives.

The technological take-over of our lives could spark a counter-revolution and a return to visiting stores rather than shopping online and posting letters instead of emailing.

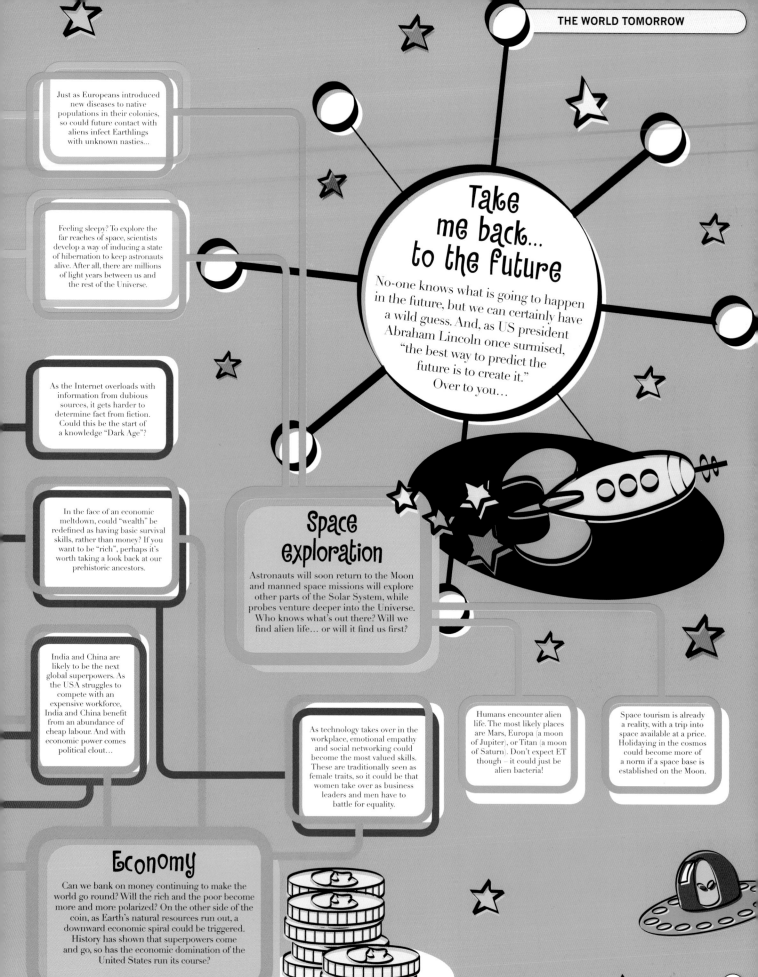

Just as Europeans introduced new diseases to native populations in their colonies, so could future contact with aliens infect Earthlings with unknown nasties...

Feeling sleepy? To explore the far reaches of space, scientists develop a way of inducing a state of hibernation to keep astronauts alive. After all, there are millions of light years between us and the rest of the Universe.

As the Internet overloads with information from dubious sources, it gets harder to determine fact from fiction. Could this be the start of a knowledge "Dark Age"?

In the face of an economic meltdown, could "wealth" be redefined as having basic survival skills, rather than money? If you want to be "rich", perhaps it's worth taking a look back at our prehistoric ancestors.

India and China are likely to be the next global superpowers. As the USA struggles to compete with an expensive workforce, India and China benefit from an abundance of cheap labour. And with economic power comes political clout...

Take me back... to the future

No-one knows what is going to happen in the future, but we can certainly have a wild guess. And, as US president Abraham Lincoln once surmised, "the best way to predict the future is to create it." Over to you...

Space exploration

Astronauts will soon return to the Moon and manned space missions will explore other parts of the Solar System, while probes venture deeper into the Universe. Who knows what's out there? Will we find alien life... or will it find us first?

As technology takes over in the workplace, emotional empathy and social networking could become the most valued skills. These are traditionally seen as female traits, so it could be that women take over as business leaders and men have to battle for equality.

Humans encounter alien life. The most likely places are Mars, Europa (a moon of Jupiter), or Titan (a moon of Saturn). Don't expect ET though – it could just be alien bacteria!

Space tourism is already a reality, with a trip into space available at a price. Holidaying in the cosmos could become more of a norm if a space base is established on the Moon.

Economy

Can we bank on money continuing to make the world go round? Will the rich and the poor become more and more polarized? On the other side of the coin, as Earth's natural resources run out, a downward economic spiral could be triggered. History has shown that superpowers come and go, so has the economic domination of the United States run its course?

Happiness lies in conquering one's enemies.

GENGHIS KHAN (1162–1227), FOUNDER OF THE MONGOL EMPIRE

Be less curious about people and more curious about ideas.

MARIE CURIE (1867–1934), FRENCH PHYSICIST AND TWO-TIME NOBEL PRIZE WINNER

I've finished that chapel I was painting. The Pope is quite satisfied.

ITALIAN SCULPTOR AND PAINTER **MICHELANGELO** (1475–1564), IN A LETTER TO HIS FATHER AFTER 18 MONTHS OF PAINTING THE SISTINE CHAPEL

We didn't land on Plymouth Rock – that rock landed on us.

MALCOLM X (1925–1965), AFRICAN-AMERICAN ACTIVIST LEADER

An army marches on its stomach.

FRENCH EMPEROR **NAPOLEON BONAPARTE** (1769–1821)

I am not a dictator. It's just that I have a grumpy face.

GENERAL AUGUSTO PINOCHET (1915–2006), CHILEAN DICTATOR, NO MATTER WHAT HE SAYS

All I was doing was trying to get home from work.

ROSA PARKS (1913–2005), AMERICAN CIVIL RIGHTS ACTIVIST ABOUT HER ARREST FOR NOT GIVING UP A BUS SEAT TO A WHITE PASSENGER – AN EVENT THAT TRIGGERED A BUS BOYCOTT

Curious Quotes

I CAME, I SAW, I CONQUERED.

ROMAN GENERAL **JULIUS CAESAR** (102–44 BCE), ON A PLACARD CARRIED AFTER A MILITARY CAMPAIGN

IN THE FUTURE EVERYBODY WILL BE WORLD FAMOUS FOR FIFTEEN MINUTES.

ANDY WARHOL (1928-1987), AMERICAN POP ARTIST

I cannot help it that my paintings do not sell. The time will come when people will see that they are worth more than the price of the paint.

DUTCH POST-IMPRESSIONIST PAINTER **VINCENT VAN GOGH** (1853–1890), IN A LETTER TO HIS BROTHER, THEO IN 1888. HIS PAINTINGS HAVE GONE ON TO SELL FOR MILLIONS OF POUNDS

I have the body of a weak and feeble woman, but the heart and stomach of a king, and of a king of England, too.

QUEEN ELIZABETH I (1558–1603) IN A SPEECH TO HER TROOPS AS THEY AWAITED THE SPANISH ARMADA

THE DEATH OF ONE MAN IS A TRAGEDY. THE DEATH OF MILLIONS IS A STATISTIC.

JOSEPH STALIN (1879–1953), LEADER OF THE SOVIET UNION AND ONE OF THE MOST POWERFUL DICTATORS IN HISTORY

An eye for an eye only ends up making the world blind.

POLITICAL AND SPIRITUAL LEADER OF INDIA, **MAHATMA GANDHI** (1869–1948)

I have a dream.

MARTIN LUTHER KING, JR, (1929–1968) AMERICAN CIVIL RIGHTS ACTIVIST

You can fool all of the people some of the time, and some of the people all the time, but you cannot fool all the people all of the time.

ABRAHAM LINCOLN (1809–1865) 16TH PRESIDENT OF THE UNITED STATES WHO LED THE COUNTRY THROUGH THE CIVIL WAR

Genius is 1 per cent inspiration, 99 per cent perspiration.

INVENTOR AND ENTREPRENEUR **THOMAS EDISON** (1847–1931)

We are just an advanced breed of **monkeys** on a minor planet of a very average star. But we can understand **the Universe**. *That makes us something very special.*

BRITISH PHYSICIST **STEPHEN HAWKING** (BORN 1942)

The only thing we have to fear is fear itself.

TAKEN FROM UNITED STATES **PRESIDENT FRANKLIN D ROOSEVELT**'S (1882–1945) FIRST INAUGURAL ADDRESS, IN 1933

MIX-UPS

WHO SAID IT: ASTRONAUT NEIL ARMSTRONG TAKING HIS FIRST STEPS ON THE MOON DURING THE APOLLO 11 MISSION IN 1969

WHAT HE SAID:

That's one small step for man, one giant leap for mankind.

WHAT HE WAS SUPPOSED TO SAY:

That's one small step for a man, one giant leap for mankind.

(MANY PEOPLE THINK NEIL GOT IT RIGHT, BUT THE "A" WAS LOST IN THE STATIC OF THE TRANSMISSION.)

WHAT HE SAID NEXT:

Yes, the surface is fine and powdery. I can kick it up loosely with my toe.

WHAT HE DIDN'T SAY:

Good luck, Mr Gorsky!

A FAMOUS URBAN LEGEND SAYS THAT WHEN NEIL WAS A SMALL BOY, HE HEARD HIS NEIGHBOURS ARGUING. ONE NEIGHBOUR, MR GORSKY, TOLD THE OTHER MAN THAT HE'D DO HIM A FAVOUR "WHEN THAT KID OVER THERE WALKS ON THE MOON."

WHO SUPPOSEDLY SAID IT: FRENCH QUEEN MARIE ANTOINETTE (1755–1793), WHEN HER ADVISERS INFORMED HER THAT THE PEASANTS WERE STARVING.

WHAT SHE SUPPOSEDLY SAID:

Let them eat cake!

WHAT SHE ACTUALLY SAID:

Let them eat brioche (bread).

OR WAS SOMEONE ELSE DOING THE TALKING? ANOTHER VERSION OF THIS QUOTE IS ATTRIBUTED TO **MARIE-THÉRÈSE,** WIFE OF **LOUIS XIV,** BUT SHE SAID,

Let them eat pastry!

WHO SAID IT (MAYBE): FRENCH WRITER AND PHILOSOPHER VOLTAIRE (1694–1778)

WHAT HE SUPPOSEDLY SAID:

I disapprove of what you say, but I will defend to the death your right to say it.

WHAT HE ACTUALLY DID SAY:

Think for yourselves and let others enjoy the privilege to do so, too.

(NOT SO CATCHY, IS IT?)

WHO SAID IT: BRITISH NAVAL HERO HORATIO NELSON (1758–1805)

WHAT HE SUPPOSEDLY SAID ON HIS DEATHBED AT THE BATTLE OF TRAFALGAR, TO HIS FLAG CAPTAIN, THOMAS MASTERMAN HARDY:

Kiss me, Hardy.

WHAT SOME PEOPLE THINK HE SAID:

Kismet, Hardy.

KISMET MEANS FATE, BUT AT THE TIME OF HIS DEATH, THE WORD WASN'T IN USE IN THAT WAY.

WHAT HE ACTUALLY SAID:

Thank God, I have done my duty. Drink, drink. Fan, fan. Rub, rub.

WHO SAID IT: COMMUNIST REVOLUTIONARY KARL MARX (1818–1883)

WHAT HE DIDN'T SAY:

Religion is the opiate of the masses.

WHAT HE DID SAY:

Religion is the sign of the oppressed creature, the heart of a heartless world, and the soul of soulless conditions. It is the opium of the people.

AND MISQUOTES

BLAGGER WITH A BEARD

HATSHEPSUT (1470s BCE)

After ruling Egypt as a regent with her young nephew, Hatshepsut decided she'd rather like his job – but female pharaohs were unheard of. So, to calm everyone down, this queen became a king. She put on the royal headdress and crown, and slapped on a fake beard. Her propaganda ploy worked, and she became one of the most powerful female rulers in Egypt's history.

MAD COW DISEASE

Nebuchadnezzar II (reigned 605–562 BCE)

As king of Babylon, Nebuchadnezzar set out to make his capital city a wonder of the world. He ordered the construction of the fabulous Hanging Gardens of Babylon and more than 50 temples. Yet something was building inside him: possibly a bout of boanthropy – where a person believes he or she is a cow. It is reported that King Neb hung out in the fields for seven years, chewing the cud.

CALIGULA (12–41 CE)

This Roman emperor was very good at being very bad. Caligula was so sensitive about his bald spot, he declared that looking down at him from above was a crime punishable by death. Caligula loved humiliating people – he made the losers of a public-speaking contest erase their wax tablets by licking them. He also enjoyed random death, chucking spectators in to fight the lions and tigers at the arena when they ran out of criminals. He adorned his horse with jewels, built a marble stable for him, invited him to dinner, and even discussed making him a senator.

NERO (37–68 CE)

THIS ROMAN EMPEROR REPORTEDLY POISONED HIS ADOPTIVE BROTHER TO ELIMINATE ANY RIVALRY FOR THE THRONE. WHEN HIS MOTHER STARTED MEDDLING, HE TRIED TO KILL HER – THREE TIMES BY POISONING AND ONCE BY ATTEMPTING TO BRING DOWN THE CEILING AS SHE LAY IN BED. IN A FOURTH ATTEMPT, NERO HAD A COLLAPSIBLE BOAT BUILT FOR HER; THE BOAT SUNK, BUT SHE SWAM TO SHORE. FINALLY, HE CALLED IN THE PROFESSIONALS, HIRING AN ASSASSIN WHO STABBED AND BEAT HER TO DEATH.

TO CELEBRATE, HE THREW LAVISH CONTESTS AND GAMES. HE EVEN GOT UP ON STAGE TO PLAY HIS LUTE AND SING AT ONE CONCERT. PEOPLE COULD NOT LEAVE THE AUDITORIUM WHILE NERO WAS ROCKING OUT. REPORTS TELL OF PEOPLE PRETENDING TO DIE JUST SO THEY COULD BE CARRIED OUT OF THE AUDITORIUM.

NOT A MOTHER'S BOY

ASHURNASIRPAL II

(ruled 884–859 BCE)

NASTY PIECE OF WORK

This brilliant Assyrian general loved boasting about his conquests in disgusting detail. An inscription at the entrance to his palace read, "I flayed all the chief men who revolted, and I covered the pillar with the skins, some I walled up within the pillar, some I impaled upon the pillars on stakes, and others I bound to the skin upon the walls; and I cut off the limbs of the officers who had rebelled…" That wasn't much of a welcome mat, was it?

MEGALOMANIAC

PEISISTRATOS
(560s BCE)

LIAR, LIAR, PANTS ON FIRE

Athens citizen Peisistratos gave himself a few minor cuts and bruises, then claimed he had been brutally attacked. The Athenians bought his story, and allowed him to put together a troop of tough guys armed with wooden clubs for defence. Peisistratos and his guards then seized Athens and he declared himself tyrant ruler.

Irene of Athens
(752–803)

MOTHER OF EMPEROR CONSTANTINE VI, IRENE HAD HER SON'S EYES GOUGED OUT SO THAT SHE COULD RULE THE BYZANTINE EMPIRE ON HER OWN. HE DIED OF HIS WOUNDS A FEW DAYS LATER.

VLAD III (1431–1476)

Feared for his bloodthirsty cruelty, Vlad III of Transylvania (nicknamed Dracula and Vlad the Impaler) marched into Bulgaria, captured some 20,000 people, and impaled them on a forest of stakes. He was very proud of his impaling, arranging the stakes in circular patterns and putting more important victims on taller stakes, so that even powerful opponents realized they could be next. He also skinned people alive, boiled them, roasted them, tortured them, and dismembered them, for his own entertainment.

A LOT AT STAKE

Loony leaders

You don't have to be mad to run a country, but it helps. Throughout the long parade of history, there were many rulers who, shall we say, marched to a different drummer. History books teem with control freaks, egocentric megalomaniacs, devious weasels, and the chronically confused.

KLEPTOMANIAC

FAROUK OF EGYPT
(1920–1965)

Even though he could buy whatever he wanted, Farouk was partial to a spot of pilfering. He nicked valuable artefacts while he was on state visits, including an expensive pocket watch from Winston Churchill. Subjects who mingled with the King often had their pockets picked by this right royal robber.

BASIL II
(958–1025)

BLIND AMBITION

After victory in battle with the Bulgarians in 1014, Emperor Basil of Byzantium ordered his troops to punish the 15,000 Bulgarian prisoners. They scooped out the eyes of 99 men per 100, and removed one eye from the 100th man. The half-blinded led the blind on the long march home.

MARIA ELEONORE OF BRANDENBURG
(1599–1655)

NOT-SO-MERRY WIDOW

When Maria's husband died in battle, she clung to his remains… literally. She hung his embalmed heart above her bed at night, while his unsealed coffin was placed in her black-shrouded chambers. For nearly a year, she locked herself and her infant daughter away with her husband's body, weeping inconsolably. When the King was finally buried in 1634, she demanded that the coffin be dug up and opened again.

TIMUR THE LAME
(1336–1404)

HEAD CASE

He may have walked with the limp that gave him his nickname, but there was nothing lame about the way this nomadic warlord from present-day Uzbekistan treated his enemies. His plan was simple: invade a country, kill anyone who offered even a hint of resistance, then take things. After capturing one city, he ordered his band of baddies to behead its 30,000 citizens. They created giant pyramids from the human heads, so everyone else could see what fate awaited them.

Writers

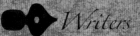

Lewis Carroll, Charles Dickens, Ernest Hemingway, and Virginia Woolf all wrote while standing up.

He may have done a lot of writing in his time, but today only seven copies of William Shakespeare's signature exist.

Mark Twain's Life on the Mississippi, written in 1883, was reportedly the first novel to be written on a typewriter.

Artists

Vincent van Gogh only sold one painting in his lifetime.

According to his mother, Pablo Picasso's first word was "pencil".

Leonardo could write with one hand and draw with another at the same time. Show-off.

In 1961, the Museum of Modern Art in New York City mistakenly displayed a Henri Matisse painting upside-down for 47 days.

ODD JOBS

Mongol ruler Genghis Khan's first job was as a goatherd.
20th-century Cambodian dictator Pol Pot was a schoolteacher.
German fascist Adolf Hitler painted postcards.
Italian fascist Mussolini was a newspaper writer.
American gangster Al Capone's business card identified him as a used furniture dealer.

FAMOUS FIRSTS
(AND INVENTIVE DISASTERS)

In 1864, afraid of getting hit by traffic as he walked to his gentleman's club, London gent Colonel Pierpoint built the world's first traffic island in St James Street, Piccadilly. When it was finished, he sprinted across the busy road to admire it, tripped, and was knocked down by a cab.

William Brodie (1741–1788) was a Scottish builder and cabinet-maker and an upstanding member of society in Endinburgh. He installed and fixed door locks and other security devices all over town, but Brodie had a double life. At night, he became a burglar. He made wax impressions of keys during his day job so he could let himself into banks later on. A bungled raid on a tax office led to Brodie's capture. He was sentenced to hang on the gallows. And who was the carpenter who had constructed the device? Brodie himself.

In 1895, French brothers Auguste and Louis Lumière ensured a front-row seat in cinematic history by giving the first public showing of a motion picture. One of the Lumière's one-shot, one-minute movies showed a steam train chugging into a French station. The audience, never having experienced the movies before, were terrified to see what appeared to be a train heading right for them. They shrieked in terror and many ran away. Hopefully they paid for the tickets on the way in.

On 10 March 1876, Scottish-Canadian inventor Alexander Graham Bell spoke the first words ever heard on the telephone. His assistant working in the next room (near the telephone receiver) heard his boss say, "Watson, please come here. I want you". These historic words were unscripted. Bell had just spilled acid on his trousers.

Insomniacs
(people that have trouble sleeping)

Galileo
(scientist and star spotter)

Napoleon Bonaparte
(French emperor)

Vincent van Gogh
(artist who cut off his ear)

Abraham Lincoln
(US president)

Caligula (mad Roman emperor)

Catherine the Great
(Russian empress)

Thomas Edison (US inventor)

Margaret Thatcher
(British prime minister)

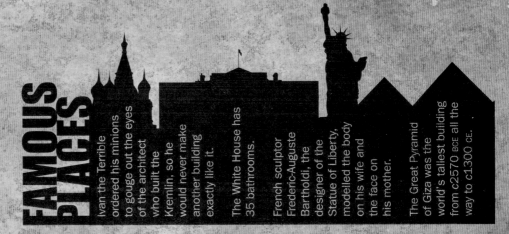

FAMOUS PLACES

Ivan the Terrible ordered his minions to gouge out the eyes of the architect who built the Kremlin, so he would never make another building exactly like it.

The White House has 35 bathrooms.

French sculptor Frederic-Auguste Bartholdi, the designer of the Statue of Liberty, modelled the body on his wife and the face on his mother.

The Great Pyramid of Giza was the world's tallest building from c2570 BCE all the way to c1300 CE.

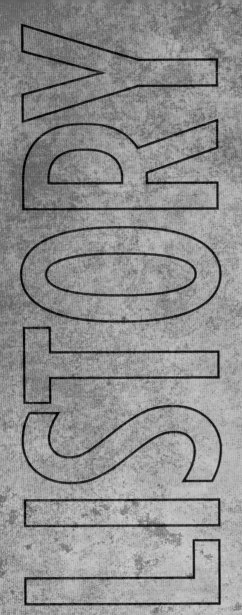

The shortest war in history was probably the one between Britain and Zanzibar in 1896. Zanzibar surrendered after 38 minutes.

Armoured knights used to raise their visors to identify themselves as they rode past the king. This custom evolved into the military salute.

The War of 1812 between Great Britain and the United States should perhaps have been called the War of Miscommunication. Two days before war was declared, the British announced that they would repeal (cancel) the laws that the US were fighting about, but news travelled slowly in those days. The greatest battle of the war, fought in New Orleans, took place two weeks after the peace treaty had been signed.

Beauty spot

Egyptian queen Cleopatra wrote a book about make-up and beauty. One of the featured ingredients in her beauty potions was burned mice. She also made red lipstick from crushed beetles and ants.

Queen Elizabeth I of England was totally bald. She lost her hair after a bout of smallpox when she was 29. She was never seen without a wig.

Soviet dictator Joseph Stalin had webbed toes.

Second wife of England's King Henry VIII, Anne Boleyn had six fingers on one hand.

US president George Washington's face was scarred from smallpox, and he wore false teeth made of walrus ivory.

FIVE KINGS WITH AWFUL NICKNAMES

KING RUDOLF THE SLUGGARD (OR THE PIOUS), KING OF BURGUNDY (933-1032)

KING MALCOLM IV THE MAIDEN OF SCOTLAND (1153-1165)

KING LOUIS VI THE FAT, KING OF THE FRANKS (1108-1137)

KING ETHELRED THE UNREADY, RULER OF ENGLAND (978-1016)

KING FERDINAND THE FICKLE, KING OF PORTUGAL (1367-1383)

FIVE KINGS WITH GREAT NICKNAMES

KING PHILIP I THE HANDSOME, FIRST HABSBURG RULER IN SPAIN (1482-1506)

KING RICHARD I THE LIONHEART, RULER OF ENGLAND (1189-1199)

KING WILLIAM II THE GOOD (HIS FATHER WAS KNOWN AS WILLIAM THE BAD), RULER OF SICILY 1166-1189

KING CHARLES V THE WISE, KING OF FRANCE 1364-1380

KING LOUIS XV THE WELL-BELOVED, RULER OF FRANCE (1710-1774)

Left-handers

Rameses II (Egyptian pharaoh)
Alexander the Great (military genius)
Julius Caesar (Roman ruler)
Joan of Arc (French heroine)
Leonardo da Vinci (all-round smart alec)
Michelangelo (ceiling painter)
Raphael (artist)
Isaac Newton (gravity definer)
Napoleon Bonaparte (fearless Frenchman)
Beethoven (deaf composer)
Queen Victoria (British monarch)
Lewis Carroll (writer of Alice in Wonderland)
Mark Twain (US author)
Henry Ford (mass car producer)
Marie Curie (scientist)
Mahatma Gandhi (Indian independence leader)
Charlie Chaplin (comedy actor)
Jimi Hendrix (rock guitarist)
Paul McCartney (one of the Beatles)
Bill Gates (rich computer dude)
Barack Obama (US President)

Famous Janes

Calamity **Jane**, American frontierswoman
Jayne Mansfield, American actress
Jane Austen, British novelist
Lady **Jane** Grey, queen of England for nine days in 1554
Jane Seymour, third wife of King Henry VIII
Jane Seymour, English actress
Jane Fonda, American actress and activist

Famous Johns

King **John**, signed England's Magna Carta in 1215
John Dillinger, American criminal
John Logie Baird, inventor of the first working television system
John Adams, second American president
John the Apostle, wrote one of the Gospels in the Bible
Johannes Brahms, German composer
Johann Sebastian Bach, another German composer
Ivan the Terrible, first tsar of Russia
John Wayne, actor best known for westerns
John Lennon, Beatle
Juan Peron, three-time president of Argentina

Sticky ends

After his death in 896, the body of Pope Formosus was dug up, dressed in papal robes, and propped up on a chair to stand trial. The verdict: he had not been a worthy pope.

Three of the first five American presidents (John Adams, Thomas Jefferson, and James Monroe) died on 4 July (not the same one).

People committed suicide in ancient China by eating 0.5 kg (1 lb) of salt.

In 44 BCE, Julius Caesar was stabbed to death in the Roman senate. The conspirators didn't want any one person to be responsible for his death, so everyone stabbed him with their daggers.

Roman emperor Caracalla was murdered in 217 when he broke away from the safety of his marching legions to answer a call of nature. As he was relieving himself, an officer of the imperial bodyguard charged at him, stabbing him in the back.

In 791, Imam Idris, the founder of an Arab dynasty in Morocco, was murdered by a poisoned toothpick sent by his enemy. The tooth will out!

Who's afraid of what?

King Henry III of France, King Louis XIV of France, Roman emperor Julius Caesar, Italian dictator Benito Mussolini, and French emperor Napoleon all suffered from ailurophobia: the fear of cats.

England's Queen Elizabeth I had a case of anthophobia, a fear of roses. It was nothing to be sniffed at.

German dictator Adolf Hitler, US actor/president Ronald Reagan, and escapologist Harry Houdini were claustrophobic, dreading small enclosed spaces.

Frederick the Great, king of Prussia, was so afraid of water he could not bathe or even wash his face or hands. Instead, his servants rubbed him with dry towels.

Author Hans Christian Andersen and composer Frederic Chopin feared being buried alive (not necessarily with each other).

Austrian psychiatrist Sigmund Freud grappled with his fear of railways, death, and ferns (pteridophobia). Wonder if he ever got to the root of his problems?

1 Fab footwear

What would we do without the shoe? The easiest way to protect bare tootsies from sharp rocks was by grabbing some bark or a few large leaves and tying them to the bottom of the feet with some vines. Later cultures wove plant fibres into sandals. But shoe design didn't stop there. Let's see what's afoot…

Roman sandals
The Roman army marched to victory on sandals named caligae. These sturdy leather shoes laced up the middle of the foot. Iron hobnails hammered into the sole made the sandals sturdier.

Moccasins
Many Native Americans wore these soft, slipper-like shoes made of deerskin sewn together with animal sinew. Because they were so light, you could walk through the woods quietly – perfect for sneaking up on a deer in case you needed a new pair.

Pointy shoes
In medieval Europe, shoe toes were sharply pointed. Known as pikes, crackowes, or poulaines, they were longer depending on the wearer's social status. The king and his court made sure they wore the longest, pointiest shoes in town. French monarch Phillip Augustus even regulated shoe length by law. People had to stuff the tips of the shoes with moss to prevent themselves tripping over.

Chopines
These stilt-like wooden platforms, all the rage in 15th-century Venice, featured a cork or wood stacked sole covered in velvet. Chopine height could soar to 50 cm (20 in), giving posh ladies a truly high and mighty look. Sadly, they were so difficult to walk in that people needed help getting down the street, let alone in and out of a gondola.

Pattens
Cleaned streets are a relatively recent innovation. To cope with the mud in the past, people wore pattens. Held on to regular shoes by a strap, they were thick wooden soles that raised the wearer above the muck.

2 Socks and tights

People invented socks because toasty toes are happy toes. The first pairs were probably made from animal skins gathered up to the ankles and tied in place. The Ancient Greeks made socks from matted animal hair. Thankfully, sock technology improved. Here's a few pairs to try on:

Hose
In the 1100s, fashion-forward European men covered their lower legs with hose, a tube-like garment of linen or wool. By the 14th century, hose had exploded with colour. Some were striped, others had a different colour for each leg. In the 1500s, a trend for shorter jackets led to longer hose, extending up to the waist. Every bump and flaw was revealed.

Knitted socks
When the craft of knitting, perfected in the Arabic world, reached Europe, toes tingled with joy. Knitted socks fit better, kept their shape, and could be created in an array of colours and styles.

Nylons
Synthetic nylon stockings were first launched in 1940, nearly causing a stampede. More than 72,000 pairs were sold in New York stores on the first day of sale, and by the end of the year 64 million pairs had been sold.

3 Underwear

Smalls have a long history. These garments, worn under other clothing, help keep outerwear clean by soaking up smells. They also keep the wearer warm and help shape and support the body. Last, but not least, they cover stuff up to preserve a person's modesty. Look away now if you are easily embarrassed…

Loincloth
The loincloth is a strip of fabric tied or wrapped around the hips and bits. In hot places, people didn't wear much else. Ancient Egyptian pharaoh Tutankhamun was buried with a pile of linen loincloths. Maybe there were no washing machines in the afterlife?

Codpiece
This strange item of clothing appeared during the Renaissance. A flap or pouch attached to the front of men's trousers, the codpiece protected the wearer's modesty and also served as a handy place to carry small items like coins. They were padded out or made in ridiculous shapes until the codpiece craze died out.

Corset
An undergarment designed to pull in and reshape the waistline, corset-wearing may have started with the Ancient Greeks. Stiffened with whalebone or iron, corsets were in widespread use over wide-spreading tums until the 20th century. Even children were laced into them.

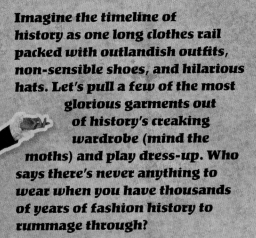

Imagine the timeline of history as one long clothes rail packed with outlandish outfits, non-sensible shoes, and hilarious hats. Let's pull a few of the most glorious garments out of history's creaking wardrobe (mind the moths) and play dress-up. Who says there's never anything to wear when you have thousands of years of fashion history to rummage through?

Dress me up

4 Outerwear

What goes over underwear? Outerwear, of course. From animal skins worn to ward off the Ice Age chill to the very latest chilled-out looks, clothing has a long and colourful history. Here are a few iconic fashions from the past.

Toga
No Ancient Roman citizen would be caught in public without his toga. This long ribbon of fabric, usually wool, wrapped around the body and was worn over a simple linen dress called a tunic.

Kimono
The national costume of Japan, this floor-length, T-shaped robe has wide, long sleeves. Kimonos are wrapped around the body and secured by a sash-like belt called an obi. Putting on a kimono is difficult (there are classes to teach people how to do it), but one pointer is to wrap the left side over the right. Wrapping right over left is only used to wrap a body for burial.

Lederhosen
A traditional garment in the mountain regions of Austria and Germany is the lederhosen – a pair of short leather trousers with a drop flap in front. Men may hold up this get-up with a pair of embroidered braces.

Kilt
This Scottish skirt for men is wrapped around the waist and fastened with buckles. Kilts are almost always woven in a pattern of coloured threads known as tartan. Some say they are called kilts because that is what happened to the last person who called it a skirt! The kilt does not have pockets, so it is traditionally worn with a sporran – a purse worn on a chain around the waist.

5 Hats

Head coverings not only provide practical protection from the elements. They can also be symbolic or decorative. Hold on to your hat as we look at the history of headgear.

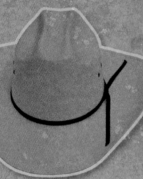

Sombrero
Its name comes from the Spanish word for "shadow", and the sombrero provides perfect protection from the hot Mexican sun. Everyday sombreros are woven from straw, while fancier ones are made from felt richly decorated with embroidery.

Tricorne
This three-cornered hat popped up everywhere in the 18th century. Its wide brim was pinned up in the front and at the back to give the hat its distinctive triangular shape. Later it evolved into the bicorne (two-cornered) hat, much favoured by Napoleon. And no, the bicorne was not replaced with the unicorn.

Ten-gallon hat
Cowboys and ranchers from the American West top their noggins with broad-brimmed felt hats. Some high-crowned styles became known as ten-gallon hats, even though most could only hold about a gallon of water. Wearing a hat that could hold ten gallons would be like walking around with a garbage can on your head… not a good look for anyone.

Fez
A small, cone-shaped red cap with a black tassel, the fez originated in Greece and became popular in the Ottoman Empire. Time to fez up: it gets its red colour from a natural dye made from Turkish berries.

Turban
These very ancient hats, made of a long length of cloth wrapped around the head or an inner hat, were worn in many cultures. Probably the largest turbans were worn in Ottoman Turkey. The cloth was wrapped over a hollow cone worn on the head to give a rounded hat as big as a pillow. Suleiman the Magnificent was famous for his mega-huge turban.

6 Hair

If you look back in history, you will be amazed at some of the hairdos (and definite hair-don'ts) that people wore. Here is a hair-raising look at historical hairstyles.

Powdered wigs
In 18th century Europe, the only way to wear a wig was to powder with starch until it turned white. Both men and women bigged up their wigs with horsehair padding or woven frames, creating a perfect nesting place for vermin, which had to bug people.

Oh, beehive!
In the late 1950s, many American women began to backcomb their hair into a massive pile resembling a beehive. Lacquered in place with enough hairspray to poke a hole in the ozone layer, these beehive hairdos became popular globally.

Moustaches
The earliest-known depiction in art of a man with a moustache is from Central Asia in 300 BCE.

7 Accessories

Want to be bang on trend no matter what date it is? Pile on the must-wear accessories of the day, and you'll never look dated.

Umbrellas
The oldest umbrellas were probably parasols, used to shade people from the heat of the Sun. An ancient Persian carving shows a slave holding an umbrella over the king's head.

Handbags
Some Egyptian hieroglyphs show people with bum-bag-like pouches around their waists, but the first mention of a handbag in literature dates from the 14th century.

Sunglasses
These protective lenses have a shady past. Roman emperor Nero was said to watch gladiators battle it out while holding emeralds up to his eyes, but it is more likely he did this for an optical effect rather than to cut Sun glare. In 12th-century China, people covered their eyes with thin sheets of quartz rock. It was not until the mid-1800s that scientists began tinkering with sunglasses.

Dear Sibyl...

Making history is not always easy. Revolts and revolutions can take their toll, not to mention the daily grind of plague and pestilence. If life is dragging you down, write to our agony aunt Sibyl to make your problems a thing of the past.

I have noticed some black spots appearing under my arms. Should I change my brand of deodorant?

Ned Smith, peasant, 1348

No, you silly sausage! This has nothing to do with personal hygiene. You have the plague. You will soon experience headaches, painful joints, vomiting, fever, purple skin patches, and will cough up blood. Unfortunately there is no cure in the 14th century so you will most likely be dead within five days. I'm surprised you didn't realize – the Black Death has wiped out one-thirds of the population of Europe!

Like any good Aztec parent, when my children misbehave I hold them over a chilli pepper fire and force them to inhale the smoke. My son has been particularly naughty of late, so can you advise which chillies produce the most eye-watering smoke?

Acolmiztli, Aztec farmer, 1500

Red chillies every time! As my wise old grandmother always said: "Green smoke's a joke; red smoke to choke."

I fly off the handle at the slightest thing. When I was young I tortured animals for fun, and when members of the Russian aristocracy made me angry, I threw their leader into a pack of hungry dogs. Boiling people alive is my latest hobby. How can I control my temper?

Ivan the Terrible, Tsar of Russia, 1580

You need to express your anger in a less destructive way. Tell the person who has upset you why you feel hurt before you rip their ribs out. Instead of butchering someone who's annoyed you, why not give him a hug? Turn that frown upside-down and, who knows, you may yet be remembered as Ivan the Terrific!

I am the shogun leader of Japan, but my nickname is "Monkey-face". My friends laugh at me and make monkey noises. How can I get them to take me seriously? Please help, or I may just disembowel myself.

Shogun Hideyoshi, Japan, 1590

Your friends are just jealous because you are in charge of the country. Keep your intestines right where they are and have the guts to stand up to the bullies. You're the boss. Remind them you can have them executed if they don't quit the monkey jibes.

I work as a cowboy on a cattle ranch in the Wild West. It's a tough job and my trousers are always getting torn. Can you recommend where I can buy trousers in a thicker fabric to stop me being the butt of people's jokes.

Trevor Pantsplit, cowboy, 1860

How embarrassing! A German merchant called Levi Strauss is selling blue denim jeans to gold-rush miners in California. He has come up with the ingenious idea of reinforcing the points of strain with copper rivets. Hopefully his trousers will be sturdy enough for you.

"Stop me from being the butt of people's jokes "

You may have heard of my brother Orville and myself? We recently built an aircraft and made the first-ever sustained heavier-than-air human flight. I know! We are amazing! The problem I have is every time I take to the air I start to feel a little sick. How can I become a truly great pioneer of flight if I turn green at the gills at every lift-off?

Wilbur Wright, aeroplane inventor, 1903

Firstly, congratulations! I have a feeling your invention is going to take off in a big way. Air-sickness is a pain, especially in your line of work. I suggest eating a dry cracker to ward off the nausea – but remember not to take your hands off the aeroplane controls!

HISTOROSCOPE

Aries (21 March – 19 April)
You have a desire to lead the way, and think actions speak louder than words. Military mastermind Otto von Bismarck carved out a German empire, but silent movie star Charlie Chaplin took the Aries trait of "doing" rather than "talking" to a whole new level.

Taurus (20 April – 20 May)
Stubborn and determined you may be Taurus, but what a mixed bag! On the one hand there is William Shakespeare and dance-floor glider Fred Astaire, but on the dark side is big-headed Russian empress Catherine the Great and nasty Nazi Adolf Hitler.

Gemini (21 May – 20 June)
You have a very inquisitive mind, Gemini. Just look at the investigative achievements of Enlightenment botanist Carl Linnaeus and Sherlock Holmes creator Arthur Conan Doyle.

Cancer (21 June – 22 July)
Quit the crabby mood, Cancer. Your sign has produced its fair share of history makers, including suffragette Emmeline Pankhurst, and civil rights campaigner Nelson Mandela.

Leo (23 July – 22 August)
As Leo artist Andy Warhol famously said, you want that 15 minutes of fame – but you plan on it lasting a lot longer. Just look at the careers of French emperor Napoleon Bonaparte, Italian dictator Benito Mussolini, and Cuban communist ruler Fidel Castro.

Virgo (23 August – 22 September)
I see travel on the horizon for Virgo… if the wanderlust of Christopher Columbus is anything to go by. Virgo women have made their mark, counting Queen Elizabeth I, Frankenstein creator Mary Shelley, and detective writer Agatha Christie in their number.

Libra (23 September – 22 October)
Libra, it is important you get the balance right. You are all about giving peace a chance, like Mahatma Gandhi and Beatle John Lennon. But you also like life to go with a bang, like naval hero Horatio Nelson and dynamite inventor Alfred Nobel.

Scorpio (23 October – 21 November)
No one can doubt your passion, Scorpio. You could be occupied in artistic pursuits like Claude Monet and Pablo Picasso, making scientific discoveries like Marie Curie, or reforming the Church like Martin Luther. Your zeal is legendary.

Sagittarius (22 November – 21 December)
"Don't fence me in" is your rallying cry as the independent spirits of writers Jane Austin and Mark Twain and war leader Winston Churchill show. Be careful not to fence anyone else in either though. Soviet dictator Joseph Stalin is not a good role model.

Capricorn (22 December – 19 January)
Whether you are busy over-achieving like inventor/scientist/statesman Benjamin Franklin, swivelling your hips like Elvis Presley, or packing a punch like Muhammad Ali, there's no doubting you cheeky goats are determined to reach the mountain top.

Aquarius (20 January – 18 February)
Unique and inventive just about sums you up, Aquarius. But take care – thinking outside the box can get you into trouble. Galileo lost his life for suggesting Earth isn't the centre of the Universe.

Pisces (19 February – 20 March)
Hmm… something fishy is going on. While some Pisceans have an artistic bent (take a bow Auguste Renoir and Michelangelo) others are more scientifically minded (yes, I'm talking about you, super-brainy physicist Albert Einstein).

A HISTORY OF BRITAIN AND IRELAND

PREHISTORIC ISLANDS

Britain and Ireland were once attached to the continent of Europe. Around 10,000 years ago, the latest Ice Age came to an end. Sea levels rose as the ice sheets melted and great seas covered the land bridge that is now known as the English Channel.

About 8,000 years ago, humans came, settled, farmed land, and built. Farming transformed the landscape of Britain from lush forests to ploughed fields. "Neolithic" people built circles of standing stones. The most famous of these is Stonehenge in Wiltshire.

The arrival from mainland Europe of the "Beaker people" (named after their distinctive bell-shaped pottery drinking vessels) brought the first metal-users to the British Isles. Bronze was used to make bowls and weapons.

By 500 BCE, the Bronze Age chieftains had to make way for a new elite — the Celts. Celtic tribes were connected by their language and culture and brought new farming methods. They came to dominate the British Isles, until the Romans decided to move in.

ut into the turf
f a hill slope, the
Uffington White
Horse in Oxfordshire
is 110 m (374 ft)
long and was
created more than
3,000 years ago.

ROMAN RULE

The Romans first raided Celtic Britain under Julius Caesar in 55 BCE, but it was not until 100 years later that permanent settlement of the grain-rich isles took place.

In just 20 years, the Romans had subdued most of the south. However, the rugged regions of present-day Scotland and Wales were not as easily settled. When Emperor Hadrian visited Britain in 122 CE he decided the Empire needed securing. He ordered a wall to be built across the northern frontier "to separate Romans from barbarians". This 117-km- (73-mile-) long structure and its forts took a decade to build and became known as Hadrian's Wall. Parts of it remain today.

Further south, Roman life prospered. The Romans were good rulers. They made sensible laws and built new towns, villas, roads, and bridges. However, the Romans didn't have it all their own way. Many native tribesmen still resisted being "Romanized". Queen Boudicca of the Iceni tribe was incensed at how her people were treated by Roman officials. After years of fighting she was defeated in 61 CE, and took poison rather than submit to Roman rule. Four hundred years after their arrival, Roman legions began departing Britain to protect a weak Rome. Those left behind had to fight new enemies.

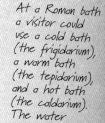

Oooh, it's a bit hot

At a Roman bath a visitor could use a cold bath (the frigidarium), a warm bath (the tepidarium), and a hot bath (the caldarium). The water was heated by underfloor furnaces.

RAIDING AND LOOTING

As the Roman hold on Britain got progressively weaker, Britain was being attacked from three directions. It was a terrifying time; so bad it became known as the Dark Ages.

The Irish attacked from the west; the Picts from the north; and various Germanic-speaking peoples from the east, across the North Sea. They included the Angles, Saxons, and Jutes, who were from northern Germany and southern Denmark. These Germanic

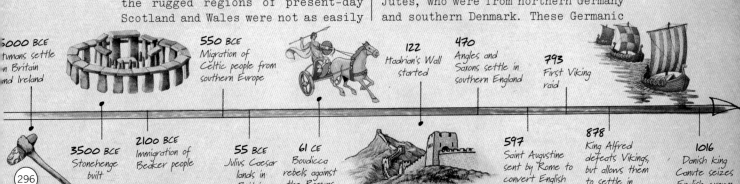

6000 BCE
Humans settle
in Britain
and Ireland

3500 BCE
Stonehenge
built

2100 BCE
Immigration of
Beaker people

550 BCE
Migration of
Celtic people from
southern Europe

55 BCE
Julius Caesar
lands in
Britain

61 CE
Boudicca
rebels against
the Romans

122
Hadrian's Wall
started

470
Angles and
Saxons settle in
southern England

597
Saint Augustine
sent by Rome to
convert English
to Christianity

793
First Viking
raid

878
King Alfred
defeats Vikings,
but allows them
to settle in
eastern England

1016
Danish king
Canute seizes
English crown

tribes became the "Anglo-Saxons" who gave to Britain and Ireland much of their tradition and language. They poured in upon the Romanized Celts of Britain, who defended themselves as best they could. According to legend, one of the Celts' military leaders was the famous King Arthur.

The Germanic tribes eventually settled, and Roman Britain was transformed into Anglo-Saxon Britain, with Celtic rule remaining in Cornwall, Wales, Scotland, and Ireland. The Anglo-Saxon areas eventually combined into kingdoms, and much of the population was converted to Christianity.

The 8th century was a time of great wealth — so much so that fearsome warriors across the water decided to steal it. The Vikings launched deadly attacks on monasteries around the coast. However, they didn't just loot — they came to stay. In Ireland, Dublin became a base, but the Vikings were prevented from being total masters of England by the heroics of King Alfred "the Great". After repelling the Vikings, Alfred began restoring the cultural and military well-being of his country.

According to legend, King Arthur led the defence of Britain against the Saxon invaders in the early 6th century.

THE MIDDLE BIT

Viking Danes began raiding again in 991, and in 1016 King Canute made England part of his Danish realm. Canute ruled well, but it was the calm before the storm.

In 1042, the English throne passed to the Anglo-Saxon King Edward the Confessor. When he died in 1066 there were several claims to the crown.

These included a powerful earl named Harold Godwinson, and his relation William, Duke of Normandy. William defeated Harold at the Battle of Hastings. The victory of the Normans was a turning point in English history. Never again would a foreign enemy take possession of English soil. William the Conqueror ruled England under the feudal system. Knights and barons were granted large estates of land in return for providing military support to the king. Having conquered England, William wanted to know how much it was worth. The Domesday Book was a survey to find out who owned what so they could be taxed on it.

A major step in the shaping of how Britain would be governed occurred in 1215 when the Magna Carta was signed. It was a series of written promises between the king and his subjects that the king would not abuse his power. Later, English kings turned their energies to attempts to gain French territories. A war against France lasted for 116 years from 1337, but despite some famous victories, England was finally defeated. It was yet another grim time. At home the Black Death of 1348 reduced the population by about one-third.

TUDOR RENAISSANCE

After the devastation caused by the Black Death, England took time to recover. The wool trade brought prosperity, and Henry VII established an efficient government, ruling in cooperation with parliament, a pattern followed by later Tudor monarchs (Tudor was their family name).

In 1536, Wales was formally united with England, and in 1542 Henry VIII declared himself king of Ireland. In 1534, Henry VIII, disturbed that he

I need a wee!

Medieval knights wore heavy armour made from riveted plates of metal to protect them in battle.

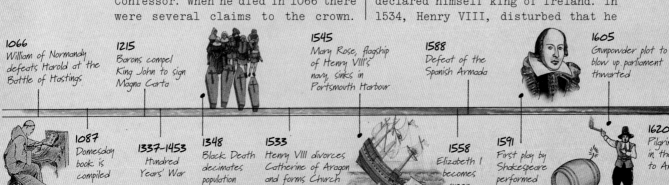

1066 William of Normandy defeats Harold at the Battle of Hastings

1215 Barons compel King John to sign Magna Carta

1545 Mary Rose, flagship of Henry VIII's navy, sinks in Portsmouth Harbour

1588 Defeat of the Spanish Armada

1605 Gunpowder plot to blow up parliament thwarted

1642 Civil War breaks out

1087 Domesday book is compiled

1337–1453 Hundred Years' War

1348 Black Death decimates population

1533 Henry VIII divorces Catherine of Aragon and forms Church of England

1558 Elizabeth I becomes queen

1591 First play by Shakespeare performed

1620 Pilgrim fathers sail in the Mayflower to America

had no male heir, broke away from the Church of Rome after the Pope refused to annul (declare invalid) his marriage to Catharine of Aragon. The Church of England came into being. Four more wives came, then went by chopping blocks, divorce, or death in childbirth. A sixth wife survived Henry.

Henry's daughter Queen Mary temporarily restored Catholic authority but, on her death in 1558, Elizabeth I came to the throne as Protestant head of Church and state. Elizabeth's reign saw England grow in strength and prosperity. There was an improvement in education, and a great age of literature and architecture produced such figures as playwright William Shakespeare and architect Inigo Jones. Abroad, brave sea captains such as Francis Drake brought trade and wealth from the Americas. In 1588, the Spanish Armada (naval fleet) was defeated in a sea battle in the English Channel. It was a golden age.

I've got a headache!

Anne Boleyn was the second wife of King Henry VIII and mother of Queen Elizabeth I. Henry ordered her execution by beheading after suspecting her of cheating on him.

FIRE AND PLAGUE

Unlike their Tudor predecessors, the Stuart kings, who were also kings of Scotland through the line of Mary, Queen of Scots, were continually clashing with parliament.

In 1605, several disgruntled men tried to blow up the king and Houses of Parliament, but the Gunpowder Plot failed. Disagreements between King Charles I and parliament eventually led to a civil war in 1642. The royalists were roundly defeated by the parliamentarian general Oliver Cromwell in 1645. The King lost his head, and Cromwell led a republican government. Chaos followed Cromwell's death in 1658, and the monarchy was

restored in 1660 with Charles II proclaimed king. Charles II ruled during a time of two great disasters. In 1665, the Great Plague killed about 70,000 people. It was brought to London by rats, and spread quickly because people lived in very close quarters and hygiene standards were low. In 1666, the Great Fire of London destroyed two-thirds of the city. It started as a small fire in a bakery in Pudding Lane, and raged for four days. To prevent such a disaster happening again, the King commanded that all new houses in London be made of stone and brick. Christopher Wren constructed St Paul's Cathedral, and Buckingham Palace was built in 1703 for the Duke of Buckingham.

RULE BRITANNIA

Catholic Stuart King James II was ousted and replaced by Protestant rulers William and Mary. England, Wales, and Scotland were united as Great Britain and German-speaking George I became king. Language difficulties at meetings led to Robert Walpole becoming the first prime minister in 1721.

Unsuccessful attempts were made by the Stuarts to regain the throne, which resulted in the defeat of Bonnie Prince Charlie at Culloden in 1746. In the second half of the 18th century, Britain fought France over control of colonial territories. France ceded most of her Indian and North American lands to Britain, which also owned sugar-producing Caribbean islands and slave-trading posts in west Africa. Captain Cook claimed Australia and New Zealand in 1769–1770.

The British Empire was expanding, and the country ruled supreme. However, Britain was more interested in trade abroad than government abroad,

Plague doctors wore primitive gas masks in the shape of birds' beaks and long black overcoats to minimize skin exposure.

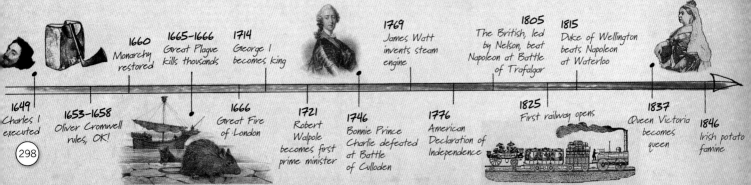

1660
Monarchy restored

1665–1666
Great Plague kills thousands

1714
George I becomes king

1769
James Watt invents steam engine

1805
The British, led by Nelson, beat Napoleon at Battle of Trafalgar

1815
Duke of Wellington beats Napoleon at Waterloo

1649
Charles I executed

1653–1658
Oliver Cromwell rules, OK!

1666
Great Fire of London

1721
Robert Walpole becomes first prime minister

1746
Bonnie Prince Charlie defeated at Battle of Culloden

1776
American Declaration of Independence

1825
First railway opens

1837
Queen Victoria becomes queen

1846
Irish potato famine

and discontent in the American colonies led to war. On 4 July 1776, 13 American colonies declared independence. An uprising was suppressed in Ireland, and Great Britain and Ireland became the United Kingdom in 1801.

EMPIRE AND INDUSTRY

During the late 18th and early 19th centuries, Britain gradually changed from an agricultural to an industrial society, a revolution brought about by inventions such as the steam engine, which mechanized and expanded industry and communications.

How do I do a wheelie?

Wars against Napoleon's France (1799–1815) ended with the Duke of Wellington's victory at the Battle of Waterloo, but were followed by unrest at home. Factory workers struggled in bad conditions, bread was expensive to buy, and there was a devastating potato famine in Ireland in 1846 that killed more than a million people and caused thousands to flee abroad. Laws were changed, and trade unions were set up to protect and fight for workers' rights.

The penny-farthing bicycle was popular in the 1870s and was named after two British coins in circulation at the time.

The wealth from trade and industry during Queen Victoria's reign (1837–1901) made Britain one of the world's most powerful nations. In 1851, the country showed off its many achievements at the Great Exhibition. Held in Crystal Palace in London, it was a chance to celebrate the nation's industrial, military, and economic superiority. The Empire kept growing, taking in large parts of Africa, including South Africa after the Boer War of 1899–1902. By the early 20th century, however, Britain's naval and trade supremacy was challenged by the USA and Germany.

CENTURY OF CHANGE

At home, a militant campaign for women's suffrage began in 1903. Women were given the vote in 1918, but not on the same terms as men until 1928. Rebellion in Ireland in 1916 led to home rule under separate governments in the north and south in 1920, and in 1921 all but the six northern counties became the Irish Free State (Eire).

Many of Britain's colonies sought independence, and the days of Empire came to an end. Twice in the first half of the 20th century Britain was involved in world wars. Both conflicts left the country victorious, but in debt. After World War II, Britain developed a welfare state and introduced the National Health Service to provide free medical care for all.

The 1960s saw an explosion of colour, fashion, style, and youth culture, but by the end of the decade the bubble had burst. There were ugly scenes of racism against the influx of mass immigration from the former colonies. In the 1970s, there were industrial strikes and high unemployment, and strife in Northern Ireland. The Irish Republican Army (IRA) led a bombing campaign seeking Irish unity.

Any shorter and I'll see your knickers!

Membership of the European Union led to closer economic and political ties with the continent. Margaret Thatcher became the first female prime minister in 1979, and the "iron lady" took Britain to war defending the Falkland Islands against invasion by Argentina. The election of Tony Blair's "New Labour" government in 1997 was accompanied by a rebranding of Britain. With the Irish "Troubles" resolved by a peace agreement, Britain could thrive as a modern, dynamic, and multi-ethnic nation. Which is how she likes to see herself today.

During the "swinging sixties" mini skirts and mini dresses were popular fashions.

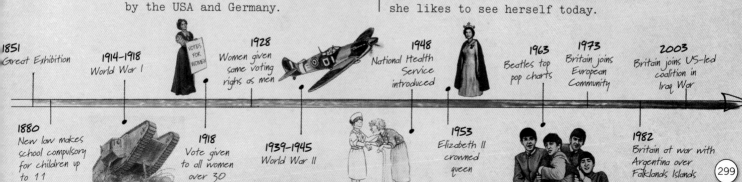

1851
Great Exhibition

1914–1918
World War I

1928
Women given same voting rights as men

1948
National Health Service introduced

1963
Beatles top pop charts

1973
Britain joins European Community

2003
Britain joins US-led coalition in Iraq War

1880
New law makes school compulsory for children up to 11

1918
Vote given to all women over 30

1939–1945
World War II

1953
Elizabeth II crowned queen

1982
Britain at war with Argentina over Falklands Islands

INDEX